LAW AND THE RESTORATION

LAW AND THE RESTORATION

Law and Latter-day Saint Thought and Scripture

Nathan B. Oman

Greg Kofford Books
Salt Lake City, 2024

Cover design by Loyd Isao Ericson.

Published in the USA.

ISBN: 978-1-58958-808-0 (paperback); 978-1-58958-811-0 (hardcover)
Also available in ebook.

Greg Kofford Books
P. O. Box 1362
Draper, UT 84020
www.gregkofford.com
facebook.com/gkbooks
twitter.com/gkbooks

Library of Congress Cataloging-in-Publication Data

Names: Oman, Nathan, author. | Oman, Nathan. Law and the Restoration ; v. 2

Title: Law and Latter-Day Saint thought and scripture / Nathan B. Oman.
Description: Salt Lake City : Greg Kofford Books, 2024. | Series: Law and the Restoration | Includes bibliographical references and index. | Summary: “Law and the Restoration: Law and Latter-day Saint thought and scripture is a comprehensive exploration of the intricate relationship between legal principles and the doctrines of The Church of Jesus Christ of Latter-day Saints. Author Nathan B. Oman delves into the profound ways in which Mormon theology intersects with legal concepts, offering readers a detailed analysis of church doctrines, their authority, and their implications for members’ daily lives. In doing so, Oman addresses foundational questions about the nature of church authority, the role of personal judgment, and the dynamic interplay between divine law and secular legal systems. The book is not just an academic treatise but a thoughtful discourse aimed at elucidating how Mormons navigate complex moral and legal landscapes in their quest to reconcile faith with modern societal norms. Each chapter serves as a deep dive into specific aspects of Mormon doctrine and its legal ramifications. From the examination of Nephi’s actions in the Book of Mormon to the contemporary debates surrounding same-sex marriage and civil disobedience, Oman provides a balanced and respectful analysis that seeks to understand rather than critique. This book is an invaluable resource for scholars, legal practitioners, and anyone interested in the intersection of religion and law, providing a rich narrative that underscores the ongoing dialogue between faith and jurisprudence within the Latter-day Saint tradition.”-- Provided by publisher.
Identifiers: LCCN 2024024185 (print) | LCCN 2024024186 (ebook) | ISBN 9781589588080 (paperback) | ISBN 9781589588110 (hardcover) | ISBN 9781589588097 (ebook)
Subjects: LCSH: Book of Mormon--Philosophy. | Christianity and law. | Latter Day Saint churches--Philosophy.
Classification: LCC BX8643.L5 O434 2024 (print) | LCC BX8643.L5 (ebook) | DDC 261.8--dc23/eng/20240730
LC record available at https://lccn.loc.gov/2024024185
LC ebook record available at https://lccn.loc.gov/2024024186

For Heather.

"The light which is in all things,
which giveth life to all things, which is the law . . ."
(Doctrine & Covenants 88:13)

". . . the law was engraven upon plates of brass . . ."
(1 Nephi 4:16)

Contents

Preface

This is the second of a two-volume work collecting essays on the relationship between law and Mormonism. The essays in the first volume focused on Mormon legal history. However, history is not the only standpoint from which one can explore Latter-day Saint legal thought. Rather than study legal aspects of the Mormon past, an alternative model for Mormon legal thought is to apply theories developed in the study of law to Mormon thought and experience. Mormonism is not a legalistic religion in the way that Islam or Judaism are legalistic; there is nothing remotely like the tradition of legal exegesis of sacred texts that one finds in the *halakah* or *usul al-fiqh* of Jews and Muslims. Mormonism is striking, however, in the relatively minor role that formal, dogmatic theology plays into Mormon thinking and the primary emphasis placed on practice over orthodoxy. Mormonism is also an authoritarian faith, in the sense that it has a well-developed ecclesiastical hierarchy and places a strong emphasis on questions of ecclesiastical and doctrinal authority. Hence, despite the absence of any formal tradition of "Mormon law," Latter-day Saint thought and experience has grappled with many of the same concepts—the regulation of behavior, authority, and hierarchy; the interpretation of authority; and so on—that have long interested legal theorists. Indeed, if we accept Lon Fuller's capacious definition of law as subjecting human behavior to the government of rules, it seems fair to describe Mormonism as a legal tradition.[1]

The structural affinity between law and Mormonism opens up two possibilities. The first is that ideas and concepts developed in the study of the law could be applied to the interpretation of Mormonism. Given the catholic nature of modern legal thought, there are dozens of different approaches that could be applied. One could apply the tools of law and economics to the analysis of Mormon ecclesiastical structures or use feminist legal theory to interpret Mormon teachings regarding gender. In the two thousand years that law has existed as a self-conscious intellectual discipline, it has produced a vast body of literature reflecting on how one

---

1. See Lon L. Fuller, "Law as an Instrument of Social Control and Law as a Facilitation of Human Interaction," *Brigham Young University Law Review* 1975, no. 1 (1975): 89–98.

interprets and understands the claims of legal authorities. One of the perennial questions that Mormon intellectuals have struggled with is how to understand the claims of Church authorities and Church doctrine. As I discuss elsewhere in this volume, these are questions that can be usefully approached using tools developed by legal philosophers such as Joseph Raz, H. L. A. Hart, and Ronald Dworkin.

The second possibility is to employ the kind of interpretive reconstruction that is frequently used to study the common law as a model for how one might extract meaning from Mormon practices. One of the drawbacks of Mormonism's orthopraxic, relatively atheological approach to religious life is the absence of a deep tradition of disciplined Mormon reflection even in those areas where there are thick Mormon practices. The result is a rich texture of norms, rules, and institutions without an accompanying tradition that seeks to systematically explain and interpret them. The Church court system provides a good example. From its earliest period, the Church has regarded adjudication through ecclesiastical courts as a key religious activity. The result has been an elaborate institutional structure that at various times has heard cases ranging from adultery to bankruptcy to theft. There is no accompanying tradition, however, of Mormon legal texts explaining and justifying the rules to be applied in these cases. Nevertheless, practical norms emerged from this practice. Like the common law, where the rule comes first and the explanation comes afterward, Mormon practices present a vast and seemingly inarticulate mass. Just as a common lawyer reconstructs legal doctrine from a myriad of individual cases and articulates the policies and choices inherent in that structure, Mormon practices may be interpretively reconstructed to reveal latent structures of thought. Hence, even if there is no tradition of disciplined Mormon reflection on legal topics such as punishment or property, there are extensive Mormon practices that can form a starting place for Mormon discourse on these topics.

A final approach to Latter-day Saint legal thought modeled in these pages is a close reading of the legal materials in Mormon scripture. Among its many other heresies, Mormonism rejects the idea of a closed canon of scripture. Latter-day Saints accept the Bible as scripture, but they believe that God has given additional sacred texts that stand beside it with equal authority. These texts consist of the Book of Mormon, the Doctrine and Covenants, and the Pearl of Great Price. Each of these books is quite different from the others. The Book of Mormon is a sprawling narrative about ancient prophets in the Americas, which Church-founder Joseph

Smith claimed to have miraculously translated from golden plates delivered to him by an angel. The Doctrine and Covenants has a structure similar to the Qur'an and consists of the text of revelations received and published by Joseph Smith during his lifetime and by his successors. It lacks an explicit narrative structure and consists of divine instructions given in response to discrete historical circumstances or questions. Finally, the Pearl of Great Price is a miscellaneous collection of texts produced by Joseph Smith, mainly containing expanded versions of biblical narratives. In addition, Latter-day Saints read the Bible in the light of these Restoration scriptures. Hence, while they accept the same scriptural text as other Christians, they frequently read that text in idiosyncratic ways.

Within this scripture is a mass of legal material that takes many forms. The Book of Mormon, for example, has numerous narratives that revolve around legal events such as trials, transfers of political power, treaties, and the like. The narrative itself is structured around various theological agendas, which means all of these legal materials are situated in contexts designed to give them religious significance. The Doctrine and Covenants, on the other hand, lacks narrative content but often speaks in a legal voice. First, in its pages God frequently speaks as a lawgiver on a cosmic scale. On a more mundane level, much of the Doctrine and Covenants consists of revelations given in the context of developing rules and procedures governing the expanding Church and, equally important, the various attempts at economic utopianism that marked nineteenth-century Mormonism.

All of this material can be grist for the legal scholar's mill. Latter-day Saint reading of scripture is overwhelmingly devotional or apologetic. There is a very limited tradition of careful exegesis of Mormon scripture divorced from the need to exhort the faithful or to defend the faith. However, a small but growing body of such literature does exist, and it demonstrates that Mormon texts will reward a close reading. There is no reason that the exegesis of Mormon texts requires that one pursue apologetic or devotional goals. Indeed, one needn't even regard the text as religiously authoritative to read it profitably. As the law and literature movement has amply demonstrated, non-authoritative literary texts can be read profitably for what they tell us about how one might think about the law.

The essays in this volume are organized around these two approaches to Mormon legal thought; although because they were all written separately over several years, I freely admit that the taxonomy is loose. Some of these essays were written for a non-Mormon scholarly audience, and some of them were aimed at observant Latter-day Saints. Some of them have been previously published in Mormon studies journals or legal fora. Several essays are published here for the first time, although some of them have circulated more or less widely on the Internet. For example, I first distributed chapter 8, which deals with a possible theology for same-sex temple sealings, though online newsletter, where I expected it to circulate at most among a few hundred friends and interested readers. I was shocked when the essay was downloaded over 20,000 times in less than six months, garnering a half-page story in the *Salt Lake Tribune*.[2] In the case of the essay "Mormonism and Conscience," I had the privilege of co-authoring the original article with Rosalynde Welch. I am grateful for permission from the various publishers to reprint the following materials:

Nathan B. Oman. "Standing Betwixt Them and Justice: War and Atonement in the Book of Mormon." In *God Himself Will Come Down: Reading Mosiah 15*, edited by Joseph M. Spencer and Andrew Smith, 121–32. Seattle, Washington: Latter-day Saint Theology Seminar, 2023.

Nathan B. Oman. "Nomos, Narrative, and Nephi: Legal Interpretation in the Book of Mormon." *British Journal of American Legal Studies* 11, no. 2 (2022): 297–322.

Nathan B. Oman. "Civil Disobedience in Latter-Day Saint Thought." *BYU Studies Quarterly* 60, no. 3 (2021): 229–40.

Rosalynde Welch and Nathan B. Oman. "Mormonism and Conscience." In *Christianity and the Law of Conscience: An Introduction*, edited by Jeffrey B. Hammond and Helen M. Alvare, 245–64. New York: Cambridge University Press, 2021.

Nathan B. Oman. "Doux Commerce in the City of God: Trade and the Mormon Ideal of Zion." In *Reapproaching Zion*, edited by Samuel D. Brunson and Nathan B. Oman, 131–66. Salt Lake City: By Common Consent Press, 2020.

Nathan B. Oman. "'I Will Give Unto You My Law': Section 42 as a Legal Text and the Paradoxes of Divine Law." In *Embracing the Law: Reading Doctrine and Covenants 42*, edited by Jeremiah John and Joseph M. Spencer. Provo: Neal A. Maxwell Institute for Religious Scholarship, 2017.

2. See Peggy Fletcher Stack, "Same-Sex Temple Sealings That Honor LDS Teachings?," *Salt Lake Tribune*, October 2, 2022.

Nathan B. Oman. "'The Living Oracles': Legal Interpretation and Mormon Thought." *Dialogue: A Journal of Mormon Thought* 42, no. 2 (Spring 2009): 1–19.

Nathan B. Oman. "A Defense of the Authority of Church Doctrine." *Dialogue: A Journal of Mormon Thought* 40, no. 4 (Winter 2007): 1–28.

Nathan B. Oman. "Jurisprudence and the Problem of Church Doctrine." *Element: The Journal of the Society for Mormon Philosophy and Theology* 2, no. 1 (2006): 1–19.

CHAPTER 1

"The Living Oracles": Legal Interpretation and Mormon Thought

"We have only an outline of our duties written; we are to be guided by the living oracles."—Wilford Woodruff[1]

"The judges in the several courts of justice . . . are the depositary of the laws; the living oracles . . ."—William Blackstone[2]

Mormon thinkers have a problem. Suppose that a Latter-day Saint were interested in learning what his or her religion has to say about some contemporary philosophical, social, or political issue. Where should a Mormon thinker begin? Consider the counter-example of Catholic intellectuals. Faced with such a question, they have the luxury of a rich philosophical and theological tradition on which to draw. They can turn to Aquinas or modern Catholic social thought and find there a set of closely reasoned propositions and arguments to apply to the questions before them. To be sure, the task of such a thinker is not simply to "look up" the answer, but Catholic intellectuals do have a religious tradition that has been digested over the centuries in intellectual categories that lend themselves easily to analysis and extension into new areas. This option, however, is not open to a Latter-day Saint. Mormonism—despite some important exceptions[3]—has largely eschewed closely reasoned systematic theology. As one sympathetic Catholic observer has written, "I have found it difficult to try to understand the complex relationships between philosophy and theology in Mormon thought."[4] To which I would respond,

---

1. Wilford Woodruff, "Necessity of the Living Oracles Among the Saints—Exhortation to Obedience to Counsel," in *Journal of Discourses*, vol. 9 (London and Liverpool: LDS Booksellers Depot, 1855–86, 1862), 9:324.

2. William Blackstone, *Commentaries on the Laws of England*, 3 vols. (Chicago: University of Chicago Press, 1979), 1:69. Blackstone's *Commentaries* was originally published in England in 1765.

3. One might point to the early work of Orson Pratt, the synthesis attempted by B. H. Roberts, or modern Mormon philosophers such as Sterling McMurrin, Blake Ostler, and David Paulsen.

4. David Tracy, "A Catholic View of Philosophy: Revelation and Reason," in *Mormonism in Dialogue with Contemporary Christian Theologies*, ed. Donald W. Musser and David L. Paulsen (Macon: Mercer University Press, 2007), 449.

"Join the club." Given the difficulties presented by what is at best a nascent philosophical tradition, Mormon thinkers interested in offering a "Mormon perspective" on an issue such as the nature of property or the proper forms of political reasoning, for example, face a methodological problem. How does one begin looking for Mormon resources from which to construct such perspectives? Indeed, on many issues it would seem that Mormon thinkers might be justified in concluding that Mormonism just doesn't have much of anything to say.

There is a voluminous body of Mormon writing on many subjects, but the overwhelming majority of this work is homiletic and is meant to inspire and motivate its audience rather than provide them with careful conceptual analysis. Furthermore, when one looks to the content of this work, one finds that much of it consists of narrative rather than exposition. Richard Bushman has observed that "Mormonism is less a set of doctrines than a collection of stories."[5] Indeed, the central obsession of Mormon intellectual life for the last half century has not been systematic theology but history. One might point to any number of things to underline the centrality of history for Mormon thought.

One example will suffice. The relationship between faith and reason is a perennial question for religious thinkers. Generally speaking, these debates are couched in the language of philosophy. The question is, as Alvin Plantinga has put it, whether or not belief is rationally warranted.[6] In contrast, the most sophisticated and prolonged debates within Mormonism on the relative claims of faith and unaided human reason have been cast as battles between "faithful history" and "secular history."[7] Where other traditions debate epistemology and theology, Mormons debate historiography and historicity. Accordingly, one response to the methodological problem facing Mormon intellectuals discussed above would be the interpretation of history in normative terms. Indeed, we can see something like this in the work of writers such as Hugh Nibley, who look to historical narratives about nineteenth-century Zion-building as a basis for social

---

5. Richard Lyman Bushman, "What's New in Mormon History: A Response to Jan Shipps," *The Journal of American History* 94, no. 2 (2007): 518.

6. See generally Alvin Plantinga, *Warranted Christian Belief* (New York: Oxford University Press, 2000).

7. For a collection of the key articles, see George Smith, ed., *Faithful History: Essays on Writing Mormon History* (Salt Lake City: Signature Books, 1992).

criticism.[8] Such efforts, however, are dogged by persistent anxieties about the intellectual respectability of using the past as a springboard for broader conceptual or normative discussions. For many professional historians and the Mormon intellectuals who take them as models, straying beyond concrete debates over sources, chronology, and their interpretation smacks of apologetics or sectarian rather than "scholarly" history.

The two quotations at the beginning of this chapter point toward a related but slightly different response to the methodological quandary of Mormon thinkers. Wilford Woodruff taught, "We have only an outline of our duties written; we are to be guided by the living oracles."[9] On its face, this seems like a fairly standard appeal to the authority of Mormonism's living prophets. The contrast between "living oracles" and the mere "outline of duties" that is actually written down, however, suggests a second point. The formal, propositional content of Mormon scripture, it would seem, provides no more than a framework in which the concrete meaning of Mormonism is worked out by the inspired fiat of Mormon leaders. While Joseph Smith produced a mass of scriptural narrative, subsequent Mormon prophets—with notable exceptions such as Joseph F. Smith's vision of the redemption of the dead (see D&C 138)—have made their weight felt less in terms of new sacred stories than in terms of new institutions and practices. Strikingly, Brigham Young's sole contribution to the formal Mormon cannon is a revelation on the structure of immigrant trains (see D&C 136). He—like most of his successors—spent the bulk of his energies on the delineation of Mormon practices and institutions.

What Mormons see in this history is the accretion of many decisions in concrete historical situations made by wise and inspired leaders. The

8. See Hugh Nibley, *Brother Brigham Challenges the Saints*, ed. Don E. Norton (Salt Lake City: Deseret Book Co., 1994). Other examples include James W. Lucas and Warner P. Woodworth, *Working toward Zion: Principles of the United Order for the Modern World* (Salt Lake City: Aspen Books, 1996), and Phillip J. Bryson, "In Defense of Capitalism: Church Leaders on Property, Wealth, and the Economic Order," *Brigham Young University Studies* 38, no. 3 (1999): 89–107. For historical works setting forth the narratives on which this work is largely based, see Leonard J. Arrington, *Great Basin Kingdom: An Economic History of the Latter-Day Saints, 1830–1900* (Urbana: University of Illinois Press, 2005), Leonard J. Arrington, Feramorz Y. Fox, and Dean L. May, *Building the City of God: Community and Cooperation Among the Mormons*, 2nd ed. (Urbana: University of Illinois Press, 1992).

9. Woodruff, "Necessity of the Living Oracles Among the Saints—Exhortation to Obedience to Counsel," 9:324.

result is a set of practices and institutions that they regard as imbued with the divine, even when the practices and institutions cannot be shown to be deduced in any unproblematic manner from sacred texts, theological first principles, or dramatic moments of charismatic revelation. The same is true of the activities of Latter-day Saint leaders who have not reached the top of the hierarchy. They, too, have been involved mainly in the execution and building up of a set of practices and institutions. Accordingly, Bushman's view of Mormonism as a collection of stories must be updated. Mormonism is also a set of practices and institutions. This fact points toward another answer to the methodological dilemma of Mormon thinkers: legal interpretation, particularly the methods of interpretation used in the judge-made common law.[10]

According to Oliver Wendell Holmes Jr., "it is the merit of the common law that it decides the case first and determines the principle afterwards."[11] Like most Holmesian aphorisms, this statement is open to multiple interpretations; however, it rightly insists that the common law is first and foremost about resolving concrete disputes. A common-law judge seldom finds himself announcing abstract principles for their own sake. Rather, he is generally concerned with the question of doing right in the particular case before him or, at most, in making minor modifications to existing laws. The resolution of the case will depend on analogies to past cases and the judge's own wisdom and intuitions about justice. It is only after the piling up of innumerable particular cases that the abstract rules of legal doctrine emerge.

Hence, it is uncontroversial to claim that, for example, in the case of conflict between a written contract and the parties' oral testimony about the content of their agreement, the writing will control.[12] This rule, how-

---

10. I have written elsewhere about the relationship between legal thinking and Church doctrine. In a sense, I am repeating many of the same arguments here, although I offer them as a way of generating identifiably Mormon perspectives rather than as a way of discovering authoritative Church doctrine. See Nathan B. Oman, "Jurisprudence and the Problem of Church Doctrine," *Element: The Journal of the Society for Mormon Philosophy and Theology* 2, no. 1 (2006): 1–19; Nathan B. Oman, "A Defense of the Authority of Church Doctrine," *Dialogue: A Journal of Mormon Thought* 40, no. 4 (Winter 2007): 1–28.

11. Quoted in Louis Menand, *The Metaphysical Club* (New York: Farrar, Straus, and Giroux, 2001), 339.

12. This is the so-called parole evidence rule, which holds, in the technical language of the American Law Institute, that "a binding integrated agreement discharges prior agreements to the extent that it is inconsistent with them . . .

ever, was never announced in a distinct, legislative moment. Rather, it is an accepted generalization that captures the outcomes of hundreds of preexisting cases. Finally, it is only after the myriad of particular cases has been organized into a doctrinal structure of abstract legal rules that a common law thinker might try to discern within, say, the law of contracts a set of normative choices, such as a general preference for economic efficiency, personal autonomy, or transactional fairness.[13] Hence, as Blackstone wrote, common law judges are "living oracles" who declare the law in particular cases rather than deducing it from first principles. In this sense, they function much like Mormon prophets and priesthood leaders.

Working within the common law system, a jurist doesn't provide a conceptual foundation from which the law is deduced. Rather, her task is to uncover the latent normative judgments that emerge spontaneously from the accretion of particular precedents. These generalized statements of legal principles and policies can then serve as a basis for either criticizing or extending current practice. They are not, however, the common law itself. Rather, the common law always continues on as a practice that is "more like a muddle than a system."[14] This process is true whether our jurist is a lawyer, a law professor, or even a judge reflecting on the law.[15]

Hence, for example, a common law lawyer would note that, in case after case, when a litigant in a contract case claims that the oral agreement of the parties was substantially different than the written contract, the judges always side with the writing over the oral testimony. This regularity might then be stated as a rule. In many cases, the theorist would note, the effect of this rule is to enforce contract terms that may differ from the subjective understanding of the parties. Such an outcome seems inconsistent with

---

[and] a binding completely integrated agreement discharges prior agreements to the extent that they are within its scope." *Restatement (Second) of Contracts* (St. Paul: American Law Institute, 1978), § 212.

13. For a brief introduction to the contemporary philosophy of contract law, see Nathan B. Oman, "Unity and Pluralism in Contract Law," *Michigan Law Review* 103, no. 6 (2005): 1483–1506.

14. A. W. B. Simpson, ed., "The Common Law and Legal Theory," in *Oxford Essays in Jurisprudence, Second Series* (Oxford: Oxford University Press, 1973), 99.

15. Admittedly, law professors are less tied than lawyers or judges to what H. L. A. Hart called "the internal point of view" described here. Nevertheless, when law professors are engaged in what is called "doctrinal scholarship" or—at a higher level of abstraction—"interpretive reconstruction," they are engaged in the sorts of activities described above. For Hart's discussion of the "internal point of view," see, e.g., H. L. A. Hart, *The Concept of Law* (Oxford: Clarendon Press, 1991), 88–91.

the notion that contract law is primarily concerned with advancing the autonomous choices of individuals. On the other hand, by privileging the written terms, the common law rule contributes to certainty in commercial transactions and reduces the cost to the courts of resolving contract disputes, throwing those costs back onto the parties who have an incentive to reduce their actual intentions to a clear writing. What emerges from this analysis is a conclusion that, at least in this area of contract interpretation, concern for economic efficiency seems paramount over concern for individual choice. This conclusion, however, is not the law. It is not even a major premise from which the law is deduced. It is simply an articulation of the latent normative logic of the law as it now stands. The case comes first, and it is only afterward that we discover principles. The "living oracles," however, with their focus on particular cases, may well move the law in a different direction in the future.

This method of interpretation can be applied to the practices and institutions of Mormonism. The goal would not be to provide first principles from which correct conclusions can be deduced. Rather it would be to articulate the inchoate normative logic of these practices and institutions. Two concrete examples can illustrate the kind of analysis that I envision. Suppose that one is interested in Mormon conceptions of property and contract. These institutions stand at the center of modern market economies, and one might wonder what Mormonism has to say about them. At first glance, Mormon theology—or at any rate, the extremely small literature on systematic Mormon theology—seems to have very little to say about either property or contracts. The analogy to legal interpretation, however, suggests that one should search for Mormon ideas not only in Mormon discourse but also in Mormon practice.

One place to look for materials would be the nineteenth-century Church court system, which among other things decided property and contract disputes between Latter-day Saints.[16] One will search the records of these cases in vain for anything that even distantly resembles a theory of property or a theory of contract. The priesthood leaders resolving these disputes decided the case without recourse to any elaborate set of first prin-

---

16. For a summary of civil dispute resolution in nineteenth-century Mormon courts, see Nathan B. Oman, "Preaching to the Court House and Judging in the Temple," *Brigham Young University Law Review* 2009, no. 1 (2009): 157–219; and Edwin Brown Firmage and Richard Collin Mangrum, *Zion in the Courts: A Legal History of the Church of Jesus Christ of Latter-Day Saints, 1830–1900* (Urbana: University of Illinois Press, 1988).

ciples. Nevertheless, in examining their practices and the institutions they sought to create, we can discern a distinctive set of normative choices that one might unapologetically label as Mormon concepts of property and contract. Consider first the case of Oliver Cowdery's excommunication.

In 1831, Joseph Smith received a revelation setting forth what became known as the "Law of Consecration and Stewardship" (see D&C 42).[17] All members of the Church were to "consecrate" their property to the Lord by executing a deed that transferred land and other assets to the Church. Each member then received in return a parcel of property as his particular "stewardship."[18] In Jackson County, Missouri, which an earlier revelation had designated as the location of the New Jerusalem to be founded by the Saints, members received their stewardships as part an effort to build up Zion. In 1833, after growing tensions with the original settlers in the country, an ad hoc militia violently expelled the Mormons from the area.[19] The loss of Jackson County precipitated a crisis for many Latter-day Saints. How were they to build up Zion if the revealed location of the New Jerusalem was held by "the Gentiles"? Coupled with other events, this loss caused a leadership crisis within the Church that came to a head in 1838.[20]

In the resulting struggle, Oliver Cowdery found himself on trial before a Church court. Among the charges levelled against him was that he had denied the faith and abandoned Zion by selling his stewardship. Oliver responded with a lengthy letter in which he refused to submit to the jurisdiction of the high council that was trying his case, insisting that no Church court could interfere in his "temporal affairs." The letter contained a revealing passage on property rights: "Now sir the lands in our Country are allodial in the strictest construction of the term, and have not the least shadow of feudal tenours attached to them, consequently, they may be disposed of by deeds of conveyance without the consent or even approbation of a superior."[21] Scholars have long found his reference to "al-

17. Richard Lyman Bushman, *Joseph Smith: Rough Stone Rolling* (New York: Alfred A. Knopf, 2005), 154–55.

18. Firmage and Mangrum, *Zion in the Courts*, 61–63.

19. Bushman, *Rough Stone Rolling*, 222–27.

20. Bushman, 346–49.

21. Donald Cannon and Lyndon W. Cook, eds., *Far West Record: Minutes of the Church of Jesus Christ of Latter-Day Saints, 1830–1844* (Salt Lake City: Deseret Book Co., 1983), 164.

lodial" land and feudal tenures puzzling.[22] Oliver's objections, however, go to the heart of how Mormon practices conceptualized property.

Feudal tenures refer to medieval doctrines in the common law by which the ownership of land created certain kinds of reciprocal social obligations. The way in which one owned property defined one's place in the social system. Every freeman "held his land of" someone else. A deed, for example, might specify that Sir Cedric held Blackacre "in knight's service" of Lord Lothgar. What this meant was that Sir Cedric's ownership of Blackacre created an obligation on his part of loyalty and military service to Lord Lothgar. In turn, Lord Lothgar—at least in theory—had obligations to protect Sir Cedric and provide him with justice in disputes with his neighbors. The result was a thick set of social duties centered on the ownership of land. As one legal historian has written: "When feudalism was at full tide, it was clearly much more than a system of providing legal title in land; indeed, the sense of mutual personal obligation between lord and vassal may have been even more essential than the granting of fiefs in return for promises of services."[23] Legally speaking, however, these were not free-floating rights or obligations. They inhered in the concept of property itself. To own Blackacre meant to have a certain set of obligations in the community where Blackacre was located. By contrast, holders of allodial land "were free from the exactions and burdens to which the holders of fiefs were subject, yet they did not enjoy the protection of a superior."[24] Hence, allodial land had no "feudal tenures," rendering its

---

22. Mormon law professor Steven D. Smith, for example, has written: "Oliver's position seems a bit bizarre. . . . I admit to being in sympathy with some of Oliver's concerns. Even from a distance, though, I think we can say that on this specific issue of property, Oliver seemed confused. . . . Why would the fact that in this country property is allodial rather than feudal (whatever that means) preclude a church from giving direction to those who choose to belong to it, even in temporal affairs?" Steven D. Smith, "The Promise and Perils of Conscience," *Brigham Young University Law Review* 2003, no. 3 (2003): 1057, 1065–66. Bushman, *Joseph Smith: Rough Stone Rolling*, 348, however, sees Cowdery as making a deeper point with his pedantry over allodial property.

23. Arthur R. Hogue, *Origins of the Common Law* (Indianapolis: Liberty Press, 1984), 94.

24. George W. Thompson and Leonard A. Jones, *Commentaries on the Modern Law of Real Property, Being a Comprehensive Treatment of Every Phase of the Subject with Special Reference to the Acquisition, Encumbrance and Alienation of Real Property with Complete Forms*, ed. John S. Grimes (Indianapolis: Bobbs-Merrill, 1980), 1:168–69.

owner free of both the social obligations and the social benefits inherent in the lord-vassal relationship.

During the period prior to his Church trial, Cowdery was following an informal course of reading of the kind standard among would-be frontier attorneys.[25] In the perennial manner of law students, he was no doubt eager to show off newly mastered jargon, but his appeal to allodial property and feudal tenures recognized that the Church was asking him to fundamentally reconceptualize property in terms very different than those that prevailed in American culture. Following the formulation given by Locke a century earlier, the American Revolution had rallied around the vindication of rights to "life, liberty, and property." In this trinity of values, however, property had a particular meaning, one mediated in part through the legal concepts that Cowdery invoked. For example, in 1765, John Adams attacked the Stamp Act in *A Dissertation on the Canon and Feudal Law* that identified the tyranny of Parliament as the latest chapter in a story of repression with its roots in feudal tenures. "All ranks and degrees held their lands by a variety of duties and services, all tending to bind the chains the faster on every order of mankind," Adams noted.[26] The dire result of this system, he continued, was "a state of total ignorance of every thing divine and human." In contrast, among those who "holden their lands allodially," a man was "the sovereign lord and proprietor of the ground he occupied."[27]

A generation later, in his widely used American edition of Blackstone's *Commentaries*, William and Mary law professor St. George Tucker noted with pride that, due to the "republican spirit," feudal tenures had been abolished by statute in America, and "it was expected that every trace of that system would have been abolished in this country when the republic was established."[28] Likewise, in his 1828 *Commentaries on American*

25. See Stanley R. Gunn, *Oliver Cowdery, Second Elder Scribe.* (Salt Lake City: Bookcraft, 1962); Richard Lloyd Anderson, "Oliver Cowdery, Esq.: His Non-Mormon Career," *Proceedings of the Utah Academy of Sciences, Arts, and Letters* 45, no. 1 (1968): 66–80.

26. John Adams, *The Revolutionary Writings of John Adams*, ed. Bradley C. Thompson (Indianapolis: Liberty Fund, 2000), 23.

27. Adams, 27.

28. St. George Tucker, *Blackstone's Commentaries: With Notes of Reference to the Constitution and Laws of the Federal Government of the United States and of the Commonwealth of Virginia, in Five Volumes* (Philadelphia: W. Y. Birch and A. Small, 1803), 3:44.

Law, Chancellor James Kent traced in detail the end of feudal tenures in America and the rise of allodial holding, marking it as a restoration of ancient lost liberties. "Thus, by one of those singular revolutions incident to human affairs," he wrote, "allodial estates . . . regained their primitive estimation in the minds of free-men."[29] As an aspiring attorney, Oliver was well aware of such standard legal texts as Tucker's and Kent's commentaries, and his rhetorical fillip on allodial land was likely a deliberate allusion to this line of thinking.[30]

The most salient feature of this "republican" vision of ownership was that it constituted a sharp limit on social obligation. Whatever a man's obligations in the public realm, once within the private space of his allodial castle, he could do as he wished. Blackstone, the most important reference work for generations of American attorneys, insisted: "So great moreover is the regard of the law for private property, that it will not authorize the least violation of it; no, not even for the general good of the whole community. . . . In vain may it be urged, that the good of the individual ought to yield to that of the community."[31] Nor were these merely "legal" categories. For a lawyer of Oliver's generation, legal positivism had not yet shattered the identification of the common law with natural law. Accordingly, this absolutist conception of property marked off more than simply the positive law of the land. It represented a fundamental feature of moral reality. In effect, to own property was to have a sphere, however limited, beyond the reach of the community.

Mormonism did not try to reinstitute feudal tenures. It did, however, reject the notion of property as a boundary or limit of communal duties. Furthermore, in common with the feudal system, it fragmented the moral concept of ownership and transformed property into a nexus of obligations to others. In Joseph Smith's revelations, nobody owns property in the absolutist way championed by Blackstone.[32] Rather, one 1834

---

29. James Kent, *Commentaries on American Law* (New York: O. Halsted, 1826), 3:412.

30. In an 1838 letter setting forth the books necessary for his study of the law, Oliver listed both Blackstone and Kent's *Commentaries*. See Gunn, *Oliver Cowdery, Second Elder Scribe*, 168.

31. Blackstone, *Commentaries*, 1:135.

32. Interestingly, however, Doctrine & Covenants 134:10–11 takes a somewhat different attitude toward property, insisting that "we do not believe that any religious society has authority to try men on the right of property" and further insisting that "we believe that all men are justified in defending . . . their . . .

revelation declared, "I, the Lord, stretched out the heavens, and built the earth, my very handiwork; all things therein are mine" (D&C 104:14). The institutions of consecrated properties and stewardships served not only to redistribute wealth among the Saints, but also to redefine their relationship to property. In the same revelation, God declared that property is given to the Saints "that every man may give an account unto me of the stewardship which is appointed unto him" (D&C 104:12). One did not hold property as a way of creating a private sphere free of communal obligations. Rather the purpose of property was to create obligations to others and to become accountable to God (see D&C 42:32). Obligations associated with ownership included the duty to "administer to the poor and needy," assisting to purchase property "for the public benefit of the church," and most inclusively for "the building up of the New Jerusalem" (D&C 42:34–35).

While the concrete institutional arrangements of "the law of consecration and stewardship" were short lived, the underlying approach to property continued within Mormon practice. For example, in 1838 Joseph Smith published a revelation that replaced the earlier system of consecrations and stewardships with a system of tithing that required Mormons to "pay one-tenth of their interest annually" into the coffers of the community (see D&C 119:4). However, the rule, which is still followed by Latter-day Saints, did not repudiate the earlier concepts of stewardship and subsidiary ownership. Rather, the revelation explicitly linked the new regime to the older rules requiring that "surplus property be put in the hands of the bishop" (D&C 119:1) and to a notion of property rights linked to the obligation to build up Zion:

> Verily I say unto you, it shall come to pass that all . . . shall be tithed of their surplus properties. . . .
>
> And I say unto you, if my people observe not this law, to keep it holy, and by this law sanctify the land of Zion unto me, that my statutes and my judgments may be kept thereon, that it may be most holy, behold, verily I say unto you, it shall not be a land of Zion unto you (D&C 119:8–9).

Thus, in a single passage, "properties" are associated with divine obligations ("my statutes and judgments") and the creation of a community defined by reciprocal obligations of love and service ("a land of Zion").

---

property . . . from unlawful assaults." This section was authored by none other than Oliver Cowdery. See Robert J. Woodford, "The Historical Development of the Doctrine and Covenants" (PhD dissertation, Provo, Utah, Brigham Young University, 1974), 1784–94.

In place of the conception of property as a bulwark of individual freedom, Mormonism offers property as a nexus of obligation to God and to one's neighbors. The 1838 revelation is particularly striking in this regard because it came in the context of a retreat from cooperative economic arrangements toward a regime of greater personal control of property. Nevertheless, it carried forward the notion that to care for the poor and to build up Zion is not something that one chooses to do with property that is truly one's own. Rather, everything one owns is a stewardship from God, given for the purpose of making one accountable to him. The obligation to build Zion inheres in the concept of property itself.

The nineteenth-century Mormon court system can be similarly mined for Mormon conceptions of contract. In contrast to their detailed discussion of matters relating to property, Mormon scriptures have comparatively little to say about contracts. In this sense, they mirror the law codes of the Old Testament, which likewise have little to say about enforcing voluntary agreements. Nevertheless, Joseph Smith's revelation on the law of consecration and stewardship clearly assumes an economic order involving commerce and voluntary exchange, commanding "thou shalt pay for that which thou shalt receive of thy brother" (D&C 42:54). Another revelation speaks of a store to be set up to serve the Saints in Zion (see D&C 57:8–10). While contracts exist only in the margins of Mormon scripture, covenants are an enormously important concept in Latter-day Saint theology. Most dramatically, an 1832 revelation suggests that sacred promises bind even God. "I, the Lord, am bound when ye do what I say; but when ye do not what I say, ye have no promise" (D&C 82:10). This reverential attitude toward the power of promises carried over into Mormon contract cases.

On December 7, 1863, a local schoolteacher filed a complaint with the bishop of a ward in northern Utah against a local farmer (both teacher and farmer were Mormons) "for unchristianlike conduct, unworthy of a Latter Day Saint, in refusing to pay me a small debt due for School teaching in wheat flour or corn." The farmer admitted to having promised to pay but insisted that "prior to his calling on me for wheat, I contracted my flour what I had to spare to raise a certain amount of money that I owed." A trial ensued, and testimony before the bishop's court revealed that the farmer had initially told the schoolteacher that he had no grain and had then tried to find a buyer who would pay for his wheat either with livestock or sufficient ready cash. When the schoolteacher found out, he demanded the wheat according to the earlier agreement, but by this time, the farmer had found willing buyers at the higher price, a group of Gentile miners. In his complaint to the bishop's court, the schoolteacher insisted that he had "very much needed" the wheat and expressed dismay that it had gone to "speculators from the Bannock Minz." Other Mormons testified that they had offered to buy the corn with cash or calves, but the farmer had refused them, either because the amount of money offered was too little or because the calves were too young. The clerk recorded that the bishop, after deliberating, "said it was a very plain case, many cases come up rather misty but this is a very plain case. . . . I think so and more than enough has been said to prove that [the farmer] has told in a number of instances that which is not true and [the bishop] moved that we disfellowship [him] until he make satisfaction."[33]

The little drama described in this case is common enough in contract litigation. Able promises Baker some commodity at a fixed price. At the time of delivery, however, the market price of the commodity has risen, and Able breaches his contract to Baker to make a better deal elsewhere. The bishop's approach to the case, however, deviates significantly from the common law of contracts. Holmes famously declared, "The duty to keep a contract at common law means a prediction that you must pay damages if you do not keep it—and nothing else."[34] While laypersons commonly speak of "enforcing" a contract, in point of fact the common law generally will not force a breaching party to literally do what he promised in his contract. Rather, the usual remedy is damages. A breaching party must—in theory, at least—compensate the disappointed promisee for the lost value of the bargain but is always free to simply breach and pay. Furthermore, the breach of contract—while giving rise to liability—is not regarded as a legal wrong in and of itself. For example, with a few extremely rare exceptions, the mere breach of contract is not a crime or even a civil wrong giving rise to a fine nor do courts inquire into the culpability of breach in any but the rarest of cases. In short, one is always free to simply walk away from one's agreements, albeit at the risk of a suit for damages.

The justifiability of the common law's preference for compensatory damages is hotly contested among legal scholars. There are at least two possible arguments. The first is that contract law's primary concern is and

33. Ecclesiastical Court Cases Collection, Disfellowship Records, 1839–1965, CR 355, 2, 1863, fd. 1, Church History Library, Salt Lake City. These restricted records are used by permission on condition of masking individuals' identity.

34. Oliver Wendell Holmes, Jr., "The Path of the Law," *Harvard Law Review* 10 (1897): 459.

ought to be to provide contracting parties with incentives to behave in economically efficient ways. In this view, society does not want people to keep all of their promises. Rather, it only wishes to see promises kept when the benefits of doing so exceed the costs. Sometimes, however, it will be economically efficient for parties to breach their contracts; and in such cases, we wish them to do so. Damages incentivize performance but not too much, encouraging so-called "efficient breaches."[35] Alternatively, some argue that, in a liberal society, the law should not concern itself with the personal morality of its citizens, confining itself to protecting them against invasions of their rights by others. The duty to keep a promise, being grounded in personal virtue, is not something that the law should concern itself with. It will provide compensation to those whose legitimate expectations have been disappointed by breach, but it ought not to act to keep the promisor from breaking his promise merely on the basis of moral objections.[36]

Thus, there is a sense in which both of these justifications treat contracts as extremely thin obligations between two essentially unrelated individuals. Both take an amoral attitude toward promises, treating them as either instrumentally useful in some cases to achieve economic goals or alternatively as matters about which a properly constituted political community ought to be indifferent. In this view, the actions of the farmer were altogether benign, even perhaps commendable from an economic point of view. To be sure, he ought to pay the schoolteacher something, but the common law would attach no stigma per se to his shopping of grain to the highest bidder, notwithstanding his prior promise to give it to the schoolteacher. The bishop, in contrast, viewed the farmer's actions in starkly moralistic terms. The farmer had not only breached his contract, but he had also lied. Furthermore, the remedy imposed was not simply an order to pay some amount of damages. Rather, he was cut off from the community until the man he had wronged determined that he was once again eligible to enter it. Under the rules that prevailed at the time, of course, the schoolteacher's power over the farmer's continued fellowship was not absolute. Someone who felt that he had been abused under a

---

35. See A. Mitchell Polinsky, *An Introduction to Law and Economics* (Boston: Little, Brown, 1989), 27–38. For reasons to doubt the economic validity of these arguments, see Nathan B. Oman, "The Failure of Economic Interpretations of the Law of Contract Damages," *Washington & Lee Law Review* 64 (2007): 829–75.

36. Randy E. Barnett, "Some Problems with Contract as Promise," *Cornell Law Review* 77, no. 5 (1992): 1022–33.

judgment from a Church court could always file a counter complaint for, in the words of one such action, "unchristianlike conduct in . . . depriving me of my fellowship in the Ch. Of J. C. of LDS."[37] Still, the bishop's resolution of the case gave more to the schoolteacher than a mere claim for money damages and had a punitive aspect foreign to the common law of contracts.

The Mormon preference for moralizing contracts shows up in other areas where Mormon adjudication differed sharply from secular legal doctrines. Where possible, Church courts required breaching parties to perform their obligations, awarding damages only when performance was no longer possible.[38] Even when damages were awarded, the Church courts took a tougher line with breaching parties than do secular courts. For example, under the rule announced in the famous English case of *Hadley v. Baxendale*, a breaching party's liability included few of the secondary negative effects of his breach because the law sharply limits so-called "consequential damages." The decisions in the Church courts were quite different.

For example, in October 1847 the Salt Lake High Council heard a complaint against a man who had apparently breached a contract to deliver some gunpowder in his possession, selling it instead to a third party. He offered to pay for it, but the council went on to hold that he "be held responsible for *any damage* that may accrue from the want of it, until paid," greatly enlarging the man's liability beyond what would be available under the common law.[39] Elsewhere, Church courts awarded punitive damages for breach of contract, something almost totally unheard of in the common law.[40] Likewise, Mormon courts regularly enforced debts that had been discharged by bankruptcy or even death, on the theory that Latter-day Saints had a moral duty to meet their obligations come what

---

37. Ecclesiastical Court Cases Collection, Disfellowship Records, 1839–1965, CR 355, 2, 1858, fd. 2.

38. See, e.g., Nicholas Groesbeck Morgan, ed., *The Old Fort: Historic Mormon Bastion, the Plymouth Rock of the West* (Salt Lake City: Nicholas Groesbeck Morgan, 1964), 55 (reproducing minutes of the Salt Lake Stake High Council in a case for "non-delivery of an ox" ordering the defendant to deliver the ox rather than pay damages).

39. Morgan, *The Old Fort*, 71–72; emphasis added. It is not entirely clear that this was a purely contractual case. The man may have been the equivalent of a bailee, holding the gun powder as an agent rather than simply promising to deliver it. Needless to say, Church courts made no attempts to draw such fine distinctions in their decisions.

40. Firmage and Mangrum, *Zion in the Courts*, 344.

may.[41] This highly moralistic approach to obligations was never tied to communitarian economic institutions and has survived in contemporary Mormon discourse, notwithstanding its sharp divergence from secular ideas of contract.[42]

Obviously, the interpretation of these two Church court cases is open to debate. They do illustrate, however, the way in which one can extract fairly abstract ideas from a concrete set of practices that do not themselves articulate the abstract ideas. Hence, Cowdery's property dispute reveals an idea of property as a nexus of communal obligations rather than as a boundary of those obligations. The dispute between the farmer and the schoolteacher shows a contract as a locus of moral testing and obligation, rather than the amoral vision of a contract as a mere facilitator of efficient behavior or as another boundary line among rights-holding strangers. In short, the analogy to legal interpretation shows how the nitty-gritty response of Mormonism to concrete questions of practice contains the germ of more generalized discussions.

Such an approach has a number of attractive features. First and most importantly, it shows that Mormonism has something to say on subjects where it appears initially taciturn. While a philosopher might view the relentlessly practical and practice-focused Mormon landscape as a mute wasteland, a legal theorist can see it as a vast reserve of material waiting to be rendered articulate.

Second, a jurisprudential approach largely sidesteps the thorny issue of authority within Mormonism.[43] At a conceptual level, it rests on the authority of the "living oracles" and their ability to invest the prosaic, practical aspects of Mormonism with the divine. The concrete confrontation over the sale of Cowdery's parcel of Jackson County land or the dispute between the farmer and the schoolteacher serve to fill in the "outlines of our duties [that] are written." They do not, however, purport to uncover the first principles that ought to guide the decisions of the living oracles. The legal analogy provides no critical leverage against the authorities of the Church. Those with ecclesiastical offices giving them stewardship over a particular practice or institution may always change it and, in so doing, will provide new cases to be interpreted and enfolded into our ongoing

41. Firmage and Mangrum, 341–44.

42. See, e.g., Dallin H. Oaks, "Brother's Keeper," *Ensign*, November 1986, 20.

43. For some thoughtful discussion of the issue, see Armand Maussa, "Alternate Voices: The Calling and Its Implications," *Sunstone*, April 1990, 7–11, and Dallin H. Oaks, "Alternative Voices," *Ensign*, May 1989, 27–31.

understanding of what Mormonism has to say about the world. Hence, even at the conceptual level, the jurisprudential analogy assumes that the practice of Mormonism is logically and normatively prior to any theory that one might have about it.

Third, this approach allows us to sharpen our normative analysis of Mormon history while sidestepping the morass of debates over historiography and historicity. If we adopt the stance of a legal theorist, successful examinations of the past no longer consist of providing an "objective," "neutral," "scholarly," or "historical" assessment of it. The jurisprudential approach can mine past practices and institutions in normative terms without intellectual embarrassment because it is, from first to last, an exercise in normative archeology rather than ostensibly disinterested history. Past practices and institutions become interesting primarily as the instantiation of a particular constellation of normative choices. It is this constellation of normative choices, rather than the concrete historical details and their interpretations, that is of interest. In a sense, institutions and practices become more akin to arguments to be appreciated and evaluated rather than events to be explained on causal or historical grounds. Finally, and most importantly, the turn to legal interpretation helps to render articulate what was previously mute and to reveal Mormon practices and institutions—and by extension Mormonism itself—as "worthy of the interest of an intelligent [person]."[44]

---

44. The phrase appears in Oliver Wendell Holmes Jr., Letter to Harold Laski. One of his goals in writing *The Common Law* was to reveal jurisprudence as a topic "worthy of the interest of an intelligent man." Oliver Wendell Holmes, *The Essential Holmes: Selections from the Letters, Speeches, Judicial Opinions, and Other Writings of Oliver Wendell Holmes, Jr.*, ed. Richard A. Posner (Chicago: University of Chicago Press, 1992), 265.

CHAPTER 2

Jurisprudence and the Problem of Church Doctrine

Mormons frequently refer to "Church Doctrine" in their theological discussions. For example, Sister Smith might express her belief that the earth is no more than five or six thousand years old and that the theory of evolution is a Satanically inspired plot. Brother Young responds by noting, "Those are just your opinions. That is not Church Doctrine." Whatever else the term Church Doctrine might mean in this exchange, it is clearly functioning as a theological authority, delineating those beliefs that have a claim on Brother Young from those that do not. Like most Mormons, Brother Young seems to be conceptualizing Church Doctrine as some set of authoritative teachings promulgated by the Church that it is possible to identify. Yet how we differentiate between Church Doctrine and mere opinion is unclear. I argue that we can analogize the problem of "What is Church Doctrine?" to the jurisprudential problem of "What is the law?" The answers offered by the philosophy of law to the second of these questions illuminates the sorts of answers that we can give to the first. Ultimately, I conclude that we discover Church Doctrine not by application of any hard and fast rule that allows us to identify it but rather through a process of interpretation. This approach to Church Doctrine, in turn, throws new light on two persistent issues in Mormon thought: the relationship between authority and independent moral judgment, and the way in which Mormons interpret their own past.

Consider the example of the Roman Catholic Church. Like the LDS Church, Roman Catholicism has an integrated ecclesiastical structure with a strong emphasis on authority. Were one interested in the "Church Doctrine" of Roman Catholicism, one would consult the *Catechism of the Catholic Church*. This is a volume of 864 pages promulgated in 1992 by Pope John Paul II which sets forth the official doctrine of Roman Catholicism.[1] The Church has no analogous volume. In the nineteenth century, John Jacques attempted to synthesize Church Doctrine into a Mormon catechism, but his work did not survive and has garnered few imitators in

1. See Catholic Church, *Catechism of the Catholic Church*, 2nd ed. (New York: Doubleday, 2003).

the century or more since it was published.[2] More recently, Elder Bruce R. McConkie attempted a complete synthesis of Church Doctrine in his book *Mormon Doctrine*, but the only thing that seems clear about the doctrinal status of that work is that it is not official Church Doctrine.[3]

In an age of correlation, we seem to have an easy solution to the problem of what is Church Doctrine. Church Doctrine is simply whatever is published by the Church, perhaps subject to the caveat that it has been properly correlated. Let's call this the correlation argument. This is where our first analogy from the philosophy of law appears. During the first half of the twentieth century, a group of American thinkers known as the legal realists adopted a similarly functional answer to the question, "What is the law?" As one representative scholar in the movement wrote:

> [D]oing something about disputes . . . is the business of law. And the people who have the doing in charge, whether they be judges or sheriffs or clerks or jailers or lawyers, are officials of the law. *What these officials do about disputes is, to my mind, the law itself.*[4]

Hopefully the analogy to the correlation argument is clear. Just as in the realist view, law is simply what the judges do; in the correlation argument, Church Doctrine is simply what correlation says. The correlation argument, however, suffers from precisely the same problem as the realist conception of law. One cannot say that the law is simply what the judges do, because the judges themselves look up the law and try to follow it in rendering their decisions. Accordingly, law as what the judges do runs into a hopeless problem of circularity. The problem with the correlation argument—and with most other arguments that seek to identify Church Doctrine as simply "what X person says"—is that those on the correlation committees (and others who speak for the Church) look to Church Doctrine as the governing standard of what they are doing. In other words, in the best of all possible worlds, correlated Church statements are not Church Doctrine because they are correlated. Rather they are correlated to conform with Church Doctrine. This assumes, however,

2. See Davis Bitton, "Mormon Catechisms," in *Task Papers in Mormon History No. 14* (Salt Lake City: History Division, Historical Department, The Church of Jesus Christ of Latter-day Saints, 1976) Copy available in the Harold B. Lee Library at Brigham Young University.

3. See Bruce R. McConkie, *Mormon Doctrine*, 2nd ed. (Salt Lake City: Bookcraft, 1966), Preface ("For the work itself, I assume sole and full responsibility").

4. Karl N. Llewellyn, *The Bramble Bush: On Our Law and Its Study* (New York: Oceana Publications, 1930), 3.

that Church Doctrine exists as some body of identifiable, authoritative teachings *independent of correlation or whoever else is expounding it.* My point is not that Church Doctrine doesn't exist or that it somehow lacks authority. Nor is my point even that we are incapable of identifying clear instances of Church Doctrine. The claims that Jesus Christ is the savior of mankind and that good Latter-day Saints should not drink coffee are both uncontroversial instances of Church Doctrine. My point is that identifying the full contours of Church Doctrine presents a puzzle—a puzzle that legal philosophy can assist us in untangling.

Jurisprudential Solutions to the Problem of Church Doctrine

Jurists and political philosophers tend to ask different questions about the law. Political philosophers are largely concerned with justification. They tend to assume that the question of what the law is, is relatively simple, and they want to spend their time thinking about what sorts of laws are justified. Jurists, in contrast, know from experience that the contours of the law are frequently unclear, and determining what the law is can be as difficult as determining whether it is justified. Ultimately, the jurists' questions are of more use for thinking about how we discover Church Doctrine than the political philosophers' questions. This is because rather than seeking to determine the extent to which the law's authority is justified, the jurists seek to determine how far the law's claim of authority extends. It is this focus on form over substance that makes the juristic arguments useful for thinking about Church Doctrine. This is because the question of how we identify Church Doctrine is a formal question rather than a substantive question. We are not interested in what Church Doctrine ought to be but rather in what it actually is. Consider analogies to three jurisprudential theories: natural law, legal positivism, and law as integrity.

The idea of natural law makes its entrance into legal philosophy in the work of the ancient Stoics, and since that time the term has followed so many twists and turns and taken on so many different meanings and nuances that it is dangerous to speak of *the* natural law account of the law. Forced to hazard a brief definition, however, I think that the core of natural law can be stated as the claim that law is defined in terms of what is actually morally justified. Perhaps more importantly, natural law involves a very strong negative claim, namely that a command or rule that is immoral, no matter how official looking, is not law. Suffice it to say that this is a gross over-simplification, and that natural law does not simply identify law and morality. Natural law thinkers acknowledge that law has certain social and institutional aspects—for example, enforcement—but what they deny is that it can be defined purely by reference to its social aspect.

What would an analogous theory of Church Doctrine look like? Joseph Smith once declared, "One of the grand fundamental principles of 'Mormonism' is to receive truth let it come from whence it may,"[5] and Brigham Young taught, "'Mormonism' embraces all truth that is revealed and that is unrevealed, whether religious, political, scientific, or philosophical."[6] Young, I take it, is making a claim about the contours of Mormonism properly understood, rather than about the status of the society of Deseret in the nineteenth century (or the society of the Wasatch Front in the twenty-first century, for that matter). Mormonism, on this view, is coextensive with truth. Applying this notion to Church Doctrine, we would say that Church Doctrine is that which is true. In other words, truth acts as our criteria for identifying Church Doctrine. Just as natural law identifies law with morality, a natural law approach to the question of what is Church Doctrine identifies it with truth. There is an appealing audacity and expansiveness to this approach, but unfortunately it suffers from some basic problems.

Saying that Church Doctrine is simply coextensive with what is true cannot make sense of some very basic ways in which the concept is used. Consider once more Sister Smith's claims about the age of the earth. Imagine that Brother Young's reaction —"That is just your opinion. It is not Church Doctrine."—is prompted by the fact that he is uncertain about the age of the earth. There would be nothing shocking about Brother Young's invocation of Church Doctrine in such a situation. Faced with a doubtful situation, he is using Church Doctrine to confirm the legitimacy of his doubt. He is not required by its authority to assent to Sister Smith's position. Furthermore, it is precisely because Brother Young seems to know the contours of Church Doctrine that he knows that he is under no obligation to accept Sister Smith's claims. Yet if Church Doctrine were truth, in identifying its contours he would necessarily have laid to rest any doubts as to Sister Smith's position. Indeed, placing it outside of Church Doctrine would be tantamount to claiming that it was false. Yet this is precisely what our doubtful Brother Young refuses to do.

---

5. Joseph Fielding Smith, ed., *Teachings of the Prophet Joseph Smith* (Salt Lake City: Deseret Book Co., 1967), 313.

6. Brigham Young, *Discourses of Brigham Young*, ed. John A. Widtsoe (Salt Lake City, Deseret Book Co., 1925), 2.

The problem of Church Doctrine as truth is further undermined if we believe—as I think we are required to do—that there are issues about which Church Doctrine is silent. For example, I take it to be fairly uncontroversial that there is no Church Doctrine on the precise location of Williamsburg, Virginia. Somewhat more controversially, one can plausibly (and correctly, in my view) claim that there is no Church Doctrine on the truth or falsity of the theory of evolution.[7] No one could plausibly argue, however, that because of this, no statement about the location of Williamsburg, Virginia, (or the theory of evolution) could be true or false. The statement that "Williamsburg, Virginia, is located on the banks of the Potomac River" is clearly false, the silence of Church Doctrine notwithstanding. Nor does it make sense of our ordinary usage of the term Church Doctrine to say, "It is Church Doctrine that Williamsburg, Virginia, is on the York-James Peninsula." One might try to save the Church Doctrine as truth approach by refining it somewhat, saying that Church Doctrine is any truth that is taught by or in the Church. The refinement runs into two problems. First, it leaves unanswered the difficult question of what constitutes teaching by the Church (more on this below). Second, it still doesn't capture the way in which the concept of Church Doctrine is used. An example illustrates both points. Suppose that I am called as the gospel doctrine teacher in my ward. I then begin teaching in class that Williamsburg, Virginia, is located on the York-James Peninsula, including in my lesson a detailed discussion of the geography of the Virginia tidewater. My bishop then instructs me to stop, telling me that I should confine my teaching to Church Doctrine. Clearly his instructions do not do any violence to the ordinary usage of Church Doctrine, even though there is nothing false about my teachings. They do suggest, however, that Church Doctrine cannot be understood as any truth that is taught in the context of the Church.

Legal positivism provides a second possible analogy for Church Doctrine. According to H. L. A. Hart, an influential legal positivist, law is a system of rules. Some rules govern human behavior; for example, the rule that murder is prohibited. Some rules govern the promulgation and validity of other rules. On this view, law is ultimately defined by what

7. For the record: I think that the theory of evolution is true. I do not think that there is anything in Church Doctrine *per se* that requires this view. See generally William E. Evenson and Duane E. Jeffery, *Mormonism and Evolution: The Authoritative LDS Statements* (Salt Lake City: Greg Kofford Books, 2005).

Hart called a "rule of recognition."[8] This is a rule that allows us to differentiate those rules that are law from other rules, such as rules of manners or the rules of golf, which are not law. For example, in the United Kingdom a statute passed by the House of Commons is law. This is a rule of recognition.

Positivism provides a seemingly elegant solution to the problem of what is Church Doctrine. All that is necessary is to identify a rule of recognition for Church Doctrine. The problem is that, as a matter of social understanding, it does not appear that any such rule of recognition exists. It is tempting to look to the scriptures and the idea of canonization as a rule of recognition. On this view, Church Doctrine would consist of whatever the scriptures say. There are at least two problems with this approach. First, it is over- and under-inclusive. There are certain things that are very clearly Church Doctrine that cannot really be found in the scriptures. For example, our current understanding of the Word of Wisdom exceeds the text of the Doctrine and Covenants. The very fact that the Word of Wisdom is regarded today as a commandment is at odds with the text itself, which clearly states that it is not given by way of commandment (see D&C 89:2). The scriptures also contain many teachings that are not Church Doctrine. For example, certain aspects of the text of the Word of Wisdom—such as the prohibition on meat except in winter or time of famine—are not regarded as normative (see D&C 89:12–13). Likewise, Christ's prohibition on divorce in the Gospel of Mark does not seem to be Church Doctrine, to say nothing of the intricate rules found in the Pentateuch (see Mark 10:6–9).

The second problem with looking only to the scriptures for Church Doctrine is the problem of interpretation. Mormonism begins with a rejection of the sufficiency of scriptural interpretation standing alone. After finding himself caught up in a war of words between the rival evangelists in Palmyra, Joseph Smith noted that "the teachers of religion of the different sects understood the same passages of scripture so differently as to *destroy all confidence in settling the question by an appeal to the Bible*" (JS-H 1:11–12; emphasis added). The new revelation of the Restoration came only after the sufficiency of scripture had been rejected. As it now stands, Mormons regularly invoke the concept of Church Doctrine as an aid to the interpretation of scripture. For example, should someone teach that the text of Doctrine and Covenants 89 requires that Mormons become

8. H. L. A. Hart, *The Concept of Law*, 2nd ed. (Oxford: Clarendon Press, 1997), 100–110.

vegetarians, the standard response would be, "That is just your interpretation; it is not Church Doctrine." This points, however, to an important function of Church Doctrine. It is something that we frequently use to identify which interpretations of scripture are authoritative and which are not. This means that Church Doctrine necessarily exceeds the Standard Works standing alone.

Finally, one might look to the statements of General Authorities as providing a clear rule of recognition for Church Doctrine. Joseph Smith, however, insisted that a prophet is only a prophet when speaking as a prophet. What we lack is a clear criterion for identifying when a prophet is speaking as a prophet. For example, should we assume that everything uttered in general conference is Church Doctrine? If so, is it because the speakers in general conference are careful to make sure that they don't say anything that contradicts Church Doctrine, or because Church Doctrine simply is what is said in general conference? Furthermore, is Church Doctrine confined to some set of public statements by high Church leaders? For example, if the *General Handbook of Instructions* was modified so that abstinence from coffee was no longer necessary to qualify as worthy for a temple recommend, would such a change constitute a shift in Church Doctrine, even if it was not announced from the pulpit in general conference? The fact that we do not have clear answers to these questions suggests to me that we lack a clear rule of recognition for what constitutes Church Doctrine. This does not mean, of course, that the words of scripture and modern prophets are without authority. It simply means that a statement does not become Church Doctrine by virtue of being uttered by any particular Church leader or even by virtue of being printed in the Standard Works. Nor does it mean that the various potential rules of recognition that we might propose are wrong per se. All of these rules can help to orient us toward Church Doctrine. However, they cannot provide a fool-proof way of identifying Church Doctrine in every case.

Law as Integrity and Church Doctrine

"Law as integrity" provides an attractive alternative to the analogy of legal positivism. This approach begins with so-called "easy cases," situations where what the law consists of and what it demands is more or less clear and obvious. For example, we know that the US Constitution's requirement that the president be at least 35 years of age can be identified as the law without recourse to any elaborate theory of what law is. Such obviously true legal propositions abound: Lower courts are bound to apply the holdings of higher courts; the 1964 Civil Rights Act clearly forbids a Hilton from refusing to serve a patron because he or she is Black; after centuries of accumulated precedent, many common-law rules, like the requirement that a will have two witnesses, are beyond serious question. The vast majority of legal disputes involve such "easy cases." We only require a theory of "What is the law?" when we are faced with what Ronald Dworkin has called "hard cases."[9] In these situations the scope of the law is unclear, and we are hard-pressed to identify its demands. Dworkin imagines how a perfect judge, who he names Hercules, would decide such a case.[10] According to Dworkin, Hercules would survey the vast mass of clear and easy law relating to the issue. He would then construct an account that makes sense of all of this material. Any theory of law must do this because the clear and easy law is binding, hence his interpretation must fit and justify it.

Dworkin gives the example of the English case of *McLaughlin v. O'Brian*.[11] The case involved a woman who sued a negligent driver for damages for emotional distress. The woman was not in the car accident and had not been physically injured in any way. Rather, she was called to the hospital where she learned that her husband and daughter had been killed. Previous English cases had awarded damages for emotional distress but only in cases where the plaintiff had actually witnessed the injury or had come upon a loved one's corpse at the scene of the accident.[12] The question presented by *McLaughlin* was whether or not these cases authorized damages in a situation where emotional distress was removed from the scene of the accident to the more antiseptic setting of the hospital.

In deciding a case like *McLaughlin*, Hercules does not simply decide whether he believes, all things considered, that recovery for emotional distress in this situation is a good idea. Rather he begins with the earlier cases. Suppose, for example, that Hercules believes that any recovery for emotional distress would be misguided. He thinks that it is a bad policy and that the moral arguments in favor of compensating emotional distress are weak. He cannot, however, simply apply this judgment to McLaughlin's case, be-

9. Ronald Dworkin, "Hard Cases," in *Taking Rights Seriously* (Cambridge: Harvard University Press, 1978), 81.

10. Ronald Dworkin, *Law's Empire* (Cambridge: Belknap Press, 1986), 239–40.

11. [1983] 1 A.C. 410, reversing [1981] Q.B. 599.

12. See Marshall v. Kionel Enterprises Inc., [1971] O.R. 177, Chadwick v. British Transport, [1967] 1 W.L.R. 912.

cause the previous decisions by which he is bound clearly reject his position by awarding damages. Nor may he simply hold that the previous decisions were mistaken and that from now on no damages for emotional distress will be awarded.[13] Rather, Hercules must look at the previously decided cases and construct the best possible argument he can to justify them. In justifying them, he looks not only at the outcomes in the cases, but also to the reasons offered by the previous judges. He must also account for these reasons, although in constructing the best possible justification for the previous cases he will necessarily recharacterize the reasoning of previous judges. Thus, the arguments in support of the holdings evolve over time. In *McLaughlin*, Hercules would draw on the best possible understanding that he has of policy and political morality to justify the conclusion that those who witness the death of a loved one should be compensated, and he would then decide if those arguments justify giving the wife and mother of accident victims compensation when she learns of the deaths in a hospital. Hercules's interpretation involves normative judgments, but it is not simply a matter of *his* normative judgments. Rather, discovering what the law requires in a particular case is a matter of giving force to the latent normative judgments of previous, controlling precedents. Put another way, to discover the law in a "hard case," a judge creates a story that makes sense of the clearly established cases and then fits the new case into that story in a way that places the whole in the best possible light.

In my view, thinking of Church Doctrine as an analogous kind of interpretation provides the best account of how we discover it. The advantage of this view is that it does not require that we have any clear idea about the rule of recognition. It simply requires that we have some easily identifiable core cases of Church Doctrine from which we can reason. This is precisely the situation in which we find ourselves. We can easily

---

13. This is true even though common-law courts can overrule previous decisions. The issue of overruling precedent is a complicated question beyond the scope of this chapter. Suffice it to say that courts do not simply reject precedent when they disagree with it, but rather they overrule a previous case only when subsequent decisions decided under it severely undermine its holding and rationale. For example, in *Brown v. Board of Education*, which struck down racial segregation in primary-level public schools, the Supreme Court reversed its previous decision in *Plessy v. Ferguson*, which announced the principle of "separate but equal." However, prior to *Brown* the Court had decided a series of cases—mainly striking down segregation in higher public education—that undermined *Plessy*'s holding.

imagine that Brother Young and Sister Smith have very different opinions about the rule of recognition for Church Doctrine. For example, Brother Young might believe that Church Doctrine consists only of texts formally canonized by a vote in general conference, while Sister Smith might regard any public sermon by a member of the Quorum of the Twelve as Church Doctrine. Both of them agree, however, that it is Church Doctrine that Jesus Christ is the savior of mankind and that Latter-day Saints should not drink coffee. When faced with a new question about Church Doctrine, rather than trying to determine which of them has the correct rule of recognition, they can simply reason on the basis of clear cases, fitting the new question into a story that will place things in the best possible light. More importantly, I think that this is how most Mormons actually use the concept of Church Doctrine. To be sure, Latter-day Saints point to authoritative statements in support of their claim that this or that proposition or rule of conduct is Church Doctrine. However, all of these claims are made against a background of teachings, experiences, and texts that they seek to accommodate and charitably characterize. It is their interpretation of the totality that produces their conclusions about what is or is not Church Doctrine.

There are obviously important ways in which Church Doctrine as integrity is different than law as integrity. A judge faced with a case does not have the luxury of not resolving the question presented. Once the parties have concluded the litigation, the judge is required to declare one of the parties a winner. In centuries gone by a judge could rule *dubitante*, simply declaring that the law was unclear and leaving the case undecided, but this is no longer allowed. Accordingly, a jurisprudential theory requires that the law be complete in the sense of providing some definitive answer to any case that can be posed to it. Even in hard cases there are answers, and the law is without gaps. Church Doctrine, however, doesn't labor under the same institutional imperatives as the law. Sometimes—often—the best interpretation of Mormon texts, practices, and history will be *dubitante*: We simply don't know. Even here, however, the process of interpretation will discipline our ignorance. Mormon texts, practices, and history will foreclose certain answers even while they make other answers more likely, all the while not definitively laying the matter to rest. Hence, on some questions—such as the location of towns in the Virginia tidewater—Church Doctrine is simply silent. On other questions, however, the answer might be something like, "Well, under Church Doctrine there are a couple of possible answers . . ."

For example, the precise meaning of the term "intelligence" as it is used in the scriptures is notoriously vague. Bruce R. McConkie suggested that "intelligence" consisted of some sort of pre-sentient stuff from which spirits are organized.[14] B. H. Roberts thought that "intelligences" were the eternal, self-existent, self-aware cores of the spirit that could neither be created nor destroyed.[15] Perhaps most esoterically, Orson Pratt suggested that "intelligence" was an elemental fluid of divinity that pervaded, to a greater and lesser extent, the entire universe.[16] (Blake Ostler has recently articulated a philosophically sophisticated modern version of Pratt's position.[17]) I take it that none of these positions can be identified as the authoritative approach of Church Doctrine to the question. They all fit and justify Mormon texts, practices, and history to a greater or lesser extent. On the other hand, Church Doctrine *does* foreclose certain theories of intelligence. For example, the consistent rejection of the doctrine of ex nihilo creation by Mormon scriptures and authorities would foreclose the idea that Church Doctrine can accommodate the view that "intelligence" refers to some spirit substance created from nothing by God through an act of divine fiat.

The question of whether Diet Coke is prohibited by the Word of Wisdom provides an example of how we discover Church Doctrine. We start with the brute fact that we all agree that the Word of Wisdom is Church Doctrine and that it forbids drinking coffee, tea, and alcohol. What would be the best story that one could tell about this? One story would be to say that it is a health code designed to prohibit the ingestion of bad substances.[18] Thus we look at alcohol and caffeine and use them as touchstones for Word of Wisdom compliance. On this view, chocolate and Diet Coke, both of which contain caffeine, are out. There are a number

---

14. McConkie's views are summarized (with sources) in Blake Ostler, "The Idea of Pre-Existence in Mormon Thought," *Dialogue: A Journal of Mormon Thought* 15, no. 1 (Spring 1982): 59, 72.

15. B. H. Roberts, "The Immortality of Man," in *B. H. Roberts Scrapbook*, vol. 2., comp. Lynn Pulsipher (Provo: Pulsipher Publishing, 1991), 21, 26.

16. Orson Pratt, "The Holy Spirit," in *The Essential Orson Pratt*, ed. David Whittaker (Salt Lake City: Signature Books, 1991).

17. Blake Ostler, "Re-Visioning the Mormon Concept of Deity," *Element: A Journal of Mormon Philosophy and Theology* 1, no. 1 (Spring 2005).

18. For an extremely influential version of this interpretation, see John Andreas Widtsoe and Leah D. Widtsoe, *The Word of Wisdom: A Modern Interpretation* (Salt Lake City: Deseret Book Co., 1937).

of problems with this interpretation. For example, the schedule of prohibited substances is strangely random from a purely health-oriented point of view. Why condemn excessive meat consumption but not excessive sugar consumption? Why explicitly include relatively harmless substances like tea or coffee but not narcotics? One might offer the argument that they didn't have such drugs in the nineteenth century when Section 89 was given. This, however, is historically inaccurate. The nineteenth century was well acquainted with narcotics like opium. Furthermore, the current interpretation of "hot drinks" as meaning tea and coffee (but not herb tea) didn't gel until the twentieth century, so it is not clear why nineteenth-century practice should control their consumption. Given these difficulties, one could conclude that the bad-substances interpretation doesn't provide the best account of the rules. A better account is that the prohibition is meant as a reminder or symbol of the covenant that one makes with God and an open-ended admonition to be healthy. This explains the seemingly arbitrary schedule of prohibited substances. As symbols, they are arbitrary in the same way that using the shape "A" to designate the sound "ahhh" is arbitrary. It also explains the rise of the Word of Wisdom as a central part of Mormon identity in the 1930s. As outward reminders of Mormons' status as a "peculiar people" in the form of things like polygamy or the United Order retreated in the face of intense outside pressure, the Word of Wisdom provided a workable mark of the covenant. On this reading, however, the prohibition of hot drinks cannot be reduced to a prohibition of caffeine that then extends to Diet Coke. It does suggest, however, that one should avoid consumption—including the consumption of Diet Coke—that is bad for one's health.

Some Implications of Church Doctrine as Integrity: Historical Interpretation

This interpretation of the Word of Wisdom may or may not be correct, but it does illustrate how applying an interpretive approach to the problem of Church Doctrine would work. This approach also casts light on two persistent intellectual issues within Mormonism: historical interpretation and the role of personal judgment in following Church Doctrine. The Word of Wisdom example illustrates how an interpretive approach makes sense of history and change in Church Doctrine. The notion of Church Doctrine as a story whose totality must be accounted for with a new chapter fits in nicely with Mormon ideas of continuing revelation (e.g., A of F 9) and with the reality of evolution in Mormon thought.[19] The requirement that the story be told in a way that places it in the best possible light also accounts for the persistent tendency of Mormons to understand their own history in the rosiest of possible terms. Generally, this approach to Mormon history has been characterized as simple apologetics and chalked up to naiveté or perhaps dishonesty.[20] Seeing the discovery of Church Doctrine as an exercise in interpretation, however, suggests that the goal of much of Mormon discussion of history is neither history nor apologetics. Rather it is a search for what is normative and what is not. In seeking to understand their past in the best possible light, Mormons are trying to understand which parts of that past have a claim on them and which parts do not. The stories function less as historical explanations or even "faith promoting" narratives than as an exercise in the discovery of Church Doctrine.

This is not meant as a historical apology for traditional Mormon history. No doubt the search for the normative in Mormon history obscures a great deal and creates a distorted view of the past. If our goal is to understand fully—in so far as we are able—the nature of historical events, then we will need to consider and offer interpretations that will not fit into the narrative of Church Doctrine. Neither historical explanations nor the doctrinal search for the normative in the Mormon past are illegitimate. They are, however, different sorts of endeavors, although Mormons are seldom clear—even in their own minds—about which exercise they are engaged in.[21] For example, the explanation for the twentieth-century rise in the importance of the Word of Wisdom offered above uses the interpretation of the past as a way of discovering the current contours of normativity. It may or may not be an accurate or compelling historical explanation. Indeed, it obscures things that a fully realized historical explanation should consider. For example, a purely historical explanation would take into account Heber J. Grant's life-long affiliation with the temperance movement and his failure to keep Utah from casting the deciding

19. See Thomas Alexander, "The Reconstruction of Mormon Doctrine," in *Line Upon Line: Essays on Mormon Doctrine*, ed. Gary James Bergera (Salt Lake City: Signature Books, 1989), 53.

20. See D. Michael Quinn, "On Being a Mormon Historian (And Its Aftermath)," in *Faithful History: Essays on Writing Mormon History*, ed. George D. Smith (Salt Lake City: Signature Books, 1992), 69.

21. Hence this chapter.

vote to repeal Prohibition.[22] It would also consider the role that the economic imperatives of pioneer Utah played into the emphasis on the Word of Wisdom.[23] And so on. However, despite superficial appearances, my interpretation of the Word of Wisdom is not offered as a historical account at all. Rather it is seeking to understand history only in a very narrow and specific way, namely as a part of the current structure of authoritative Church Doctrine. To paraphrase Dworkin:

> [The discovery of Church Doctrine] begins in the present and pursues the past only so far as and in the way its contemporary focus dictates. It does not aim to recapture, even for present [Church Doctrine], the ideals or practical purposes of the [authorities] who first created it. It aims rather to justify what they did (sometimes including what they said) in an overall story worth telling now, a story with a complex claim: that present practice can be organized by and justified in principles sufficiently attractive to provide an honorable future.[24]

Some Implications of Church Doctrine as Integrity: Obedience and Personal Judgment

This approach also provides a more nuanced understanding of the relationship between individual judgment and following Church Doctrine. To see how, we must understand that on this view Church Doctrine is inherently contestable. This doesn't mean that doctrinal questions are without correct answers.[25] Indeed this interpretive approach necessarily assumes that many aspects of Church Doctrine are clear. Rather, it means that we can always have disagreements about certain aspects of what

---

22. For a discussion of Heber J. Grant's involvement in temperance politics and Prohibition, see Loman Franklin Aydelotte, "The Political Thought and Activity of Heber J. Grant, Seventh President of The Church of Jesus Christ of Latter-Day Saints" (master's thesis, Brigham Young University, 1965).

23. See Leonard J. Arrington, "An Economic Interpretation of the 'Word of Wisdom,'" *Brigham Young University Studies* 1, no. 1 (1959): 37. Arrington argues that Brigham Young emphasized compliance with the Word of Wisdom as a way of dealing with excessive imports of tobacco and other products from outside of Utah.

24. Dworkin, *Law's Empire*, 227–28 (substituting the term "the discovery of Church Doctrine" for "law" and "authorities" for "politicians").

25. Dworkin argues that there are right answers to inherently contestable legal questions in Ronald Dworkin, "Is There Really No Right Answer in Hard Cases," in *A Matter of Principle* (Cambridge: Harvard University Press, 1985), 119.

Church Doctrine requires and that the only way of doctrinally settling these disagreements will be by resorting to complex arguments about the best possible story to be told. It is important to understand that when I say that certain aspects of Church Doctrine are inherently contestable, I am not talking about disagreements over whether Church Doctrine is true or whether it should be followed. Rather I am talking about disagreements over the *content* of Church Doctrine itself. This inherent contestability is illustrated by the fact that the Church's solution to the practical problems created by doctrinal disputes is not a clear and mechanical rule for discovering what is Church Doctrine. We lack an intellectual formula for escaping the demands of interpretation. Instead, the coping mechanisms are essentially moral and institutional.

Morally, we are to discuss Church Doctrine with charity and unity, avoiding "contention." In the Book of Mormon, the risen Christ teaches, "For verily, verily I say unto you, he that hath the spirit of contention is not of me, but is of the devil, who is the father of contention, and he stirreth up the hearts of men to content with anger, one with another" (3 Ne. 11:28–29). This is not a philosophical Rosetta Stone that allows us to transparently identify authoritative Church Doctrine. This fact suggests that the primary danger of the contestability of Church Doctrine is not epistemic. It is not that we will be mistaken. Rather, it is moral and social. It is the danger of rancor, discord, and a loss of unity. Accordingly, we have a solution in the form of a moral injunction about social interactions—in this case doctrinal discussions—rather than an intellectual method for resolving doctrinal disputes.

In addition to a morality of doctrinal discussion, we have institutional solutions to the practical difficulties of doctrinal disagreements. Return once again to the initial disagreement between Sister Smith and Brother Young. Imagine that Sister Smith is called as a gospel doctrine teacher and begins vociferously teaching her anti-evolution views during class. Brother Young suggests to her that she should stop teaching her opinions as Church Doctrine. Sister Smith indignantly replies that her views on the age of the earth *are* Church Doctrine, insisting that she holds them precisely for this reason. Both parties take the dispute to their bishop. He asks that Sister Smith confine her lesson more closely to the text of the assigned scriptures. Such a solution to Sister Smith's and Brother Young's doctrinal disagreement is entirely institutional. Indeed, it needn't take a doctrinal position at all on the resolution of the dispute. The bishop's decision controls in this situation not because he has privileged access to Church Doctrine per se but simply because he is the bishop. In this sense, the hierarchy of the Church, with its accompanying notions of stewardship and jurisdiction, renders a theory that incontestably identifies Church Doctrine unnecessary.[26] The success of the ethical and institutional methods of coping with doctrinal disagreement underscores the inherent contestability of Church Doctrine. Given the proper attitude and institutional structure, the contestability seems to be something that we can live with. Nevertheless, the contestability remains.

The source of this inherent contestability lies in the fact that we can only discover Church Doctrine by finding the best possible story that can be told about the texts, practices, and history of Mormonism. Not only is this process of interpretation complicated, but the principle of charity means that it necessarily involves normative judgments that are inherently contestable. This does not mean, however, that discovering Church Doctrine is a free-wheeling exercise in normative reasoning. Such a view fails to appreciate the difference between judging what would make the best story about a particular set of phenomena and simply judging what would be best. Discovering Church Doctrine requires that we make sense of clear instances of Church Doctrine and their context (contemporary and historical). This interpretive requirement forecloses certain possibilities. For example, suppose that I come to believe—after careful consideration—that the best way of memorializing gospel covenants in our lives would be to eat only white food, since whiteness denotes purity and ingestion is a powerful way of symbolizing how we take the gospel into our very being.[27] Whatever the merits of this practice, it is not Church Doctrine. It does not purport to offer an interpretation of the teachings and practices of the Church. In contrast, the interpretation of the Word of Wisdom

---

26. Robert Cover made an analogous legal point about the interaction of institutions and interpretation, arguing for what he called a jurispathic theory of law. On Cover's theory, citizens produce a vast welter of interpretations about what their laws require. The role of the courts is to kill off some of these interpretations in order to resolve concrete disputes. Ironically, Cover used—inter alia—the example of Mormon interpretations of the Constitution. See Robert M. Cover, "Foreword: Nomos and Narrative Supreme Court 1982 Term," *Harvard Law Review* 97, no. 1 (1983): 51 ("The long process leading up to Utah's statehood was, from the Mormon perspective, an exploration of the degree of resistance required by religious obligation and the realities of power").

27. Something like this view was common among early Christians.

that I offered above assumes that the Word of Wisdom is an authority that forecloses, for example, the modest and healthy consumption of wine.

The precise nature of the link between the authority of Church Doctrine and the need to tell the best possible story about it is complicated. The search for the best possible story is not offered as an account of the authority of Church Doctrine. It does not aim at fully justifying it. Such a justification must come from elsewhere, and its nature is beyond the scope of this chapter.[28] Suffice it to say that the source of the authority of Church Doctrine likely lies in covenants, priesthood power, the privileged access of prophets to the divine, and the needs of the Saints as a community. These are all normative grounds separate from the particular stories that we tell about particular doctrines.[29] However, the authority of Church Doctrine does require that we look at it in the best possible light. Such an approach acknowledges that Church Doctrine is something with a claim upon us, something normative.

Hence, following Church Doctrine does not constitute an abdication of independent moral judgment, as has been so often suggested. Following Church Doctrine does mean subordinating one's independent substantive judgments on an issue to which Church Doctrine speaks. Yet understanding what Church Doctrine requires is not a mechanical process. Acknowledging the authority of Church Doctrine means committing oneself to discovering its demands. Yet this process of discovery will necessarily involve making independent judgments about what provides the best possible story to be told about the totality of known doctrines. Put another way, independent of its legitimacy or justification, *discovering* the bounds of authority is at least in part a normative inquiry that requires our independent judgment. Even in obedience we "must be as gods, knowing good and evil" (Moses 4:11).[30]

---

28. See Nathan B. Oman, "A Defense of the Authority of Church Doctrine," *Dialogue: A Journal of Mormon Thought* 40, no. 4 (Winter 2007): 1–28.

29. Although to be sure, the grounds of Church Doctrine's authority no doubt have their role to play in understanding this or that question about its contours.

30. To be clear, I do not claim that the discussion offered above exhausts the issues presented by the interaction of personal judgment and authority, or even that it answers all of the most pressing questions raised by it. Rather, my claim is that it puts to rest the notion that following Church Doctrine is intellectual or morally lazy, involving an abdication of personal judgment. Such judgment is always necessary.

Conclusion

My goal in this chapter has not been to reform or critique the way that Mormons use the concept of Church Doctrine. Rather, I have tried to elucidate what I take to be the underlying logic of their practice. Hence, the interpretive approach that I draw by analogy from the philosophy of law is not offered as something new. Rather, I think that on this point Mormons are rather like the man who discovers that he has been speaking prose all his life. Analogizing the question of how we know if something is Church Doctrine to the question of how we know if something is law, however, does allow us to bring certain issues into sharper focus. First, it allows us to recognize that we lack a rule of recognition for what is Church Doctrine. Second, it provides us with a way of understanding why this is not a serious theoretical objection to our current practice. Finally, by revealing the inherently interpretive nature of discovering Church Doctrine, it hopefully sheds light on some of our other institutional and theoretical practices.

CHAPTER 3

A Defense of the Authority of Church Doctrine

Authority is a key concept in Mormonism. If one were to ask most Mormons what makes their religion different from ordinary Christianity, many—perhaps most—would respond that Mormons believe in continuing revelation, modern prophets, additional scripture, and the restoration of priesthood powers. All of these stock elements in Mormonism involve claims of one sort or another to special authority. Given the central place that the concept of authority occupies in Mormonism, there has been surprisingly little disciplined reflection about the concept among Mormon intellectuals and scholars.[1] This chapter seeks to begin filling this gap by asking a fairly simple question: "Can the authority of Church Doctrine be justified?" My conclusion is that, given a fairly weak[2] set of assumptions, a number of arguments justify the authority of Church Doctrine over believing Latter-day Saints.

In exploring these arguments, I hope to illuminate some of the issues with which Mormon thinkers must grapple if they are to make sense of the important concept of authority in their theology. My project in this chapter, however, is limited. I do not purport to be talking about all aspects of authority within Mormonism. In particular, I am not addressing the personal authority of the leaders of the Church per se, nor am I trying to grapple with the idea of priesthood. Rather, this chapter

1. To be sure, many good and eloquent things have been said by Mormon thinkers about the tensions between authority and the intellect. Indeed, there is something of a cottage industry among Mormon intellectuals in talking and thinking about their relationship with the authorities of the Church. For a particularly thoughtful example of the genre, see Armand L. Mauss, "Alternate Voices: The Calling and Its Implications," *Sunstone*, April 1990.

2. I use the term "weak" here in its logical sense of meaning assumptions that apparently contain very little content in relationship to the conclusions that they support. In contrast, "strong" assumptions virtually restate the conclusion that they are meant to support. An argument based on "strong" assumptions shows us very little beyond the initial premises themselves. In contrast, an argument based on "weak" assumptions shows us much more. My hope is that the assumptions on which the arguments in this chapter are based are "weak" enough for the arguments themselves to be independently illuminating.

is concerned with a particular kind of authority—namely, the authority of Church Doctrine. Finally, I do not seek to justify the authority of Church Doctrine to religious skeptics. My goal is not to convert the unconverted but rather to show that many of the intuitions and implicit assumptions of ordinary Latter-day Saints with regard to the authority of Church Doctrine can be made explicit and justified by arguments resting on premises that are widely shared among Mormons.

Mormons regularly invoke the idea of Church Doctrine to differentiate between those teachings and practices that have some claim on them and those teachings and practices that are merely opinions or suggestions. For example, Heber might claim that evolution is a false and evil teaching. Brigham then responds by saying, "That is just your opinion. That is not Church Doctrine." Likewise, Brigham might suggest that the Word of Wisdom, properly understood, requires abstention from all meat. Heber then responds by saying, "That is just your interpretation. That is not Church Doctrine." The clear implication in both exchanges is that, were the opinion or practice in question Church Doctrine, it would have a claim on Heber or Brigham that it does not otherwise have.

I have presented arguments elsewhere about the problem of identifying what is or is not Church Doctrine.[3] Rather than restating those arguments here, I will simply restate my conclusions. Mormons lack a clear rule that allows them to identify what is or is not Church Doctrine. The various possibilities—teachings that have been formally added to the standard works, statements that have been formally accepted in general conference, statements that have been made by prophets and apostles in the appropriate context, etc.—all turn out to be over- or under-inclusive when examined in detail. To be sure, all of these proposed rules are useful in orienting us toward Church Doctrine, even if they are not foolproof methods for identifying it. Nevertheless, we do have unambiguous cases of Church Doctrine. It is clearly Church Doctrine that Jesus Christ is the Savior of humankind and that Mormons should not drink coffee or alcohol. Rather than relying on a rule of recognition for identifying Church Doctrine, Mormons rely on a hermeneutic approach. We determine what is or is not Church Doctrine by offering interpretations—stories, if you will—that seek to make sense of clear instances of Church Doctrine against the backdrop of Mormon scriptures, teachings, history, and prac-

3. See Nathan B. Oman, "Jurisprudence and the Problem of Church Doctrine," *Element: The Journal of the Society for Mormon Philosophy and Theology* 2, no. 1 (2006): 1–19.

tices. In offering this interpretation, we seek to present Mormon texts, practices, and history in the best possible light, not for any apologetic purpose but rather because, in seeking what is normative, we reject interpretations that we would regard as normatively less attractive. This does not mean that Church Doctrine is simply a matter of what we think is best. It is not. It is a matter of charitably interpreting Mormon practices, texts, and experience.

Because this is a complicated and inherently normative task, the precise contours of Church Doctrine are always contestable. This characterization needn't imply that there are no right answers to the question of whether something is Church Doctrine. It simply means that we are unlikely to arrive at a formula that will allow us to definitively answer the question in every circumstance. Rather than relying on an intellectual formula, the Church seems to cope with the potential problems of doctrinal disagreements ethically and institutionally. Ethically, we are told not to contend in anger about points of doctrine. Institutionally, the practical difficulties of doctrinal disagreement can be resolved by the fiat of whoever has the stewardship for a particular institutional setting. Thus, doctrinal discussions in a ward Sunday School class are "managed" by an ethic of being charitable to one another in our disagreement and by the bishop's ability to direct teachers to teach in a particular way or to release them from their callings. Neither of these coping mechanisms, however, requires that we have a formula for incontestably laying to rest what is or is not Church Doctrine in every case.

Given this understanding of Church Doctrine (and it is the understanding that I will assume for the rest of this article), can its authority be justified? Ultimately, I believe that the answer is yes, but to understand why, we must first have a clearer notion of what we mean by authority.

The Nature of Authority

Ultimately, authority is a form of reason giving. The manifest successes of philosophical modernism and philosophical liberalism, both of which rest to a greater or lesser extent on overt hostility to the notion of authority, however, can make it difficult to recognize this fact. Indeed, for some people authority seems like the antithesis of reason giving. The oddity of authority as a form of reason giving comes from the fact that authority offers a peculiar kind of reason. Consider the following dialogue.

Heber: I think that drinking wine should be fine for everyone. Alcohol needn't be destructive if it's consumed in moderation, and science has shown that modest amounts of wine are good for your heart.

Brigham: True enough, and I suppose that makes sense. However, as a matter of Church Doctrine, Mormons must abstain from alcohol. Therefore, Mormons ought not to drink wine.

Heber offers two reasons for his conclusion, namely that moderate alcohol consumption isn't destructive and can actually help one's heart. Brigham denies his conclusion, but he doesn't deny Heber's reasons. Indeed, he concedes that they are true. Rather, he offers Church Doctrine as a reason for reaching the opposite conclusion. Yet on its face, Church Doctrine does not consist of a denial of the truth of Heber's reasons. Rather, the way that Brigham invokes Church Doctrine suggests that Heber's reasons simply don't matter. The authority of Church Doctrine excludes them.

In his classic work on the concept of authority, Oxford philosopher Joseph Raz focused on this exclusionary quality of authoritative reasons. When one offers authority as a reason, he argued, it interacts with other reasons in a special way. It simply excludes them. For this reason, Raz spoke of authority as an "exclusionary" reason. He wrote: "There is a sense in which if one accepts the legitimacy of an authority one is committed to following it blindly. One can be very watchful that it shall not overstep its authority and be sensitive to the presence of non-excluded considerations. But barring these possibilities, one is to follow the authority regardless of one's view of the merits of the case (that is blindly). One may form a view on the merits but so long as one follows the authority this is an academic exercise of no practical importance."[4]

Hence, the denial of authority consists not in disagreement with it, but rather in the denial that an authority has the ability to exclude other reasons. Likewise, to accept an authority involves more than simply agreeing with it. Paradoxically, one can agree with everything that an authority claims and nevertheless deny that it is an authority. At the same time, one can disagree with everything that an authority says and yet still accept it as authoritative.

---

4. Joseph Raz, *The Authority of Law: Essays on Law and Morality*, 2nd ed. (New York: Oxford University Press, 2009), 24–25. I take it that, in the quoted paragraph, Raz is using "practical" in its philosophical sense of "relating to action" rather than in its more general sense of "useful." Nothing about Raz's theory suggests that thinking about authority is useless.

We can identify Church Doctrine as a species of authority precisely because it purports to be an exclusionary reason. This fact provides us with a structure for our arguments about its possible authority. In order to show that the authority of Church Doctrine is justified, we need to have arguments for why it should act as an exclusionary reason. This, in turn, means that we cannot justify the authority of Church Doctrine solely by reference to its substantive content. For example, one cannot defend the authority of the Word of Wisdom by marshalling arguments for its beneficial health effects. Indeed, if it were possible to compile an exhaustive catalog of every Church Doctrine and then one by one offer arguments in support of their substantive content, one would not have demonstrated the authority of Church Doctrine. In a sense, each of these arguments would consist of a rejection of the question of authority, and all that their success would produce would be accidental agreement with Church Doctrine. Put in concrete terms, a person who abstains from tobacco because he or she believes that it is harmful does not thereby accept the authority of the Word of Wisdom.

The key question for the authority of Church Doctrine thus comes in justifying its claims in those cases where we are otherwise disposed to reject its substantive conclusions. The question is vital for both practical and philosophical reasons. Practically, it is of importance because it is precisely in those cases that Church Doctrine is potentially the most valuable. To the extent that Church Doctrine simply tracks my substantive beliefs, there is a sense in which it is not really all that practically important to me. Furthermore, if I am willing to grant legitimacy to the claims of Church Doctrine only in those cases where I already substantively agree with it, there is a sense in which it lacks any power to teach or change me. It is those instances where I find myself in disagreement with the substantive content of Church Doctrine that it has the real possibility of altering or changing my beliefs and behaviors.

Philosophically, the point at which we disagree with the substantive content of Church Doctrine is key because this is the point at which we are confronted with the question of its authority. Accordingly, any argument for the authority of Church Doctrine must meet a simple test. It must justify the claim of Church Doctrine over Latter-day Saints in precisely those cases where they are otherwise disposed to believe or act differently. Such an argument must therefore be independent of the substantive content of Church Doctrine in any particular instance. Only by being substance-neutral can the argument provide an exclusionary reason. For example, suppose that one believes that—all things being equal—women should have absolutely symmetrical institutional authority with men. An argument for the authority of Church Doctrine would justify the denial of the priesthood to women without reference to why the practice is substantively desirable.

There are at least three such arguments for the authority of Church Doctrine that meet this criterion of substantive neutrality: the argument from covenant, the argument from epistemic advantage, and the argument from community participation.

The Argument from Covenant

The first basis for the authority of Church Doctrine is covenant. Promises, like authority, provide exclusionary reasons for acting. Consider another dialogue between Heber and Brigham.

> Brigham: We should go to Emma's birthday party. She has been very kind to us, and I think that it would make her happy if we went.
>
> Heber: I agree. Unfortunately, I have already promised to attend Eliza's birthday party, which is at the same time.

The structure of the reasons in this dialogue should be familiar. Brigham has offered reasons for acting that Heber accepts in the abstract. Yet his abstract agreement has become "an academic exercise of no practical importance." The reason is that Brigham's reasons have been excluded from Heber's consideration by the force of Heber's promise. Promises, however, have other qualities beyond the exclusionary nature of the reasons that they offer. Most prominently, they seem to have the ability to transform wholly unrequired action into an obligation. Even assuming that Heber has no other relationship with Eliza, his promise is sufficient enough to create an obligation to attend her party.

Some theorists of promising have found this bootstrap quality of promising unacceptable, proposing theories of promise-keeping that link the obligation to keep a promise to the promise's substantive content. For example, medieval jurists argued that, in making a promise, we are always seeking some end. The obligation to keep a promise is linked to the end that the promise-maker is pursuing. Hence, for example, a promise that has the goal to further the torture of innocent babies does not create an obligation. On the other hand, a promise whose end is the expression of some virtue, such as generosity or kindness, does create an obligation.[5]

Other theorists have embraced promissory bootstrapping. In particular, writers in the tradition of liberal political philosophy have argued that the force of a promise is an extension of a commitment to personal freedom, allowing people the liberty of, in effect, creating their own moral universe.[6] Indeed, promise-making has proved so attractive a normative basis for liberal thinkers that those in the social contract tradition have sought to show that virtually *all* political obligations—and perhaps social obligations as well—can be founded on the power of promises.[7]

Both of these approaches, however, see promises as providing exclusionary reasons.[8] It is true that the teleological theories of promise-making offered by medieval jurists did not see the obligations of promises as independent of their ends. This doesn't mean, however, that they believed that promissory obligations lacked the ability to trump other reasons. Rather, in effect they claimed that to promise for an unworthy end constituted a kind of failure, analogous to the person who attempts to make a promise but because of some misadventure does not do so. The wicked-ended promise attempts to create obligations but fails to do so. On the other hand, a morally successful promise does, in this view, create ordinary promissory obligations. The liberal theory of promising, of course, is premised on acceptance of the exclusionary nature of promises. It simply disagrees with the older, medieval theory about the conditions necessary to create a morally successful promise.

At numerous points in their religious lives, Mormons make covenants, which, at least in part, take the form of promises. Provided that we can legitimately interpret those covenants as containing a promise to accept the normative claims of Church Doctrine, then they provide an argument that meets the conditions set forth above for a successful theory of Church Doctrine's authority. A promise explains why Church Doctrine requires

---

5. For the most detailed modern discussion of the development of these ideas, see James Gordley, *The Philosophical Origins of Modern Contract Doctrine* (New York: Oxford University Press, 1993).

6. See, e.g., Charles Fried, *Contract as Promise: A Theory of Contractual Obligation* (Cambridge: Harvard University Press, 1981).

7. See, e.g., John Locke, *Two Treaties of Government*, ed. Peter Laslett (New York: Cambridge University Press, 1989).

8. They do not, of course, necessarily use the terminology used here, which was developed by Joseph Raz in the 1970s.

us to reject otherwise compelling reasons and does so independent of the particular content of Church Doctrine—although, in the teleological view of promising, the underlying end for which one enters covenants does matter.

We are therefore presented with two questions. First, do Mormon covenants contain a promise to accept Church Doctrine? Second, do Mormons in fact successfully make such promises? The first question goes to the meaning of the covenants that Mormons make. The second goes to conditions under which they enter their covenants.

There are three main contexts in which Mormons make covenants: baptism, the sacrament of the Lord's Supper, and the temple. A fourth possibility is when Mormons sustain their leaders in ward, stake, and general conferences. The first and most obvious objection is to point out that nowhere in any of these rituals do words to the effect "I promise to submit to Church Doctrine" explicitly appear. Despite its initial plausibility, however, this objection is considerably less powerful than it appears. Its problem lies in the fact that the meaning of our linguistic acts frequently—indeed, almost always—exceeds our explicit statements. There are at least two important ways in which this happens. First, there may simply be a well-established but implicit understanding of certain actions. Second, linguistic action will include some assumptions that are necessary for it to be successful, even if these assumptions are not necessarily a part of our social understanding.

Consider two separate situations. In the first situation, Heber, Brigham, Eliza, and Emma are sitting around. Heber suspects that one of them has earlier received a plane ticket to New York in the mail, but he does not know which one it was. He asks, "Are any of you going to New York?" Brigham replies, "Yes. I will go to New York next week." In the second situation, Heber asks Eliza if she will go to New York and find his lost friend. He extends his hand to Eliza and asks, "Will you go to New York next week for me?" She shakes hands with him and responds, "Yes. I will go to New York next week." Both Brigham and Eliza uttered precisely the same words, yet their actions have quite different meanings. Brigham has merely made a statement that predicts his future actions. Eliza, in contrast, has made a commitment that includes going to New York and finding Heber's lost friend. We can infer this latter meaning not only from the context in which it was given—Heber's concern for his friend and his manifest desire to extract a commitment from Eliza—but also from the fact that they shook on it, a ritual with a well-understood meaning of commitment. In other words, the unstated meaning is implicitly understood on the basis of context and social convention.

The second way in which the meaning of some linguistic act can exceed its explicit words has to do with the necessary assumptions involved in what we say. It is a matter of content that is logically necessary for some linguistic act to have the meaning (explicit and implicit) that it does. Legal philosopher Lon Fuller gave the analogy of an absent-minded professor who walks out of his office door. The professor doesn't explicitly assume that the floor outside his office door will be there, yet the floor's existence is a necessary assumption of his actions.[9] When Brigham says, with complete earnestness, that he is going to New York City, his statement carries a host of assumptions. For example, it assumes that New York City has not been utterly destroyed by a gigantic, rampaging ape, even though the absence of rampaging apes is not part of our implicit understanding of Brigham's statement. Rather, it is a logical necessity for the statement to be true. Brigham can't go to New York City if New York City no longer exists. Hence, in understanding the meaning of linguistic acts, we must also look to the implicit understanding of the meaning in the context in which the linguistic acts are used and to the assumptions that are logically necessary for both our explicit and implicit understandings—in addition to the literal meaning of the words.

In understanding whether baptism involves a promise to follow Church Doctrine, we must first establish the social meaning of baptism, since promises are fundamentally social acts. While the scriptures do not explicitly state that at baptism one promises to be bound by Church Doctrine, what they do say about baptism, coupled with common teachings within the Church, seems sufficient to support an implicit understanding of such a promise. Restoration scriptures contain several prominent discussions of baptism. In the Book of Mormon, Nephi teaches that Christ's baptism was necessary to show an example to all. In explaining the meaning of baptism, Nephi states that it shows a willingness to keep commandments (see 2 Ne. 9:14). Later, Alma the Elder teaches that baptism is a covenant to serve God and keep his commandments (see Mosiah 18:8–10). Finally, Moroni notes that baptism causes one to be numbered among the Church and notes that one loses this status by an act of the Church itself (see Moro. 6:4,7). Section 20 of the Doctrine and Covenants also provides a summary of the procedure and meaning of baptism. Pointedly, the pas-

9. Lon L. Fuller, *Basic Contract Law* (St. Paul: West Publishing Co., 1947), 666. This is the first edition.

sage on baptism begins with a colophon stating, "Duties of the members of the Church after they are baptized," (D&C 20:68) implying that baptism creates obligations for Church members.

Church publications also support the idea that baptism contains an implicit promise to follow Church Doctrine. For example, the Church's *True to the Faith* booklet, a brief compendium of Church teachings, states: "When you are baptized, you enter into a covenant with God. You promise to take upon yourself the name of Jesus Christ, keep His commandments, and serve Him to the end. . . . When you take upon yourself the name of Jesus Christ, you see yourself as His. You put Him and His work first in your life."[10]

More pointedly, in *Preach My Gospel,* the manual that provides the basis for instructing prospective converts, baptism is explained as bringing with it an obligation to keep a host of commandments commonly associated with Church Doctrine, including following the prophet and obeying the laws of chastity, tithing, and the fast, and conforming to the provisions of the Word of Wisdom.[11] In citing these sources, I am not offering them as authorities on the meaning of baptism, but as evidence of a particular social understanding—namely, that when one is baptized, one promises to be bound by Church Doctrine.[12]

One can make a second kind of argument that baptism involves a covenant to follow Church Doctrine. Rather than arguing that baptism involves an unstated but well-understood promise to follow Church Doctrine, one can argue that the presence of such a promise is a necessary assumption of what is in fact baptism's well-understood meaning. I take it to be uncontroversial that baptism creates obligations. A person who is baptized is now a member of the Church and as such has a host of obligations that he or she did not previously have. The question thus becomes how one accounts for the fact that these obligations, which did not exist before, are now thought to exist. Put another way, because baptism is unquestionably seen as a gateway to certain kinds of obliga-

---

10. The Church of Jesus Christ of Latter-day Saints, *True to the Faith* (Salt Lake City: The Church of Jesus Christ of Latter-day Saints, 2004), 23.

11. The Church of Jesus Christ of Latter-day Saints, *Preach My Gospel: A Guide to Missionary Service,* 2004 edition (Salt Lake City: Intellectual Reserve, 2004), 75–81.

12. This does not mean, of course, that these sorts of sources cannot function as authorities about the true meaning of baptism. However, to the extent that we are interested in obligations arising from promises, what matters is how a concept is actually understood rather than how it should be understood.

tions, as an analytic matter, it necessarily involves something that creates these obligations. This "something" is a necessary assumption of the act of baptism in the same way that the floor is a necessary assumption of the absent-minded professor who steps out of his office, regardless of what the professor thinks or understands. Promise-making seems like a particularly good candidate for this obligation-creating something. What we need is a concept that allows us to explain why something that was previously unobjectionable or non-obligatory—such as the moderate consumption of wine or fasting on the first Sunday of the month—now becomes forbidden or obligatory. The concept of promise would fill this role perfectly, precisely because one of the things that promises do is make obligatory what was previously not obligatory.

There is, however, a very powerful conceptual competitor to promise: divine command. In this view, the obligations associated with baptism do not exist because of any kind of promise on the part of the person being baptized, but rather because God commands them. The divine command argument can take one of two forms. Under the strong divine command argument, all of the obligations associated with baptism are actually universal, and the unbaptized are either sinning in ignorance or willfully disregarding divine demands. This position, however, is ultimately untenable. For example, for the obligations associated with baptism to be universal, it would have to be the case that the moderate consumption of wine is wrong for all people. Not only is there no support for such a proposition in the text of the Word of Wisdom, which is explicitly directed to Church members (see D&C 89:1), but it seems to be rejected by other scriptures indicating that the responsible consumption of alcohol is unobjectionable. Most prominent, of course, are Jesus's apparently positive attitude toward wine, witnessed by the miracle at the feast of Cana (see John 2:1–11) and the accounts of his drinking wine with his apostles (see Matt. 26:26–29). Hence, even if one thinks that some of the obligations commonly associated with baptism are universalizable, it is difficult to believe that all of them are.

Under the weak version of the divine command argument, the obligations associated with baptism are not necessarily universal—it really was just fine to drink wine before becoming a Mormon—but nevertheless find their basis, not in promises but in divine commands. In this view, some of God's commands, rather than taking the form of "thou shalt," take the form of "Mormons shalt" or "those who have been baptized shalt." For certain behaviors, this argument seems entirely adequate, but if applied to all of the uniquely Mormon obligations associated with baptism, it runs into two problems. First, in many instances our understanding of what is or is not a divine command is decisively mediated by Church Doctrine. The Word of Wisdom and temple work provide two striking examples. One can plausibly argue that the text of the Word of Wisdom endorses the drinking of beers and ales. Verse 17 commends the use of "barley for all useful animals, and for mild drinks" (D&C 89:17). In historical context, one might claim, "mild drinks" are opposed to "hard drinks." The distinction being drawn was between beers or ales and higher alcohol-content beverages such as whiskey or bourbon. Yet any Latter-day Saint who invokes verse 17 to justify drinking beer will be met with the objection that, whatever its merits, this interpretation of verse 17 is not Church Doctrine.

Likewise, Latter-day Saints view themselves as having an obligation to perform temple ordinances on behalf of the dead. Yet there are no scriptural passages commanding that vicarious sealings and endowments be performed. Only baptism for the dead makes an appearance in the scriptures (see D&C 128). The obligation to perform vicarious sealings and endowments is derived by expansively interpreting scriptural passages in light of later historical practice and consistent teachings within the Church. In other words, we discover the obligation to perform endowments and sealings on behalf of the dead, not from any unmediated divine command or even from a clear sacred text, but from Church Doctrine itself. Yet this process suggests that we have some sort of background obligation to follow Church Doctrine that then makes it possible to identify particular obligations as divine commands. Put another way, the obligation to follow Church Doctrine seems to be logically prior to any of the various interpretations that we use to discover particular divine commands.

Second, even if certain obligations might be plausibly—if problematically—traced back to a divine command, some of our obligations seem to have no basis other than Church Doctrine itself. There are many aspects of Church government that fall into this category. For example, there does not seem to be a strong basis for thinking that there is a direct divine command that the president of a ward Sunday School should be a priesthood holder. Yet these are nevertheless practices that seem to be embedded in the structure of Church Doctrine, such that a bishop who called a woman to be a Sunday School president would plausibly be deemed to have violated an obligation to follow Church Doctrine. In the absence of some reason for supposing that God has commanded in general terms that Mormons should follow Church Doctrine, a promise to obey Church Doctrine seems the better way of accounting for such obligations.[13]

To the extent that baptism involves a promise to follow Church Doctrine, one might nevertheless object that, when one is baptized, one fails to make a binding promise. For example, the words "I promise to pay you $1,000 next Thursday" unambiguously purport to create an obligation. One could nevertheless say that these words fail to create any obligation. No one would claim, for instance, that saying these words in response to a threat to torture your only son creates a morally binding obligation. Likewise, if we were to trick an Esperanto speaker with no understanding of English into saying these words, assuring him—in Esperanto—that they actually mean, "I enjoy eating fresh oysters with my Diet Coke," no obligation to pay the $1,000 has been created.

There are, of course, many different ways in which one might fail to make a promise by being baptized. For example, presumably children baptized by over-zealous missionaries in a "swimming party" have not made any sort of a binding promise. Likewise, a person who is baptized in the mistaken belief that in so doing he is becoming a Zen Unitarian or joining the Priory of Zion has probably failed to make a promise to follow Church Doctrine. Such idiosyncratic failures to promise, however, present no real challenge to the authority of Church Doctrine because they go only to the absence of obligation in particular cases. Of far greater concern are objections suggesting that there is some systemic failure in the practice of baptism itself that keeps it from creating obligations in most cases. It seems to me that there are two main such objections.

---

13. Of course, this argument implicitly assumes the coherence of our pre-reflective understanding of the obligations associated with being a member of the Church. It may simply be the case that this pre-reflective understanding is mistaken and ought to be rejected. The problem becomes that there is a certain circularity involved in either affirming or rejecting the coherence of our pre-reflective beliefs. If we reject their coherence, then assuming a promise to follow Church doctrine at baptism is a philosophical deus ex machina, invoked gratuitously to save the coherence of what is incoherent. On the other hand, if one accepts the coherence of pre-reflective understanding, then rejecting the assumption of a promise to follow Church doctrine at baptism seems to rest on little more than the *a priori* rejection of any theory that renders such understandings coherent. I am skeptical of our ability to escape from this basic circularity. My own view is that the best we can hope for is a kind of reflective equilibrium in which we constantly measure our pre-reflective beliefs against our theories and vice versa, oscillating between them and adjusting each in light of the other until the two converge.

First, one could argue that, when a person is baptized, he or she doesn't really understand Church Doctrine and therefore cannot intend to be bound by all of its strictures. It is a mistake, however, to think that the meaning and obligation of a promise is exhausted by our conscious intentions. Consider a promise to care for an ailing loved one. When one makes such a promise, it is entirely possible that one has no conscious understanding of the precise nature of the obligations that one has undertaken. The nature of the ailment, its progress, and the course of treatment may all be unknown. Yet one's promise is neither meaningless nor limitless. One has simply undertaken the specific—but unknown—obligations that flow from one's promise, an obligation undertaken with the understanding that it would have unforeseen requirements. If the arguments offered thus far are correct, persons being baptized should understand that they are becoming a member of the Church and are committing to following Church Doctrine. Like the promise to care for an ailing loved one, the specific obligations of the promise may be unknown, but they flow from a fairly straightforward and well-understood commitment.

The second systemic objection is that, because many Mormons are baptized as children at age eight, they lacked the capacity to make a promise so important as the promise associated with baptism. This objection could take at least two forms. First, one could argue that an eight-year-old cannot understand the obligations associated with baptism. Second, one could argue that, given the fact that most eight-year-olds likely received baptism at the instigation of adults whom they are practically unable to resist, any promise made at baptism is coerced. There are two responses to both arguments. First, one can simply deny that eight-year-olds lack freedom or understanding. In this view, while eight-year-olds lack sophisticated theological understanding, they nevertheless grasp that, by being baptized, they agree to be bound by Church Doctrine. Likewise, eight-year-olds who are baptized to please adults nevertheless do so willingly.

This line of argument, however, is somewhat less than compelling. The second response is to reject the idea that the promises associated with baptism necessarily occur at the discrete moment of baptism. In contract law, for example, it is possible to make a legally binding promise even if the discrete moment of promising cannot be located. Rather, the promise can arise out of a course of dealing whose cumulative effect can be understood as giving rise to a legitimate and identifiable commitment. Participation in the Church, especially the ordinance of the sacrament, can likewise become a kind of cumulative promising. It is a commonplace of Mormon teachings that, when we partake of the sacrament, we renew our baptismal covenants. Hence, even a member of the Church baptized as a child without full freedom or understanding has an opportunity each week to make—or not make—the same promises that he or she may have failed to make at the time of baptism. Emerging from this process of repeated rituals comes a promise to follow Church Doctrine that is both fully voluntary and sufficiently informed to create binding obligations.[14]

The Argument from Epistemic Advantage

Many Mormons, if asked to justify the authority of Church Doctrine, would likely reply that Church Doctrine has authority because it is given by God.[15] This claim is problematized by the fact that Church Doctrine can be identified only by recourse to a complex set of interpretive arguments. We lack a clear rule that allows us to identify Church Doctrine in all cases, let alone one that will vouchsafe to us the assurance that every aspect of Church Doctrine is dictated directly by God. Church Doctrine emerges from our interpretation of Mormon texts, practices, and history. Whatever the role of God in the production of these texts, practices, and history, they always and necessarily involve more than simply the divine mind, and accordingly they cannot be unproblematically identified with the literal word of God.

Nevertheless, despite these necessary concessions, we can still craft an argument for the authority of Church Doctrine based on revelation from God. Ultimately, the objection to justifying the authority of Church Doctrine on these grounds lies in its apparent fallibility. Even granting that God is infallible, so the objection goes, Church Doctrine is always and necessarily mediated through fallible human beings. Given its fallibility, Church Doctrine cannot operate as an authority. The argument for the

14. My argument here is wholly separate from the argument of community participation that I make below. Here the claim is not that participation in the rituals of the Church creates an obligation to follow Church doctrine. Rather it is a purely promissory argument. It rests on the inherently promissory meaning that we assign to the repeated taking of the sacrament. The argument from community participation, on the other hand, does not rest on any implicit promise.

15. I ignore here the question of why it is that we ought to obey God, taking this assumption as given. For a fuller philosophical treatment of the issue in the context of Mormon theology, see Blake T. Ostler, *Exploring Mormon Thought: The Problems of Theism and the Love of God*, 1st ed. (Salt Lake City: Greg Kofford Books, 2006), chapter 3.

fallibility of Church Doctrine is, in my opinion, quite strong. The scriptures themselves declare that they contain errors. It is a fairly easy matter to locate statements by prophets that have been proven to be mistaken. Church practices change, and some of these policies have been mistaken. To the extent that Church Doctrine consists of an interpretation of texts, history, and practices that are fallible, it will itself be fallible.

To be sure, the process of interpretation can exclude certain mistakes and errors from Church Doctrine. For example, one can dismiss mistaken prophetic statements by insisting that they represent personal opinions rather than binding Church Doctrine. But as long as humanity is involved in the production of the materials from which Church Doctrine emerges, it will be fallible. Even when Church Doctrine is identified according to the most charitable possible interpretation, it will no doubt contain errors, some of which we may be able to identify and many of which we cannot see. The final step of the argument is to claim that fallibility precludes authority. To be sure, one may still agree with much of Church Doctrine, and one may find it a useful source of ideas and insights, but it cannot function as an exclusionary reason on the basis of its connection to God for the simple reason that, notwithstanding any divine connection, it might be wrong.

The problem with this objection is that fallibility need not be fatal to authority. In other words, one can accept something as providing exclusionary reasons even while acknowledging that it may sometimes be mistaken. Suppose that, while granting that Church Doctrine is fallible, one has two other beliefs. First, one believes that despite its errors, on average Church Doctrine is likely to be more reliable than one's own conclusions in the absence of Church Doctrine. Second, one believes that one cannot identify with any certainty when Church Doctrine is likely to be mistaken, particularly in light of the fact that the interpretive process of discovering Church Doctrine involves difficult normative choices. In other words, if, after looking at all of the evidence, one finds oneself in disagreement with Church Doctrine, one cannot be certain whether it is oneself or Church Doctrine that is mistaken. Under these conditions, the best way of maximizing the number of situations in which one arrives at correct conclusions is to follow Church Doctrine in every case, including those cases where one believes it to be mistaken.[16]

---

16. I am indebted to Frank McIntyre for this argument. Although its presentation here is mine, the underlying insight is his.

To understand why, imagine that we are gambling on horse races. I can pick the right horse in about 60 percent of the cases. Sitting next to me is an experienced bookie who can pick the right horses in about 90 percent of the cases. I have two options. First, I could choose to follow the bookie only when I agree with his conclusions about which horse will win. If I do this, then I will pick the right horse about 60 percent of the time. Second, I could choose to follow the bookie on every single race, even when the bookie and I disagree. This may mean that sometimes I will bet on a horse other than the one that I would have chosen on my own, and the horse that I would have chosen will win. However, so long as, on average, the bookie is right 90 percent of the time and I am right only 60 percent of the time, by following the bookie blindly I will increase my total payoff by 30 percent.

The bookie example demonstrates that even a fallible authority can act as an exclusionary reason. We don't need to believe that Church Doctrine is infallible to follow it in cases where we would otherwise reach different conclusions. We only need to believe that it is, on average, more reliable than our independent conclusions. Suppose, however, that one believes that there are certain cases where we are particularly good at identifying errors in Church Doctrine, such that, in cases of disagreement in this particular area, we can be more confident that our own conclusions are correct and Church Doctrine is mistaken. This would not mean that Church Doctrine can no longer act as an authority. In other words, even if we can identify areas where Church Doctrine is more likely to be mistaken, we can still be justified in following it blindly.

To understand why, return to the bookie example. Suppose that I notice that the bookie has a fondness for black horses. If a black horse is in the race, he seems to always bet on the black horse, and his bets on black horses are less reliably correct than his bets on other horses. Would it then follow that, when the bookie bets on a black horse, I should simply bet on the horse that I think will win? The answer is that it depends. So long as the bookie's bets on black horses are more likely to be correct than my own bets, then I am still better off following the bookie blindly, even when he indulges in his fondness for black horses. If, however, when it comes to black horses, my bets are more likely to be right than the bookie's bets, then I ought to follow my own conclusions *as to black horses.*

Ironically, the fact that I know that the bookie is less accurate when it comes to black horses means that I should be more rather than less willing to follow him blindly in other circumstances. To understand why, imagine that I am betting on one hundred races. Ten of the races involve black horses. As to all of the races, I can pick the winners 60 percent of the time, and the bookie can pick the winners 90 percent of the time. However, when it comes to black horses, the bookie picks the winning horse only 50 percent of the time, while I pick the winning horse in black-horse races 60 percent of the time. This means that in the races where there is no black horse, the bookie will pick the correct horse slightly more than 94 percent of the time. The numbers here, of course, give an illusion of precision that does not exist. They do, however, usefully illustrate the relationship between different variables. If I believe that, on average, the bookie is more accurate than I am, this belief can be maintained only if I believe that the bookie is especially accurate in those cases that do not fall within the set where I know that I am more accurate, on average, than the bookie.

To return to Church Doctrine, even if we believe that we can identify areas where it is more likely to be mistaken, we should still follow it blindly so long as we believe that, on average, it has an advantage over our own conclusions in that weakened area. Furthermore, to the extent that we have a rough sense of how much more reliable Church Doctrine is, on average, than our own conclusions, the fact that we might be able to identify areas where the chances of mistakes are higher, strengthens rather than weakens the case for following Church Doctrine in other areas. The argument against the authority of Church Doctrine on the basis of fallibility ultimately makes a simple mistake. It assumes that to follow something in the face of one's own differing conclusions requires that it be perfect. This is wrong. To be justified in following something, one must only believe that it is more reliable than the alternatives. Comparative rather than absolute advantage is all that is required. Accordingly, to make an epistemic argument in favor of Church Doctrine, one need only assume advantage, not perfection.

Recall that ultimately, we have no rule that allows us to identify Church Doctrine simply and unproblematically. We cannot simply look it up. Rather, Church Doctrine consists of the conclusions that emerge from our best efforts to charitably interpret Mormon texts, history, and practices. Because Church Doctrine necessarily seems to exceed the text of the scriptures, it cannot be reduced to the charitable interpretation of scripture alone. Nevertheless, the scriptures provide a useful model for thinking about the epistemic advantage of Church Doctrine. Mormons believe that the standard works contain the word of God, and for that reason, they provide privileged access into the divine mind not available in other texts. But we do not believe that scriptural texts are inerrant. We believe that the Bible is the word of God "as far as it is translated correctly" (A of F 8), a capacious concept that can include wholesale changes and additions to the biblical text unconnected to any known biblical manuscript. We believe the Book of Mormon to be the word of God despite the fact that the title page itself refers to the "errors of men" contained within its covers. We believe that the Doctrine and Covenants is the word of God even though it explicitly provides a description of revelation in which a prophet is a coauthor with God, rather than a divinely inspired automaton (see D&C 9). And so on. In short, the ability of the scriptures to reveal the mind of God is not a function of their infallibility. Rather, they are revelatory because, despite the "errors of men," God was decisively involved in their creation in a way that gives them special theological advantages over other texts.

Church Doctrine is like the scriptures. It does not consist of some sort of pure and wholly unmediated access to the mind of God. Nevertheless, for believing Latter-day Saints, God is at work in the Church. This does not mean that he is not at work elsewhere. For Mormons, he is decisively involved in the Church in ways that he is not involved elsewhere. This does not mean that the texts, practices, and history of Mormonism are infallible. Far from it. Yet they instantiate the divine will, albeit in a form inevitably shaped and mediated by human beings. The unifying interpretation of these texts, history, and practices through which we discover Church Doctrine therefore gathers together and seeks to capture the divinity in the restored Church. It is this faith in the special involvement of God in Mormonism that provides to believing Latter-day Saints the basis for assuming the epistemic advantage of Church Doctrine.

The Argument from Communal Participation

The final justification for the authority of Church Doctrine is the argument from communal participation. Stated in its simplest form, this argument amounts to the claim that, for a practicing Mormon, the failure to follow Church Doctrine is a kind of cheating. Consider a formalized game like chess. The game is made possible by certain rules. Indeed, in some sense, chess simply consists of moving pieces around a sixty-four-square board according to certain rules. If a person plays chess with another person, these rules become obligatory for the second player such that willful flouting of the rules is deemed to be morally objectionable. It is cheating.

There are two things worth noting about cheating at chess. First, the rules of chess become obligatory for a player by virtue of playing the game. Prior to sitting down to the pieces, neither player pledges to follow the rules. Certainly, if one were to attempt to castle out of check, nudge a pawn forward when an opponent was not looking, or otherwise break the rules, it would be no defense to argue that one never promised to obey the rules. Nor does the obligation flow from any inherent evil in the act itself. Moving a knight from a black square to a black square is not inherently immoral. It becomes cheating—and therefore wrong—only when done by a person playing chess. It is participation itself in the game that makes the rules obligatory.

Second, the misdeed of cheating does not consist of harm to the other player. Suppose, for example, that I was to play chess against Gary Kasparov, widely regarded as the strongest chess player in history. Somehow, I manage to distract Kasparov momentarily and intentionally make an illegal move, say, pushing a pawn forward two squares on its second move. Notwithstanding my cheating, however, Kasparov is able to defeat me easily. The wrongfulness of my illegal move cannot consist of depriving Kasparov of his rightful victory. Indeed, given his massive preponderance of skill and ability, Kasparov's victory was not in the least doubtful. Nevertheless, it was wrong for me to cheat by illegally moving my pawn.

These two features suggest some reasons for cheating's immorality. The rules of chess are what make chess possible. In philosophical terms, the rules of chess are constitutive to the practice of chess.[17] To flout the rules of chess while playing chess undermines the game itself. Notice, however, that disobeying the rules of chess undermines the game of chess only if one is playing chess. When one plays checkers, one moves pieces on a sixty-four-square board in ways that violate the rules of chess, but playing checkers does not undermine the practice of chess. There is also a personal aspect to the immorality of cheating. To play a game necessarily conveys a willingness to abide by the rules of the game. In a very real sense, to play a game simply *is* to follow the rules of the game, as it is the rules that make play possible. To cheat while playing, then, negates the very commitment inherent in play itself. One's actions become fundamentally incoherent. It is not that one lies, for it is possible to cheat without deceiving. The con-

17. For a discussion of the distinction between constitutive and regulative rules, see John R. Searle, "How to Derive 'Ought' From 'Is,'" *The Philosophical Review* 73, no. 1 (1964): 43–58.

cept that best conveys this aspect of the misdeed of cheating is hypocrisy. To cheat while playing a game is to be a hypocrite.

To be a member of the Church is to participate in an inherently normative activity. The Church is more than simply a community defined by a particular history. Rather, it is an activity defined by certain constitutive norms. For example, to receive baptism as a Mormon simply consists of the actions defined by the rules governing baptism. An act similar to Mormon baptism—for example, a Baptist baptism—is not a Mormon baptism for the fully sufficient reason that it fails to comply with the rules that define Mormon baptism. In this sense, to participate in the Church as a member is to play a kind of game. One may, of course, participate in Mormonism as simply a community, culture, and history. Such participation is not ultimately normative. It views the structure of Mormon beliefs and practices as essentially a matter of historical accident and participation in that structure as an exercise in taste, nostalgia, or perhaps solidarity. A normative activity, in contrast, is one that is defined not by memory, but by rules and norms. One may know the history of chess and participate in the community of chess players without playing chess. Likewise, one may play chess without knowing anything about the history and community of chess players. The difference is participation in the activity defined by the norms of chess rather than simply by the history or community of chess players. The ecclesiastical structure, ordinance, and rituals of Mormon life are constituted by norms that find their source in Church Doctrine. To participate in these aspects of Mormonism is normative. It is how we "play the game" of Mormonism.

Participation in the game creates an obligation to follow Church Doctrine. Like the rules of chess, Church Doctrine is what makes the Church as a normative practice possible. Willful flouting of Church Doctrine by one who participates in "the game" is a form of cheating. It abuses the practice of Mormonism by undermining what makes Mormonism as a practice possible. Furthermore, any disclaimers aside, it is not possible to participate in the normative practices of Mormonism without conveying a willingness to submit to the norms that make the practice possible. To then flout those norms is hypocritical and, in that sense, morally objectionable.

It might be objected at this point that, even if cheating is blameworthy, the obligation to follow the rules of the game one is playing cannot create exclusionary reasons. Consider this dialogue. Heber and Brigham are playing chess.

Heber: Hey! That's an illegal move. A knight on a black square cannot move to another black square.

Brigham: I know, but an odd chess-phobic millionaire has just pledged his entire fortune to keep innocent children who would otherwise slowly starve to death from their terrible fate provided that I move my horsey to a black square.

Heber: But this is chess!

Brigham clearly has the better of this exchange. Whatever moral lapse is involved in Brigham's cheating clearly cannot justify allowing the children to starve. This example, however, seems to suggest that mere participation in an activity is insufficient to transform its norms into exclusionary reasons.

A further testing of our intuitions about cheating, however, suggests that we should not be too hasty in rejecting the exclusionary power of game playing. Imagine that Brigham and Heber are once more playing chess, but this time there is no pledge from a chess-phobic millionaire. Brigham makes an illegal move.

Heber: Hey! That's cheating!

Brigham: But by making this move, I choose to express my disapproval of allowing children to starve.

Heber: So what? We're playing chess right now. You can express your views on child starvation without cheating.

Heber clearly has the better of this exchange, just as Brigham had the better of the exchange in the preceding paragraph. Yet in both cases, Brigham's actions were motivated by a moral revulsion against starving children; and in both cases, Heber simply invoked chess as his reason for disapproving of Brigham's action. The decisive difference lies in the significance of Brigham's action. In the first case, his action saved innocent lives, which is clearly more important than chess. In the second case, he merely made a statement in one way rather than another, an act that does not seem to be more important than chess (although it may be more important than lesser games such as checkers or Monopoly). There is a certain asymmetry involved in cheating for some goal beyond the game. The good accomplished by cheating must be reckoned in the particular, i.e., the actual children saved or the particular manner of merely making a statement. The evil of cheating, however, must be reckoned in terms of the value of the game itself rather than, say, the value of moving a pawn backward. This reckoning suggests a kind of limiting hierarchy in the reasons excluded by the requirement to avoid cheating. *Acts* that are less important than the *practice* are excluded, while *acts* that are more important than the *practice* are not. All other things being equal, Brigham would prefer to make a statement about child hunger by making an illegal chess move. By playing chess, however, he has excluded this consideration because chess is more important than his desire to make a statement in an idiosyncratic way. However, the rules of chess do not exclude all reasons. Saving a starving child is not a reason for action excluded by the rules of chess.

If this analysis is correct, then participation in the Church can justify treating Church Doctrine as an exclusionary reason. Consider the logic of this dialogue:

> Heber: I'm very hungry this morning, and last night I bought some strawberries that must be eaten soon or they'll rot. Let's eat them for breakfast.
>
> Brigham: That makes sense, but it's fast Sunday and the Church is more important than your strawberries.

Notice how Brigham's response deals with Heber's reasons. He does not try to argue that the act of fasting alone is more important than Heber's strawberries (although he might have). Rather, Brigham appeals to a doctrine of the Church—the law of the fast—to justify ignoring Heber's reason. He then defends this appeal to authority by pointing out that the Church is more important than Heber's strawberries. The implication is that Heber's failure to fast would either undermine the Church or reflect poorly on his character. Both of these implications, however, make sense only in the context of Heber's participation in the Church. The same argument could not be made to a Russian Orthodox priest for the simple reason that he is not playing the Mormonism "game." Furthermore, by implicitly invoking the obligations created by Heber's participation, Brigham throws the value of the Church as a practice—rather than the discrete act of fasting—into the balance. This strategy, in effect, claims that Church Doctrine excludes any consideration less important than the Church itself as a practice.

The Limits of Authority

At this point it is easy to misunderstand the import of the arguments that I have offered. In particular, it is tempting to suppose that claiming authority for Church Doctrine is tantamount to claiming that the obligation to follow Church Doctrines is absolute. This is a mistake. The argument from covenant, the argument from epistemic advantage, and the argument from community participation are all meant to provide plausible justifications for supposing that Church Doctrine can provide an exclusionary reason for action and belief. Yet to say that something is an exclusionary reason does not imply that its claims are absolute.

Once again the law provides a useful illustration. It is entirely coherent to believe that the law has authority—i.e., that it provides exclusionary reasons for action—without believing that the claims of the law are absolute. Consider the example of John Adams. An accomplished attorney with a deep respect and love for English law, he regarded the law as providing exclusionary reasons for action. That is, he believed that one had an obligation to obey the English law even if one regarded some of its particular commands to be misguided or unreasonable.[18] Regardless, in the summer of 1776, Adams found himself willingly committing high treason by signing the Declaration of Independence, the ultimate repudiation of loyalty to English laws. For Adams, his decision to repudiate English law flowed from the nature of his commitment to the law itself. When the basis for that commitment—the implied contract between sovereign and subject—was dissolved, the law ceased to act as an exclusionary reason.

Sir Thomas More—at least as he is presented in Robert Bolt's play *A Man for All Seasons*—provides another example. In one memorable passage, More debates with his son-in-law, Roper, over whether or not he would give the Devil the benefit of law. Roper insists that he would gladly tear up any law to get at the Devil.

> Roper: So now you'd give the Devil benefit of law!
>
> More: Yes. What would you do? Cut a great road through the law to get after the Devil?
>
> Roper: I'd cut down every law in England to do that!
>
> More: (*Roused and excited*) Oh? (*Advances on Roper*) And when the last law was down, and the Devil turned round on you—where would you hide, Roper, the laws all being flat? (*He leaves him*) This country's

---

18. See, e.g., Hiller B. Zobel, *The Boston Massacre* (New York: W. W. Norton & Co., 1970). He recounts John Adam's politically unpopular defense of the soldiers indicted for murder as a result of the Boston Massacre and explains his attitude toward English law.

planted thick with laws from coast to coast—man's laws, not God's—and if you cut them down—and you're just the man to do it—d'you really think you could stand upright in the winds that would blow then? (*Quietly*) Yes, I'd give the Devil benefit of law, for my own safety's sake.[19]

This exchange is ultimately about the authority of the law. Roper denies the authority, insisting that it has no claim when one is engaged in the pursuit of the Devil. More's response is a pragmatic argument for the law's authority. He has no brief for the Devil but insists that even "getting" him—an admirable goal—is excluded by the law. Later in the play, however, More finds himself confronted by a law—Henry VIII's assumption of supremacy over the Church of England—to which he cannot submit. In the clash between his loyalty to the law and his loyalty to the Church of Rome, More found a reason that the law's authority could not exclude, and he went to the executioner for high treason.

Adams and More illustrate the ways in which the claims of authority are defeasible. Both acknowledged that the law excluded certain considerations, but neither took the authority of the law as absolute. They had quite different sorts of reasons, however, for limiting the law's authority. Adams found a limit in the foundation of the law's authority itself. When the basis for treating the law as an exclusionary reason failed, so did the authority of the law. In contrast, More's rejection of the law's authority came because of the claims of an even higher authority. Hence, the actions of the king in Parliament could exclude some reasons, but even those acts could be excluded by the higher authority of the Pope as the successor of Saint Peter. Hence, on the scaffold, Bolt's More says, "I die the king's good servant, but God's first."[20] These examples suggest two ways in which authority may be limited without rejecting the idea that authority acts as an exclusionary reason. The reasoning that Adams and More went through did not involve a weighing of the claims of the law's authority against other reasons. Rather they offered reasons that either showed that authority no longer had the power to exclude other reasons or that one authority was excluded by a higher authority.

Both of these strategies may be used to limit the authority of Church Doctrine. The three arguments offered above for the authority of Church

19. Robert Bolt, *A Man for All Seaons: A Play in Two Acts* (New York: Vintage Books, 1962), 66.

20. *A Man for All Seasons*, a video recording of the movie, adaptation by Paul Schofield, Columbia Pictures Associated (1966).

Doctrine—the argument from covenant, the argument from epistemic advantage, and the argument from communal participation—all rest on certain assumptions. When these assumptions fail, then the arguments can no longer justify treating Church Doctrine as an exclusionary reason.[21] For example, the argument from epistemic advantage rests on two assumptions. First, Church Doctrine is systematically more likely to be correct than our own conclusions. Second, we cannot identify areas where Church Doctrine is likely to be less reliable than our own conclusions. However, when either of these assumptions fails for whatever reason, the argument from epistemic advantage can no longer justify treating Church Doctrine as an exclusionary reason. Thus, if we are able to identify some area where we are justified in concluding that our own judgments are systematically superior to the teachings of Church Doctrine, then the argument from epistemic advantage no longer holds. Such a failure of a basic assumption is analogous to John Adams's rejection of the English law's authority in the American Revolution.

Alternatively, one might believe that there are certain kinds of authority or other exclusionary reasons that could trump Church Doctrine. For example, one might believe that personal loyalty to a presiding authority should trump Church Doctrine so that one should be willing to follow directions from such an authority even when they contravene Church Doctrine. Likewise, one might believe that there are certain moral injunctions that have a Kantian absoluteness that allows them to exclude the lesser authority of Church Doctrine. Both of these examples share the notion that there is a class of exclusionary reasons that excludes the authority of Church Doctrine. In that sense, they are analogous to More's rejection of the authority of the law when it conflicted with the authority of the Church.

Such examples do three things. First, they defend the concept of authority that I offer in this chapter from the charge that it recognizes no limits. Such is not the case. Second, it shows that accepting limits on authority does not mean that the idea of authority as an exclusionary reason is mistaken. Exclusionary reasons can be defeasible without altering their basic conceptual structure. Third, it serves to discipline the analysis of arguments offered by anyone suggesting that one can accept the authority of Church Doctrine while simultaneously refusing to follow it. Such claims

21. Because the arguments are essentially redundant, a complete rejection of the authority of Church Doctrine would have to involve some sort of simultaneous failure of assumptions for all three arguments.

are not prima facie contradictory, but they can be justified only by using a fairly limited set of arguments that will need to have a structure that acknowledges the basic legitimacy of authority as an exclusionary reason.

Conclusion

Church Doctrine is a central but under-analyzed concept in Mormon discussions. We discover Church Doctrine by offering the best possible interpretation of Mormon texts, practices, and history. Accordingly, Church Doctrine is a necessarily interpretive concept and a contestable one at that. It is neither a perfect reflection of the mind of God nor a clear and complete set of theological and ethical propositions. Nevertheless, I conclude that covenants, divine involvement in the production of Church Doctrine, and participation in the Church all justify treating Church Doctrine as an authority. Furthermore, while I think that Mormons are, in some sense, under an obligation to follow Church Doctrine "blindly," I do not believe that this means that the claims of Church Doctrine on Latter-day Saints are absolute or limitless. Arguments for ignoring Church Doctrine in the context of continued allegiance to its basic authority, however, must take the conceptual structure of that authority seriously and, accordingly, will be limited by it.

CHAPTER 4

Civil Disobedience in Latter-day Saint Thought

The twelfth Article of Faith declares, "We believe in being subject to kings, presidents, rulers, and magistrates, in obeying, honoring, and sustaining the law" (A of F 12). On its face, this statement seems to be an unqualified acceptance of legal authority, one that would suggest that Latter-day Saints ought to shun civil disobedience. However, a closer look at Restoration scripture, teachings, and experience reveals a more complicated picture. To be sure, law-abidingness has long been central to the Saints' identity, particularly in the twentieth and twenty-first centuries, and like the New Testament, Restoration scripture generally accepts the need to "render to Caesar the things that are Caesar's" (Mark 12:17) and affirms the legitimacy of the "powers that be" (Rom. 13:1). However, there has never been a clear consensus among Latter-day Saint authorities on the precise extent to which the Saints owe deference to secular law. From the beginning, members of The Church of Jesus Christ of Latter-day Saints have insisted that there are limits on the duty of obedience that Latter-day Saints owe to Caesar.

The Authority of Law in Restoration Scripture

While the Articles of Faith have been included in the Church's canon, they were not received by revelation like most of the sections in the Doctrine and Covenants. Rather, the Articles of Faith formed the conclusion of a document known as the "Wentworth Letter," which was prepared by Joseph Smith and his associates at the request of a Chicago newspaper editor who sought a summary of Latter-day Saint history and beliefs.[1] The Articles of Faith themselves are largely modeled on an earlier statement of the Saints' beliefs in a missionary pamphlet penned by Orson Pratt.[2] Interestingly, however, while most of the Articles of Faith have an-

1. According to the Joseph Smith Papers editors, "it is not known how much of the history was originally written or dictated by [Joseph Smith]." "'Church History,' 1 March 1842, Page 706," accessed January 30, 2023, https://www.josephsmithpapers.org/paper-summary/church-history-1-march-1842/1.

2. See David J. Whittaker, "The 'Articles of Faith' in Early Mormon Literature and Thought," in *New Views of Mormon History: Essays in Honor of Leonard J.*

tecedents in the Pratt pamphlet, the twelfth Article of Faith is unique to the Wentworth Letter. The letter itself was penned in 1842, when political and legal controversy around the Saints in Illinois was intense. Joseph Smith was resisting extradition efforts by the state of Missouri, efforts that Latter-day Saints assumed would result in his murder if successful. Accusations of lawlessness against the Saints were common. Not surprisingly, for a document aimed at a nonmember audience, the Wentworth Letter was at pains to emphasize the civic loyalty of Latter-day Saints.

Other Restoration scripture, however, offers a more nuanced take on legal obedience. The most extensive discussion of secular government in the Doctrine and Covenants comes in section 134. Strikingly, this document was also not given as a revelation. Rather, it was written by Oliver Cowdery and adopted by a Church conference in Joseph Smith's absence. Again, the context was public controversy around accusations of Latter-day Saint lawlessness, this time amid the growing tensions and persecution in Missouri. Section 134 states, "We believe that all men are bound to sustain and uphold the respective governments in which they reside," but immediately qualifies this duty by saying, "while protected in their inherent and inalienable rights" (D&C 134:5). Those rights include "free exercise of conscience, the right and control of property, and the protection of life" (D&C 134:2). In contrast to the apparently unqualified duty of legal obedience later announced in the twelfth Article of Faith, section 134 gestures toward a limited conception of legal authority, reminiscent of the kind found in the Declaration of Independence.

The earliest of Joseph Smith's revelations to address the topic of law suggests that ultimate legal authority lies with God, not the secular state. In January 1831, the Lord declared that "in time ye shall have no king nor ruler, for I will be your king. . . . And you shall be a free people, and ye shall have no laws but my laws when I come, for I am your lawgiver" (D&C 38:21–22). With the gathering of the Saints to build up Zion, many converts took this promise literally, believing that at best, secular law would shortly fade away in the imminent Second Coming of Christ. Accordingly, the Lord declared later the same year, "Let no man break the laws of the land, for he that keepeth the laws of God hath no need to break the laws of the land. Wherefore, be subject to the powers that be,

---

Arrington, ed. Davis Bitton and Maureen Ursenbach Beecher (Salt Lake City: University of Utah Press, 1987); Orson Pratt, *A Interesting Account of Several Remarkable Visions, and the Late Discovery of Ancient American Records* (Edinburgh: Ballantyne and Hughes, 1840).

until he reigns whose right it is to reign" (D&C 58:21). However, as mobs were expelling the Saints from Jackson County, Joseph Smith received a revelation that significantly qualified the claims of legal authority: "And that law of the land which is constitutional, supporting that principle of freedom in maintaining rights and privileges, belongs to all mankind, and is justifiable before me" (D&C 98:5). The revelation continued, "And as pertaining to law of man, whatsoever is more or less than this, cometh of evil" (D&C 98:7).

Taken as a whole, Restoration scriptures suggest that there is a strong prima facie obligation to obey the law. However, this is an all-things-being-equal obligation, not an all-things-considered obligation. The voice of the Lord in latter-day revelation insists that ultimate authority lies with God, not the state. Human laws demand human respect so long as they are broadly congruent with the laws of God and, at a minimum, protect "free exercise of conscience" (D&C 134:2) and other "inherent and inalienable rights" (D&C 134:5). Any law that fails to meet these standards "cometh of evil" (D&C 98:7). Alongside this theology of law, however, are defensive claims made to an often-hostile world that insist on nearly unlimited allegiance of Latter-day Saints to secular authority. The roots of this broader obligation to obey the law lie in the need for vulnerable Latter-day Saint communities to assure legal authorities that they are not a threat and therefore not fit objects of legal and political attacks. Importantly, this more defensive posture suggests that Latter-day Saints have an obligation to obey the law so as to protect the community of the Saints in precisely those cases where the state fails to meet its minimum obligation to protect "free exercise of conscience" (D&C 134:2).

Conscientious Objection and Civil Disobedience

The term "civil disobedience" doesn't have any precise, technical meaning. It entered the modern lexicon largely through Henry David Thoreau's short essay, "Civil Disobedience," in which he justified his refusal to pay federal taxes that were going to be used to support the Mexican-American War and the enforcement of the fugitive slave laws.[3] As Thoreau's usage suggests, civil disobedience involves deliberate law breaking, but not necessarily lawlessness or criminality. Rather, civil disobedience refers to some morally

3. See Henry David Thoreau, "Civil Disobedience," in *Collected Essays and Poems*, ed. Elizabeth Hall Witherell, Library of America 124 (New York: Library of America, 2001), 203–24.

serious decision to disregard the law. Civil disobedience thus is not the same thing as a general rejection of the moral authority of the law. Those who engage in civil disobedience are not philosophical anarchists. Rather, as in Thoreau's case, civil disobedience is directed against particular laws.

It is useful to differentiate between the two different ways in which the rejection of legal obedience might figure in one's moral calculations. We can refer to these different ideas as "conscientious objection" and "civil disobedience." This distinction is important because the Latter-day Saint tradition has been more congenial to the former than to the latter.

Conscientious objection refers to the idea that one refuses to obey the law because of deep moral scruples about the act of individual obedience to a particular law. This might be because the law requires one to do something that deeply offends one's sense of right moral action. The classic case of conscientious objection in American law is the case of the religious pacifist who refuses to serve in the military, even when the law demands that he be drafted into the army. There is a tradition of accommodating such objections, for example, allowing Quakers drafted into the military to serve in the medical corps. A closely related objection has to do with the idea of complicity. Thoreau, for example, did not regard the payment of taxes as immoral in and of itself. Rather, he objected to the payment of taxes when doing so would make him complicit in some greater evil, an aggressive war of conquest against a neighboring country. The Quaker who serves in the ambulance corps, in contrast, may be willing to be complicit in his country's war machine, so long as he is not required to take a human life himself. Both are examples of conscientious objection. Crucially, conscientious objection is not a political tactic. It is not directed toward achieving some concrete goal. Rather, it is an assertion of personal morality and is directed not at a social outcome but rather at the morality of individual conduct.

Civil disobedience, in contrast, *is* a political tactic. Calling it a political tactic does not imply any lack of moral seriousness, only that the moral concern is directed toward the community at large and the shape of its laws. The classic example of civil disobedience in this sense is the civil rights movement of the 1950s and 1960s. Taking their inspiration from the example of Mahatma Gandhi, Martin Luther King Jr. and his followers deliberately violated segregationist laws. By riding on buses or sitting at lunch counters reserved by law for white people, African American protesters invited criminal prosecution in order to dramatize the injustice of those laws and work for their abolition. In practice, of course, there is often no neat distinction between conscientious objection and civil disobedience. One might refuse to become complicit in some wicked law from a sense of personal moral integrity, while at the same time courting prosecution as part of a campaign to repeal that wicked law. However, the moral logic of each approach is conceptually distinct.

Latter-day Saint experience provides examples of both conscientious objection and civil disobedience. However, the strong prima facie obligation to obey the law, particularly in contemporary Latter-day Saint thought, means that both activities have required special justifications. Furthermore, of the two, Church teachings and history have proven more hospitable to conscientious objection than to civil disobedience.

The Latter-day Saint Tradition and Conscientious Objection

The most striking example of conscientious objection in Latter-day Saint history came in the 1880s, when thousands of Saints deliberately flouted federal laws against polygamy. Joseph Smith introduced the doctrine of plural marriage during the Nauvoo period (see D&C 132). He taught that polygamy was a way in which the Saints should imitate the ancient patriarchs and obtain eternal blessings. Unsurprisingly, the practice was hugely controversial, and the prophet initially tried to keep its practice secret. Hostility toward plural marriage, however, was one of the contributing factors to his murder in 1844 and the expulsion of the Saints from Illinois a few years later. In 1852, the Church, having established itself in the remoteness of the Great Basin, publicly endorsed the practice, and four years later, the newly formed Republican party declared polygamy one of the "twin relics of barbarism" (the other was slavery) that had to be expunged from US territories.

Congress responded in 1862 with the Morrill Anti-Bigamy Act, which criminalized polygamy. For over a decade, the law was unenforced until the Supreme Court upheld its constitutionality in 1879. The Latter-day Saints, however, insisted that plural marriage was a religious commandment, that the Supreme Court had erred in holding that the Morrill Act did not violate the Constitution's protections for the free exercise of religion, and refused to comply with the law. Congress responded in the 1880s with a series of increasingly punitive laws and a policy of mass prosecution and incarceration aimed at Latter-day Saint polygamists. The legal crusade against plural marriage ended with the 1890 Manifesto, although the Church did not decisively move to end polygamy until the early twentieth century. The "Raid," as the Saints called this period, marked the most intense period of legal hostility toward the Latter-day Saints and continues to stand as the most prolonged confrontation between law and religion in American history.

Church members in the 1880s were keenly aware of the twelfth Article of Faith and the passages in Restoration scripture that enjoined members to honor and sustain the law. Nevertheless, Latter-day Saints insisted that they were justified in refusing to obey the anti-polygamy laws. They deployed a number of arguments to justify their position. First, they insisted that anti-polygamy legislation was itself illegal because it violated the US Constitution. When the Supreme Court held otherwise, the Saints insisted that it might at some future time reverse its decisions. Next, Latter-day Saints argued that the anti-polygamy laws were being unfairly administered, singling out Latter-day Saints because of their religious beliefs, despite the protestations of federal officials that they were aiming only at criminal behavior and were not motivated by religious animus. Finally, many insisted that they were justified in resisting the law because of their loyalty to the higher law of revelation.

Future apostle Rudger Clawson provided a succinct statement of the Latter-day Saint case for conscientious objection in 1884. He had been found guilty of violating federal anti-polygamy laws and was asked at sentencing what he had to say in mitigation of his offense. He told the court: "Your Honor, . . . I very much regret that the laws of my country should come in contact with the laws of God; but whenever they do I shall invariably choose the latter. If I did not so express myself I should feel unworthy of the cause I represent."[4] He went on to make the by-then rejected argument that the Morrill Act violated the First Amendment. After all of the legal and rhetorical maneuvering, for Clawson the anti-polygamy laws created a stark choice between obeying the laws of God and obeying human laws, and he insisted that he had to choose the divine commands over secular commands.

The Latter-day Saint Tradition and Civil Disobedience

It is more difficult to find instances of Latter-day Saint civil disobedience. However, such instances exist. In part, the resistance to the Raid can be thought of as involving a strategy of civil disobedience. Latter-day

4. "Sentence of Rudger Clawson, and His Speech Before the Court," *Millennial Star,* 1884, 741.

Saints were not simply refusing to obey laws that they insisted required them to violate divine commands. They also claimed that if the Saints ignored such laws en masse, it would convince the nation of the laws' injustice, or at least their impracticability. In 1856, as the Republican Party launched its attacks on plural marriage, Brigham Young insisted, "They will have to expend about three hundred millions of dollars for building a prison, for we must all go into prison. And after they have expended that amount for a prison, and roofed it over from the summit of the Rocky Mountains to the summit of the Sierra Nevada, we will dig out and go preaching through the world."[5] In his hyperbolic way, President Young was making a classic tactical argument in favor of civil disobedience. By violating an objectionable law en masse, the Latter-day Saints would make enforcing the law so expensive that it would be abandoned.

President Young gave his speech at the very beginning of the federal government's anti-polygamy crusade, before Congress had passed any laws against polygamy. Three decades later, when the Raid was at its height, hundreds of polygamist Saints had been sent to prison, and numerous plural wives had been prosecuted for perjury and other crimes when they refused to cooperate with law enforcement officials in convicting their husbands. A First Presidency letter to the Saints signed by John Taylor and George Q. Cannon again invoked the idea of deliberate law breaking as a means of legitimate expression: "Every man who goes to prison for his religion, every woman who, for love of truth and the husband to whom she is bound for time and eternity, submits to bonds and imprisonment, bears a powerful testimony to the world concerning the falsity of the views they entertain respecting us and our religion. If such noble and heroic sacrifices as men and women are now called upon to make for their religion by Federal courts do not teach the world the truth concerning us, then woe to the world."[6] Of course, the strategy of changing hearts and minds by deliberately violating the law and then submitting to its punishments proved ineffective for nineteenth-century Latter-day Saints. Minds were not changed. Indeed, the Saints' resistance only further enraged anti-polygamist activists, who responded with increasingly punitive laws until the Latter-day Saints were faced with a choice between submission or the institutional annihilation of the Church.

---

5. *Journal of Discourses*, 26 vols. (London and Liverpool: LDS Booksellers Depot, 1854), 4:39 (Brigham Young, August 31, 1856).

6. "An Epistle from the First Presidency," in James R. Clark, ed., *Messages of the First Presidency* (Salt Lake City: Bookcraft, Inc., 1965), 3:35.

Perhaps because of the spectacular failure of civil disobedience as a political strategy for nineteenth-century Latter-day Saints, contemporary Church leaders have tended to endorse Jeremy Bentham's maxim for dealing with unjust or unwise laws: "to obey punctually; to censure freely."[7] For example, in the wake of World War II, the United States considered universal, compulsory military service for all young men. The First Presidency issued a strongly worded statement in 1945 attacking the proposal. Such a measure, the First Presidency argued, would "deprive [young men] of parental guidance and control at this important period of their youth," derail the educational plans of young men, "teach our sons . . . to kill," deprive them of "adequate religious training and activity," and encourage a host of other evils.[8] "What this country needs and what the world needs," they insisted, "is a will for peace, not war."[9] Notwithstanding these objections, however, the First Presidency also instructed leaders and members to cooperate with the peacetime military draft.

During the social upheavals of the 1960s and 1970s, the term "civil disobedience" came to be associated in Church discourse not only with peaceful protest but also with lawlessness and contempt for authority in general. Accordingly, it is easy to find condemnations of "civil disobedience" in official publications, although the term is generally used imprecisely. However, civil disobedience, in the more precise way we have been using it here, has also been discouraged as a political tactic, even in favor of positions that have been endorsed by the Church. In 1995, for example, James E. Faust of the First Presidency gave a public address in which he discussed a member who urged "that the Church resort to civil disobedience and violence because of the moral wrongness of abortion."[10] President Faust responded, "Civil disobedience has become fashionable for a few with strongly held political agendas. Even when causes are meritorious, if civil disobedience were to be practiced by everyone with a cause our democracy would unravel and be destroyed. . . . I tried to explain that when we disagree with a law, rather than resort to civil disobedience or

---

7. Jeremy Bentham, "Preface to A Fragment on Government," in *The Works of Jeremy Bentham*, ed. John Bowring (Edinburgh: Simpson, Marshall, 1843), 230.

8. "Statement by the First Presidency Regarding Universal Compulsory Military Training," December 14, 1945, in James R. Clark, ed., *Messages of the First Presidency* (Salt Lake City: Bookcraft, Inc., 1965), 6:240–41.

9. "Statement by the First Presidency," 6:242.

10. James E. Faust, "The Integrity of Obeying the Law," *Vital Speeches of the Day*, September 1995.

violence, we are obliged to exercise our right to seek its repeal or change by peaceful and lawful means."[11]

Legal Obedience and Latter-day Saints as a Vulnerable Minority

Since World War II, the twelfth Article of Faith's insistence that Latter-day Saints believe in "obeying, honoring, and sustaining the law" (A of F 12) has emerged as a consistent theme in official teachings about secular authority. This period corresponds with the massive missionary outreach resulting in the appearance of Latter-day Saint temples and stakes around the world. It has now been several generations since the typical member of the Church was an American citizen living in the predominantly Latter-day Saint regions of the Intermountain West. Today the majority of members of record live outside the United States, and Latter-day Saints are generally a tiny minority in the societies in which they live. Suspicion and hostility toward Church members remains, and Latter-day Saints have frequently been the targets of hostile governments and political leaders. During the 1980s and 1990s, leftist guerilla movements across Latin America murdered Church missionaries, and the Sandinista government in Nicaragua was complicit in the confiscation of Church buildings. For a time, the government of Ghana banned the Church, and Latter-day Saints have been the targets of legal harassment from Venezuela to Russia. Given this reality, the emphasis on legal obedience can be seen as part of a deliberate strategy to protect Latter-day Saint communities by convincing at-times hostile governments that Church members do not pose a political threat.

This means, however, that Latter-day Saints have often found themselves emphasizing legal obedience in precisely those contexts where legal regimes have been the most hostile. Rather than encouraging conscientious objection or civil disobedience, the Church has tried to formulate the minimum legal conditions for living as a faithful member and has refrained from missionary efforts in regimes that cannot meet even these basic standards. Those standards were articulated by David Kennedy, a former US Treasury Secretary who was tapped by President Spencer W. Kimball to act as a special ambassador for the First Presidency. Kennedy wrote, "So long as the government permits me to attend church, so long as it permits me to get on my knees in prayer, so long as it permits me to baptize for the remission of sins, so long as it permits me to partake the sacrament of the Lord's Supper, and to obey the commandments of

11. Faust, "The Integrity of Obeying the Law."

the Lord, so long as the government does not force me to commit crime, so long as I am not required to live separately from my wife and children, I can live as a Latter-day Saint within that political system."[12] While Kennedy's formulation contains a certain amount of ambiguity—specifically regarding what precisely is involved in "obeying the commandments of the Lord" or "committing crime"—in practice, this statement means that Latter-day Saint have endorsed legal obedience to odious regimes, such as the German Democratic Republic of Erich Honecker and the death-squad-wracked Chilean regime of Augusto Pinochet.

The ultimately ambiguous position of the Church and the difficult situation in which this stance can place Latter-day Saints is vividly illustrated by the case of Helmuth Hübener. Born in 1925, Hübener lived in Hamburg, Germany. He was raised as a Latter-day Saint and was active in his local branch. During the 1930s, German Latter-day Saints tried to allay Nazi suspicion of the American church by emphasizing the commonalities between the teachings of the Church and those of the new Germany, seizing on the Nazi hostility to tobacco and drunkenness. However, the Nazi government suppressed missionary pamphlets making this claim, the Gestapo investigated Church branches, one man was sentenced to a concentration camp for developing pictures of American missionaries disrespectfully holding a Nazi flag, and at least one convert of Jewish ancestry was sent to the Theresienstadt death camp. Latter-day Saints responded by emphasizing their obedience to secular law and trying to avoid official attention. In 1941, Hübener began listening to war news on the BBC, in violation of wartime German laws. Based on what he learned, he authored and secretly distributed anti-Nazi pamphlets with three friends. In 1942, a coworker denounced Hübener to the Gestapo, and the seventeen-year-old was eventually tried for treason and executed. Before Hübener's execution, his nonmember stepfather falsely fingered another Latter-day Saint as the instigator of the plot, and Gestapo agents held him for four days and interrogated him before releasing him. Hübener's pro-Nazi branch president excommunicated him, and the temporary mission president approved the action. However, after the war, the First Presidency reviewed the excom-

12. Quoted in Martin B Hickman, *David Matthew Kennedy: Banker, Statesman, Churchman* (Salt Lake City: Deseret Book Co., in cooperation with the David M. Kennedy Center for International Studies, 1987), 340–41.

munication and posthumously reversed the local leaders' decision, restoring all of Hübener's blessings.[13]

The entire incident illustrates the way that Latter-day Saint obedience to the law can be a defensive reaction to an ultimately illegitimate regime rather than an affirmation of the regime's legitimacy. There was nothing in official Church teachings that overtly encouraged Latter-day Saints to resist the Nazi regime. Rather, there was widespread distaste for Nazism—along with some scattered local supporters—and an effort to avoid the attentions of the Gestapo. Hübener's opposition to the regime was undoubtedly fueled by his moral indignation against Nazism, a moral indignation that flowed from his upbringing as a Latter-day Saint. Nevertheless, Hübener's actions endangered his co-religionists. The reaction of the Church as an institution was ambiguous, first cutting Hübener off, in large part as a defensive measure, and then posthumously acknowledging the justice of his actions through reinstatement.

Conclusion

In the end, there is no simple answer to the question of whether or not Latter-day Saints may engage in civil disobedience. The twelfth Article of Faith suggests an almost unlimited obligation to comply with secular law.[14] The Articles of Faith, however, are not the only place where Restoration scripture discusses the obligation to obey the law. The Doctrine and Covenants suggests a more limited duty of obedience, one that is contingent on the legal system being what might be called "a nearly just . . . regime."[15] In practice, Latter-day Saints and their leaders have en-

---

13. The details in this paragraph are taken primarily from Joseph M. Dixon, "Mormons in the Third Reich: 1933–1945," *Dialogue: A Journal of Mormon Thought* 7, no. 1 (Spring 1972): 70–78. See also Blair R. Holmes, Alan Keele, and Karl-Heinz Schnibbe, eds., *When Truth Was Treason: German Youth against Hitler* (Urbana: University of Illinois Press, 1995); Alan F. Keele and Douglas Tobler, "The Fuhrer's New Clothes: Helmuth Hubener and the Mormons in the Third Reich," *Sunstone*, December 1980.

14. It is striking, for example, that the text of the twelfth Article of Faith goes out of its way to insist that the obligation to sustain the law is not contingent on the particular form of government, insisting that Latter-day Saints are to be "subject to kings, presidents, rulers, and magistrates" (A of F 12).

15. This term is borrowed from the political philosopher John Rawls, who uses it in his discussion of the obligation to obey the law. See John Rawls, *A Theory of Justice*, revised edition (Cambridge: Belknap Press, 1999), 293.

dorsed both conscientious objection and civil disobedience in some cases. When pushed by a hostile state, some Saints have been willing to declare, as Rudger Clawson did, that if "the laws of my country should come in contact with the laws of God, . . . I shall invariably choose the latter."[16] However, history also reveals that the calculus for Latter-day Saints has never been as simple as Clawson suggested. Church leaders have generally counseled obedience to unjust laws coupled with engagement to improve them. More tellingly, in the face of at-times suspicious and vicious governments, Latter-day Saints have been counseled to obey the law as a way of protecting themselves and their community from predatory state actors. In short, the Restoration does not provide us with any neat or clear answer to the perennial question of where to draw the line between the claims of God and the claims of Caesar. Rather, it gives Latter-day Saints a native tradition within which they may consider such questions.

16. "Sentence of Rudger Clawson, and His Speech before the Court," 741.

CHAPTER 5

Mormonism and Conscience

(co-authored with Rosalynde Welch)

Introduction

While Mormons occasionally invoke the idea of conscience, it has played a muted role in Mormon thought and experience at best. To organize our account of conscience in Mormonism, we frame our definition around two separate but related functions. First, conscience can refer to a subjective moral sense that gives one access to moral truths about right and wrong; we call this the epistemic function. Second, it can be used as a source of subjective moral authority, in which the integrity of individual morality is asserted against a collective source of moral authority like the church or the state; we call this the moral-practical function. While traces of both conceptions of conscience can be found within Mormon discourse and practice, Mormon theology and experience has mitigated against both the epistemic and the practical claims of conscience.

Mormonism is not without conceptual resources for thinking about the tensions between individual moral choice and the claims of collective authority. However, Mormonism primarily addresses these concerns using different language and concepts, notably personal revelation, communal integrity, and a divine immanence known as the light of Christ. In comparison to other Christian traditions, the Mormon approach to the conundrums of conscience is unusually communal and deferential to claims of religious and secular authority. This is particularly true of the limited authority of Mormon private conscience vis-à-vis internal ecclesiastical authority. Nevertheless, particularly when it comes to legal authority, Mormon experience and theology provide some resources for religious conscience to challenge the claims of the law.

The low profile of conscience in Mormon thought is best grasped in the context of the idea's development in Protestantism, the religious environment within which Mormonism originated and the theological tradition from which it often departs. Since its first full Christian formulation in the writings of Thomas Aquinas, the idea of conscience has acquired a wide range of meanings as a consequence of changing religious and political uses. Practical moral judgment, psychological introspection, moral inhibition, and subjective antinomianism all inform the word's use.

In this chapter, we draw on these diverse meanings as they touch on the concept's development in Mormon thought, but we will focus primarily on conscience as an arbiter of competing claims of authority. Our interest is not in the morality of human freedom or the limits of institutional authority per se. Rather, in exploring conscience in Mormonism, we are inquiring into *a subjective way of producing authority.*

This chapter will first examine the idea of conscience in Western thought with an emphasis on how it claims subjective epistemic and moral authority. We will then explore how conscience is worked out in Mormon thought in relation to ecclesiastical and public authority. Ultimately, the claims of conscience within Mormonism are muted. Mormons do have an idea of subjective epistemic authority, but it is limited. They have very little idea of subjective moral authority. Rather, they tend to mediate the claims of authority using other ideas, such as personal revelation, stewardships, free agency, and the importance of ecclesiastical independence.

Conscience in Western Thought

What follows is not an exhaustive review of the development of Protestant conscience; rather, we focus on the epistemic and moral functions of conscience, in order to better characterize the unique contours of Mormon thinking about conscience. During the modern period, conscience evolved from a practical disposition of the soul witnessing divine and natural law to a subjective source of binding subjective moral direction.[1] As C. S. Lewis put it, "*conscience*, so to speak, passed from the witness-box to the bench and even to the legislator's throne."[2] A brief account of this process provides a useful background for understanding Mormon approaches to the idea of conscience and how they diverge from other traditions.

---

1. Of course, any account of the religious and political development of conscience must acknowledge historical complexity. No simple trajectory, whether intellectual history of the early modern passage from scholasticism to Enlightenment self-awareness or a triumphal narrative of the emergence of sovereign individuality, does justice to the development of a category as contested as private conscience. As an arena of conflict between notions of public and private, spiritual and temporal, law and anarchy, equality and pluralism, the social function of conscience has shifted over time. For recent scholarly reckoning with the complexity of conscience in the early modern period, see Harald E. Braun and Edward Vallance, "Introduction," *Renaissance Studies* 23, no. 4 (2009): 413–22.

2. C. S. Lewis, *Studies in Words*, 2nd ed. (Cambridge: Cambridge University Press, 2013), 191.

The ideological transformation of conscience in the modern West opens with Thomas Aquinas's definition of conscience. The scholastic formulation, drawing on biblical and classical accounts of morality, divided conscience into two parts: *synderesis*, an internal disposition toward natural law that inherently inclines to general principles of moral good; and *conscientia*, the application of these general principles to one's personal situation and the exercise of practical judgment to allow or prohibit particular acts.[3] Two tensions present in the Thomistic formulation proved salient in subsequent Protestant and Mormon iterations of the concept. First, *synderesis* as a "storehouse" of natural law is a universal and permanent disposition of every human soul, Christian or pagan, and never errs in exposing the soul to good; whereas *conscientia* is a subjective faculty of cognition and is thus capable of error in understanding the situation, applying the law, or drawing a conclusion. For Aquinas, "one should not act contrary to conscience, even in the case of erroneous reason."[4] For later thinkers, the contradictions implicit in the authority of erroneous conscience became a confounding locus of debate. Secondly, within the Thomistic distinction between *synderesis* and *conscientia*, one can identify the fundamental conceptual divide that emerged. On one hand, there is a negative, inhibitory, rule-oriented conscience tied to the objective content of natural law. On the other hand, there is a positive, action-oriented, subjective conscience empowered to validate personal choices against external claims. The antinomian character of conscience engaged the Protestant religious mind. Conscience stood both inside (as *synderesis*) and outside (as *conscientia*) systems of law, sometimes as subservient enforcer of law and sometimes as magisterial judge of law itself. For Luther, "conscience represented an antinomian rupture with the Thomistic tradition of natural and divine law."[5] Protestant thinkers wished to bolster conscience as the source of binding moral precept; yet in doing so, the authority of conscience inevitably collided with the authority of the Bible, and the

3. Thomistic conscience has been well explored in secondary literature. See, e.g., Edward G. Andrew, *Conscience and Its Critics: Protestant Conscience, Enlightenment Reason, and Modern Subjectivity* (Toronto: University of Toronto Press, 2001); Richard J. Regan, *The American Constitution and Religion* (Washington, DC: Catholic University of America Press, 2013).

4. Regan, *The American Constitution and Religion*, 245.

5. Andrew, *Conscience and Its Critics*, 20.

anarchic energies of antinomianism were released.[6] One historian has observed that "In the sixteenth century the most persistent and determined law-breakers were the godly who—like twentieth century conscientious objectors in wartime—claimed to be obeying a higher authority [conscience] than that of the state."[7] The Bible could be marshalled to check the excesses of conscience, both by supplying *synderesis* with the content of divine law and by disciplining its antinomian energies, as a standard against which erroneous conscience may be refuted. Yet even as Luther attempted to evade unbridled subjectivism by grounding conscience in the Bible, his teachings privileged individual interpretation over the authority of the church to declare the meaning of the canon. The uncertainty surrounding the status of the inviolable yet fallible conscience thus persisted in all post-Reformation treatments of the subject. Indeed, Mormon notions of conscience may be understood to respond to this dilemma by siding against the antinomianism of subjective conscience, with ecclesiastical authority assuming the authority of the Bible.

The antinomian energies of Protestant conscience stood opposite another approach, in which conscience acts not as moral legislator but as moral prosecutor, accusing the soul, discouraging unlawful acts, and punishing with guilt and shame. Conscience resides in the heart as a kind of demi-urge presaging the final judgment of God. Influential Puritan sage William Perkins wrote that conscience is "a little God sitting in the middle of men's hearts."[8] The influence of this prosecuting "little God" was twofold: first, it raised the subjective status of conscience above community and canon, as the highest human authority under God; second, it reduced private conscience to an internal enforcer of external authority, limiting its effects to self-censorship.[9] This second function is evident in Hamlet's famous lines, "Thus conscience does make cowards of us all";

---

6. See James Calvin Davis, "William Ames's Calvinist Ambiguity Over Freedom of Conscience," *The Journal of Religious Ethics* 33, no. 2 (2005): 333–55.

7. Christopher Hill, *Liberty Against the Law: Some Seventeenth-Century Controversies*, 1st ed. (London: Viking Adult, 1996), 181. Cited in Andrew, *Conscience and Its Critics*, 26.

8. Mika Ojakangas, *The Voice of Conscience: A Political Genealogy of Western Ethical Experience* (New York: Bloomsbury Academic, 2015), 84 (quoting William Perkins, *Discourse of Conscience*, 9).

9. See Camille Wells Slights, "Notaries, Sponges, and Looking-Glasses: Conscience in Early Modern England," *English Literary Renaissance* 28, no. 2 (1998): 231–46.

or, as Shakespeare's Richard III puts it more pointedly, "For Conscience is a word that Cowards use, / Devis'd at first to keep the strong in awe." Both impulses—to elevate the subjective status of conscience and to reduce its function to internal law enforcement—decisively shifted the locus of moral authority to the individual's interior world. The subjectivity of conscience proved to be an enduring feature of the idea, as deployed to broker the religious and political dilemmas of the Reformation and the emergence of religious pluralism. Just as it eschews the antinomian conscience, Mormonism largely abandons the self-accusing internal conscience, outsourcing to community norms the functions of encouraging good behavior and penalizing bad behavior.

The subjectivity of early modern ideas of conscience was important in English debates over public and private authority. The Elizabethan religious settlement required public participation in the state religion but allowed a degree of private dissent. Elizabeth I's mythic statement, "I would not open windows into men's souls," suggests one compromise between public and private authority: a public space under the public authority of church and state and a private space under the private authority of conscience. Ideas of conscience internalized and "privatized" moral deliberation, encouraging practices of exhaustive self-examination and personal self-fashioning. The private dictates of conscience were practiced in the private spaces of the prayer closet or, more dangerously, the priest hole, a secret harbor for outlaw Catholic priests in recusant homes. Yet boundaries between what was public and what was private had to be negotiated. Elizabethan Catholic recusants and Puritan radicals, including and especially women, assessing their place in the private sphere, enlisted conscience to enlarge its frontier. In one sense, the public/private compromise contained conscience, depriving it of public authority; in another sense, conscience burnished the cultural prestige of subjective experience and encouraged individuals and groups to expand the jurisdiction of private authority. As one scholar has noted, "the individual and the collective intersect in the conscience."[10] While discussions of conscience tend to portray the conscientious individual alone against the world, the protection of "private" conscience was often claimed by collective members of minority religious groups, instead of by isolated individuals. Private conscience could thus be deployed as a shield for group religious practice against the authority of a hostile state, rather than as a celebration of sub-

10. Slights, 231.

jective individualism. It is this corporate sense of private conscience that most directly informs the Mormon discourse of conscience, such as it is.

In the societies of early modern Europe, the fragmentation of the Catholic Church threatened to fragment the political unity of the state. Hobbes and Locke proposed radically different solutions to this challenge. The American republic, with no national established church, sided with Locke, whose vision of distinct, limited domains for government and religion informs the First Amendment. Government's domain is the safety of person and property in this world; religion's domain is private conviction relating to the next world. Like the Elizabethan settlement, the Lockean settlement neutralizes the antinomian energies of religious conscience by confining it to a separate sphere of private opinion. Thus, Locke "restricted the operation of conscience, at least for the most part, to negative judgments of reason from religious premises that were only opinion. In this respect, he was a forerunner not only of the modern Western settlement in favor of religious tolerance, but of modern subjectivist interpretations of conscience, as well."[11] Yet conscience rarely limits its dictates to beliefs and private opinions; since its first Thomistic formulation, it has also entailed practical judgment that directly influences behavior. America's religious diversity adds a further dimension: a structural division between public and private matters may function in the context of Reformed religion, which heavily privileges private personal experience over communal and ritual observance but makes little sense for religions that require external markers of membership. Like other compromises based on non-overlapping jurisdictions, the American settlement invites negotiation and contest over the boundaries between this world and the next, between behavior and belief, and between the authority of Congress and the authority of conscience.

From this historical account, we distill two conceptual categories that will organize our treatment of Mormon conscience. First, the *epistemic* authority of conscience is grounded in its putative witness of some concept of the good, variously conceived as natural law, divine law, communal norms, or privately felt conviction. From the beginning, theorists of conscience have struggled to identify and defend the precise content of *synderesis*; in a pluralistic society committed to egalitarianism, the task may be impossible. Jocelyn Maclure and Charles Taylor argue that the epistemic privilege of conscience originates in the state's "recognition of the limits of rationality,

11. Regan, *The American Constitution and Religion*, 256.

its inability to decide the questions of ultimate meaning of existence and the nature of human fulfillment in a decisive way."[12] Epistemic pluralism mediated through private conscience is thus a mechanism to accommodate ideals of both social diversity and social equality.

Second, we observe the *moral* authority of conscience as a privileged subjective faculty; that is, its status as a "little God" within the soul issuing binding mandates that overrule the external authorities of state or ecclesia. The possibility that conscience may err does not meaningfully vitiate this moral authority. While in theory conscience may be substantively mistaken, external authorities can offer no objective basis on which to determine its error. Thus conscience provides a compelling moral reason for action independent of its epistemic authority, and its internal moral authority overrules external injunctions. The moral authority of the conscience resides near the center of the modern (Protestant) self. To violate the dictates of conscience is to threaten the coherence of the self. As we have seen, the anarchic potential of conscience has been a persistent anxiety for Christian Anglo-American thinkers, and several mechanisms for its containment have emerged. Given the ideological parameters under which the modern conscience has developed, there is no easy, uncontestable solution to such quandaries. It seems that the ultimate force of conscience lies in its appeal to our deepest will. As William Earle puts it, the dictates of conscience "are neither correct nor incorrect, but affirmed or rejected."[13]

Conscience in Mormon Thought

While Latter-day Saints occasionally use the word conscience in their sermons and writings, it plays a limited role in Mormon thought.[14] When it comes to moral epistemology, Mormons tend to speak in terms of personal revelation from God rather than innate moral faculties such as *synderesis* and *conscientia*. The primacy of divine revelation in Mormon thought is reinforced by the fact that, for Latter-day Saints, the paradigmatic case of revelation is not transcendental union, as it is in the mystical traditions of Christianity, Judaism, and Islam, but what one Mormon

12. Jocelyn Maclure and Charles Taylor, *Secularism and Freedom of Conscience*, trans. Jane Marie Todd (Cambridge: Harvard University Press, 2011), 10.

13. William Earle, "Some Paradoxes of Private Conscience as a Political Guide," *Ethics* 80, no. 4 (1970): 312.

14. For example, the term "conscience" appears repeatedly in section 134 of the Doctrine and Covenants, which is discussed below (see D&C 134:2–4).

writer has labeled "dialogic revelation," which places emphasis on the propositional content of religious experience and the discrete personhood of God.[15] In this framework, conscience tends to be identified with revelation of the Holy Spirit, understood as a distinct personified being rather than with an inherent moral faculty. Furthermore, the need to contain the antinomian tendencies of personal revelation resulted—early on in Mormon history—in a series of concepts that severely limits its ability to act as a basis for challenging either ecclesiastical or political authorities. The absence of a well-developed conception of conscience in Mormon thought, however, does not mean that the tradition is without resources to limit the claims of legal authority. It does mean that Latter-day Saints have tended to invoke ideas such as the special moral status of human freedom or the importance of communal independence and integrity rather than the moral sovereignty of subjective conscience.

Conscience and Epistemic Authority

The development of Christian conscience may be imagined in broad terms as a relocation from the confessional box of Catholicism to the private prayer closet of Protestantism, transforming along the way from a largely epistemic function that testifies of right and wrong action, to a morally authorizing function that elevates private judgment in relation to other kinds of authority. Mormonism does not fit neatly on this historical-ideological spectrum from Catholic to Protestant. Broadly, Mormonism rebuffs the antinomian, subjective moral authority of conscience, while it recognizes in limited ways the epistemic functions of *synderesis*.

The idea of conscience as an internal witness of right and wrong that accuses the soul of wrongdoing and provokes guilt as a spur to repentance is present, albeit sparingly, in Mormon scripture. The Book of Mormon speaks in several passages of "remorse of conscience" as the consequence of knowingly breaking the commandments of God (see Alma 29:5, 42:18.). Like the scholastic notion of *synderesis*, the Book of Mormon emphasizes humanity's knowledge of divine law and the punishment that is justly affixed to transgression. Divine law emanates from a heavenly source and must be made available to the human mind to guide its actions. Conscience is a minor vector of that knowledge, and preaching and communal norms are the primary means of transmitting divine law and encouraging obedi-

---

15. See Terryl L. Givens, *By the Hand of Mormon: The American Scripture That Launched a New World Religion* (New York: Oxford University Press, 2003), 209–39.

ence in Mormon scripture and practice. Mormonism imposes strict behavioral requirements on its adherents, and it is rather surprising that Latter-day Saints rely so little on the language of conscience to enforce those requirements internally. Mormon teaching tends instead to appeal to the relational force of communal and sacramental covenants to encourage obedience. When serious transgression occurs, the consequences are mediated through ecclesiastical discipline and curtailment of communal worship participation rather than through the torments of conscience. The idea of conscience as a teacher and deputy of divine law appears infrequently and plays a minor role in Mormon teachings.

An analogue in Mormon theology for the idea of conscience as an epistemic authority is what Latter-day Saints call "the light of Christ."[16] The Book of Mormon contains a passage stating, "Wherefore, I beseech you, brethren, that you should search diligently in the light of Christ that you may know good from evil; and if you will lay hold upon every good thing, and condemn it not, you certainly will be a child of Christ" (Moro. 7:19). As it developed in Mormon theology, the light of Christ became identified with a universal infusion of divine revelation that gives to all people the ability to discern right and wrong. It thus represents a universally available manifestation of the Holy Spirit. As Brigham Young insisted:

> I do not believe for one moment that there has been a man or woman upon the face of the earth . . . who has not been enlightened, instructed, and taught by the revelations of Jesus Christ. . . . [I] am far from believing that the children of men have been deprived of the privilege of receiving the spirit of the Lord to teach them right from wrong.[17]

Other Mormon leaders and theologians have identified the light of Christ with human conscience. A widely used twentieth-century theological reference declares that "every man has a conscience and knows more or less when he does wrong, and the Spirit guides him if he will hearken to its whisperings."[18] More recently, a prominent Mormon leader has written, "Conscience affirms the reality of the Spirit of Christ in man. It affirms, as well, the reality of good

---

16. See C. Kent Dunford, "Light of Christ," in *The Encyclopedia of Mormonism*, ed. Daniel H. Ludlow (New York: Macmillan Publishing Company, 1992).

17. Brigham Young, *Discourses of Brigham Young*, ed. John A. Widtsoe (Salt Lake City: Deseret Book Co., 1983), 32.

18. Joseph Fielding Smith, *Doctrines of Salvation*, ed. Bruce R. McConkie (Salt Lake City: Bookcraft, 1974), 38.

and evil, of justice, mercy, honor, courage, faith, love and virtue, as well as the necessary opposites—hatred, greed brutality, jealousy."[19]

The light of Christ, however, differs from Protestant ideas of conscience in ways that tend to diminish claims to subjective moral authority. Where some Protestants saw conscience as a "little God" at the center of the self, endowing personal moral judgment with an inviolable status, Mormons understand the light of Christ quite differently. First, the light of Christ is not linked with a conception of the self that emphasizes its subjective moral sovereignty or the overriding importance of personal moral commitments. For Latter-day Saints, human freedom is seen primarily in terms of a moral test, in which human beings either choose to follow God or reject Him. Human freedom is thus given a high moral status, but not because it is tied to a thick conception of moral self-authorship or personal authenticity. Thus, the light of Christ comes from beyond the self as a moral demand imposed on the individual by God, even if the individual does not believe in God or recognize his or her moral intuitions as divine revelation.

Second, while the moral sense that every person gains through the light of Christ is a species of divine revelation, it is not the only form of personal revelation. Indeed, within Mormonism's revelation-centric theology, there is a hierarchy of revelatory forms that are mediated in part through the institutional authority of the Church. Thus, while the light of Christ is universally available, Mormons also believe in what they call the "gift of the Holy Ghost,"[20] which is a special spiritual gift available only to those who covenant with God through baptism. It promises the "constant companionship of the Holy Spirit" to those who are worthy, a companionship that is, in some not fully specified sense, superior to the light of Christ. In some ways, this hierarchy of moral guidance resembles Protestant attempts to negotiate questions of universality and confessional exclusiveness. Some Protestant thinkers acknowledge the universal influence of "natural conscience" or *synderesis* but privilege the Christian conscience that has been nourished by biblical precept.[21] The Bible, and one's interpretation thereof, prioritizes various claims and forms of conscience.

---

19. Boyd K. Packer, "The Light of Christ," *Ensign*, April 2005, https://www.lds.org/ensign/2005/04/the-light-of-christ.

20. See Bruce Douglas Porter, "Gift of the Holy Ghost," in *The Encyclopedia of Mormonism*, ed. Daniel H. Ludlow (New York: Macmillan Publishing Company, 1992).

21. See discussion in Davis, "Calvinist Ambiguity," 342.

Mormonism's solution to these questions departs in an important respect, substituting ecclesiastical authority for individual interpretive authority. Crucially, in Mormon practice one receives the gift of the Holy Ghost through a ritual—or "ordinance" in Latter-day Saint parlance—that must be administered through "the laying on of hands" by someone holding the Mormon priesthood. The effect is to link personal revelation to the disciplining force of the Church's claims to exclusive priestly authority.

Finally, the scope of the authority of personal revelation received through the gift of the Holy Ghost or the light of Christ is limited by the concept of "stewardship."[22] The concept of stewardship is in some respects analogous to, though ultimately distinct from, the notion of separate secular and religious spheres often deployed to manage the antinomian impulses of Protestant conscience against the authority of the state. For Mormons, a stewardship is a circumscribed realm of responsibility entrusted to an individual by God. The idea can be employed in an institutional or ecclesiastical sense. With an almost entirely lay ministry, most Mormons are given some ecclesiastical role—known as a "calling"—such as leading a congregation, teaching in the Church, or perhaps serving for a time as a missionary. These roles are stewardships. However, the idea can be applied more loosely to personal roles. Hence, for example, Latter-day Saints mothers and fathers speak of having a stewardship over their families. One is entitled to revelation for one's own stewardships, but not for the stewardships of others. Furthermore, those within the ecclesiastical hierarchy can have stewardship "over the Church" in their area, giving their revelation primacy in Church government over the revelation of others. For this reason, Mormon stewardships are seldom subject to the contest and negotiation that characterize Protestant attempts to sequester conscience within a circumscribed sphere. Thus, when the light of Christ is seen within the broader economy of Mormon revelation, it yields a distinctly anemic conception of individual conscience. The subjective moral sovereignty of the self is subordinated to the revelatory authority of God and the ecclesiastical ideas and structures that order the potentially antinomian potential of personal revelation. This limited epistemic authority is coupled with limited practical authority against the claims of both church and state.

---

22. See J. Lynn England, "Stewardship," in *The Encyclopedia of Mormonism*, ed. Daniel H. Ludlow (New York: Macmillan Publishing Company, 1992).

Conscience and Ecclesiastical Authority

Mormonism is a highly institutionalized and hierarchical religion. The Church of Jesus Christ of Latter-day Saints is a tightly integrated ecclesiastical polity. In contrast to the decentralized, congregational structure that is most common in American Protestantism, every Mormon congregation is nested in a hierarchical ecclesiastical structure with ascending priesthood authorities. One can analogize the Mormon Church to the Catholic hierarchy, but in practice the Mormon Church is far more tightly integrated and disciplined than the Catholic Church, which tolerates a fairly wide range of regional variation in teaching and practices. Mormonism is far more centralized and unified.

At the apex of the ecclesiastical structure are the Church's presiding councils, the Quorum of the Twelve Apostles and the First Presidency, whose members are accepted by Latter-day Saints as "prophets, seers, and revelators." These leaders not only have a great deal of practical administrative authority, but they also make strong claims to priestly and revelatory authority. Mormon theology insists that the performance of certain ordinances is a necessary component of salvation, and such ordinances can only be performed by those holding proper priesthood authority. The high Mormon hierarchy claims the exclusive authority to direct the use of that priesthood. Additionally, Mormonism's open canon means that the hierarchy always has the ability to add additional scripture, something that has happened rarely since 1844. Of greater practical significance, the hierarchy claims the ability to receive less formalized divine guidance on behalf of the Church as a whole. Mormon leaders frequently make claims to moral and ecclesiastical authority, and one of the persistent issues in Latter-day Saint experience has been the extent to which concepts of private conscience and personal revelation may be legitimately invoked against the authority of the Church and its hierarchy.

Paradoxically, the hierarchical nature of the Church exists alongside a theology that celebrates personal revelation and the ability of each individual to receive very specific divine instructions. From the very beginning, the idea of dialogic revelation meant that Latter-day Saints expected personal revelation to deliver more than simple moral discernment. It could contain detailed and specific commandments that went well beyond any subjective capacity to discern right from wrong.

The necessity of reconciling the competing claims of individual revelation and hierarchical and communal authority appeared early in Mormon history. Joseph Smith launched the Mormon movement with the publication of the Book of Mormon, which declared among other things that in the last days the faithful were to gather and build up the New Jerusalem somewhere on the American continent.[23] The question arose of where the city of Zion was to be built. One of Smith's associates, Hiram Page, declared that he had received a revelation declaring the location of the New Jerusalem.[24] Many of the members of the infant Church initially accepted Page's revelations as authoritative, and the issue threatened to split the community. Events came to a head at the Church's second general conference. Smith responded to Page's claims to authority by an appeal to the recently adopted "Articles and Covenants"—a constitutional document for the Church—biblical arguments, and a new revelation declaring, "[N]o one shall be appointed to receive revelations and commandments in this church excepting my servant Joseph Smith, Jun., for he receiveth them even as Moses" (D&C 28:2) The conference sided with Smith, declaring "Brother Joseph Smith Jr. was appointed by the voice of the Conference to receive and write Revelations & Commandments for this Church."[25] This settlement has largely held through Mormon history: each individual is entitled to revelation for themselves, but personal revelation cannot be invoked against the authority of the Church and its leaders.

From the time of Hiram Page to the present, Mormonism has periodically struggled with the schismatic tendencies inherent in the claims of revelation. At various times, charismatic figures have arisen, claiming authority based on some special revelation.[26] Generally, Mormon leaders and

23. See 3 Ne. 16, 3 Ne. 21:17, Ether 13:4–8. For the role of the Book of Mormon in the earliest LDS theologies, see Grant Underwood, "The Earliest Reference Guides to the Book of Mormon: Windows into the Past," *Journal of Mormon History* 12 (1985): 69–89; Grant Underwood, "Book of Mormon Usage in Early LDS Theology," *Dialogue: A Journal of Mormon Thought* 17, no. Autumn (1984): 35–74.

24. The incident is recounted in Richard Lyman Bushman, *Joseph Smith and the Beginnings of Mormonism* (Urbana: University of Illinois Press, 1984), 167–68; Bruce G. Stewart, "Hiram Page: An Historical and Sociological Analysis of An Early Mormon Prototype" (master's thesis, Provo, Utah, Brigham Young University, 1987), 112–43.

25. Donald Cannon and Lyndon W. Cook, eds., *Far West Record: Minutes of the Church of Jesus Christ of Latter-Day Saints, 1830–1844* (Salt Lake City: Deseret Book Co., 1983), 3.

26. The most dramatic example of this tendency is the persistence of polygamy among "Mormon fundamentalists" after The Church of Jesus Christ of Latter-day

theologians have responded with the limiting strategies outlined above, strategies that are widely accepted by Latter-day Saints. The result is a religious discourse that abounds with stories and discussions of divine instructions on the details of individual lives. However, it sharply limits the ability of such personal religious experiences to claim any broader moral authority over others or against the religious authority of the ecclesiastical hierarchy. Likewise, dissenters in Mormon history have occasionally invoked the idea of personal revelation and conscience against the authority of the Church.[27] However, such claims have more often than not been met with suspicion and hostility by both rank-and-file Latter-day Saints and the Church hierarchy. LDS theology offers relatively few resources for articulating such claims against communal authority in terms of Mormon concepts. Thus, when dissenters and others have used the language of conscience or individual rights in asserting their claims against the authority of the Church, they are generally seen by other Latter-day Saints as rejecting Mormon theology rather than elaborating on it.

Conscience and Public Authority

If anything, Mormonism is even more hostile to claims that personal revelation or subjective conscience justifies disobeying the law. Latter-day Saints insist that they have a religious duty to obey the law. Here again, Mormonism sides decisively against radical Protestantism by discounting the moral status of personal conviction relative to the moral status of civil law. The Mormon position seems to hearken back to an earlier Pauline notion of conscience as an internalized deputy of the divine authority that ordains government: "Let every soul submit itself to the higher powers. For there is no power but of God, and the powers that be are ordained of God. . . . Therefore it is necessary that ye be subject, not only for punishment, but also for conscience sake" (Rom. 13:1,5). Yet Mormons almost

---

Saints abandoned polygamy around the turn of the twentieth century and began systematically excommunicating those who continued to practice polygamy. The result has been a profusion of charismatic polygamist leaders founding new Mormon sects. See generally Newell G. Bringhurst and Craig L. Foster, eds., *The Persistence of Polygamy, Vol. 3: Fundamentalist Mormon Polygamy from 1890 to the Present* (Independence: John Whitmer Books, 2015); B. Carmon Hardy, *Solemn Covenant: The Mormon Polygamous Passage* (Urbana and Chicago: University of Illinois Press, 1992).

27. See generally Roger D. Launius and Linda Thatcher, eds., *Differing Visions: Dissenters in Mormon History* (Urbana and Chicago: University of Illinois Press, 1994).

never cite these verses. Rather, scriptural support for the Mormon duty to obey the law comes from two texts authored in the 1830s and 1840s and added to the Mormon canon. Early Mormonism operated in a millenarian world in which the end times were assumed to be imminent. Accordingly, the Latter-day Saints were to build up Zion, a New Jerusalem that was to be located in Jackson County, Missouri, at the extreme western edge of American settlement in the 1830s. This was to be an independent Mormon polity with its own laws that would await the imminent second coming of Jesus Christ. "[V]erily I say unto you that in time ye shall have no king nor ruler, for I will be your king and watch over you . . . ye shall have no laws but my laws when I come, for I am your lawgiver," the Lord declares in one of Joseph Smith's earliest revelations (D&C 38:22).[28] However, in part because of this frontal assault on the secular state's monopoly over legal authority, mobs drove the Saints first from Jackson County and then from Missouri. In the face of these reverses, Mormon revelations and theology turned toward secular law as a bulwark for the Saints against the extra-legal violence of their persecutors.[29] During the course of the nineteenth century, Mormons never fully abandoned their dream of a sovereign Zion, and secular law proved an imperfect protection for the Saints at best.[30] The key Mormon texts on legal authority, however, emerged from this turn toward secular law.

The first is a document entitled "Of Governments and Laws in General."[31] It was written in the 1830s and states:

---

28. For a discussion of the conception of divine law contained in this and other early revelations, see Nathan B. Oman, "'I Will Give Unto You My Law': Section 42 as a Legal Text and the Paradoxes of Divine Law," in *Embracing the Law: Reading Doctrine and Covenants 42*, ed. Jeremiah John and Joseph M. Spencer (Provo: Neal A. Maxwell Institute for Religious Scholarship, 2017); Mark Ashurst-McGee, "Zion Rising: Joseph Smith's Early Social and Political Thought" (PhD dissertation, Tempe, Arizona, Arizona State University, 2008), 207–49.

29. See Mark Ashurst-McGee, "Zion in America: The Origins of Mormon Constitutionalism," *Journal of Mormon History* 38, no. 3 (2012): 90–101.

30. See, e.g., Dallin H. Oaks and Marvin S. Hill, *Carthage Conspiracy: The Trial of the Accused Assassins of Joseph Smith* (Urbana: University of Illinois Press, 1975) (recounting the murder of Joseph Smith and the law's anemic efforts to punish his murderers and protect his followers).

31. For a brief summary of the background to the statement, see Steven Craig Harper, *Making Sense of the Doctrine & Covenants: A Guided Tour through Modern Revelations* (Salt Lake City: Deseret Book Co., 2008), 493–94.

> We believe that governments were instituted of God for the benefit of man; and that he holds men accountable for their acts in relation to them, both in making laws and administering them, for the good and safety of society (D&C 134:1).

The document went on to insist that "We believe that all men are bound to sustain and uphold the respective governments in which they reside" (D&C 134:5) The statement was formally included in the Mormon canon in the 1835 edition of the Doctrine and Covenants and has remained part of Mormon scripture to the present.[32] The second text comes from a statement of Mormon beliefs entitled the "Articles of Faith," published by Joseph Smith in 1842. The twelfth of these articles states, "We believe in being subject to kings, presidents, rulers, and magistrates, in obeying, honoring, and sustain the law" (A of F 12).

Neither of these texts claims a revelatory provenance. The first was likely written by one of Joseph Smith's close associates and presents a theology of the state that is largely indistinguishable from contemporary republican and Protestant ideas.[33] The Articles of Faith were prepared as part of a letter to a newspaper editor and drew extensively on early Mormon pamphlets.[34] Nevertheless, they have emerged as the key texts supporting a Mormon duty to obey the law. With the exception of their stronghold in the Intermountain West, Latter-day Saints are always a tiny minority of the societies in which they live. Accordingly, Mormon leaders have insisted on the duty of legal obedience as a way of making the community as small a target as possible.

The most dramatic example of this dynamic can be seen in the case of Helmuth Hübener, a young German Mormon who was executed by the

---

32. It is canonized as Section 134 of the current edition of the Doctrine and Covenants.

33. See Rodney K. Smith, "James Madison, John Witherspoon, and Oliver Cowdery: The First Amendment and the 134th Section of the Doctrine and Covenants," *Brigham Young University Law Review* 2003, no. Spring (2003): 891–940.

34. See Karen Lynn Davidson et al., eds., *Histories: 1832–1844*, The Joseph Smith Papers (Salt Lake City: The Church Historian's Press, 2012), 489–91. Compare Orson Pratt, *A Interesting Account of Several Remarkable Visions, and the Late Discovery of Ancient American Records* (Edinburgh: Ballantyne and Hughes, 1840), 24. For a detailed discussion of the relationship between the Articles of Faith and Pratt's pamphlet, see Breck England, *The Life and Thought of Orson Pratt* (Salt Lake City: University of Utah Press, 1985), 67–71. Interestingly, however, the twelfth Article of Faith does not have an analogue in Pratt's earlier pamphlet.

Gestapo during World War II for writing and distributing anti-Nazi pamphlets.[35] Among modern Germans, Hübener is remembered as one of the heroic handful of "good Germans" who resisted Nazi tyranny. However, his official treatment by the LDS Church has been more ambivalent. Frightened of becoming an object of the Nazis' wrath, Hübener's local ecclesiastical leaders immediately excommunicated him from the Church for failing to "honor, obey, and sustain the law." While his story has been repeatedly told by various Latter-days Saint writers as an example of moral courage, it has seldom been mentioned in official Church publications, and that only recently. This is no doubt because his act of resistance endangered the Church and his co-religionists, and Mormons in other repressive regimes who followed his example could place their religious community in danger. In the twentieth century in particular, Mormon allegiance to the law has been a key part of the Church's efforts to avoid the hostility of suspicious foreign governments worried about Latter-day Saints fomenting political unrest.[36]

Despite this tradition, Mormonism does have resources for challenging secular authority. It has seldom done this, however, in the name of individual conscience. The most dramatic example of Mormon resistance to the law came in the nineteenth-century battles over the practice of polygamy.[37] Joseph Smith secretly introduced "plural marriage" toward the end of his life as a restoration of the ancient practices of the biblical patriarchs. After his death, the Church publicly proclaimed the practice in 1852, and Congress responded with the Morrill Anti-Bigamy Act of 1862, which criminalized polygamy in Mormon Utah. Latter-day Saints refused to comply with the law. They first challenged the constitutionality

35. For a discussion of the relationship between Hübener and modern Mormon theologies of legal authority, see Frederick Mark Gedicks, "The Embarrassing Section 134," *Brigham Young University Law Review* 2003, no. Spring (2003): 960–63. Interestingly, the modern Church has formally eradicated the effect of Hübener's excommunication. Mormons believe that it is possible for living people to posthumously perform ordinances on behalf of the dead. Accordingly, the First Presidency of the Church has "restored the blessings" of Hübener, which constitutes a posthumous reversal of his excommunication. See Gedicks, 959n9.

36. See Nathan B. Oman, "International Legal Experience and the Mormon Theology of the State, 1945–2012," *Iowa Law Review* 100 (2015): 715–50.

37. See Sarah Barringer Gordon, *The Mormon Question: Polygamy and Constitutional Conflict in Nineteenth-Century America* (Chapel Hill: University of North Carolina Press, 2002).

of the Morrill Act in the US Supreme Court on free exercise grounds.[38] When that appeal failed, they simply refused to obey the law. Congress responded with ever more punitive legislation, which the Mormons challenged in the Supreme Court, generally unsuccessfully.[39] Eventually, the federal government pursued a policy of mass incarceration of Mormon polygamists, revoked the right of Mormon women to vote, disenfranchised Mormon polygamists, and moved to confiscate Mormon temples and other assets. Faced with institutional annihilation and permanent political disenfranchisement, Mormon Church President Wilford Woodruff officially abandoned polygamy in 1890, beginning the torturous process that resulted in the early twentieth century with the Church's full embrace of monogamy. Thus, for roughly four decades, Mormons actively resisted federal law.

To be sure, in their prolonged battle with the federal government, the Mormons at times invoked the language of conscience before the Supreme Court, and incarcerated Mormon polygamists referred to themselves as "prisoners for conscience sake."[40] However, Mormons never justified their resistance to federal law primarily in terms of the moral sovereignty

---

38. See Reynolds v. United States, 98 U.S. 145 (1879) (upholding the constitutionality of the Morrill Act).

39. See, e.g., Murphy v. Ramsey, 114 U.S. 15 (1885) (upholding the disenfranchisement of polygamists); United States v. Cannon, 116 U.S. 55 (1885) (adopting a relaxed definition of unlawful cohabitation in order to facilitate prosecution of Mormon polygamists); In re Snow, 120 U.S. 274 (1882) (defining the scope of unlawful cohabitation charges against Mormon polygamists); The Late Corporation of The Church of Jesus Christ of Latter-Day Saints v. United States, 136 U.S. 1(1890) (upholding the disenfranchisement of the Mormon Church and the federal government's confiscation of its property). In addition to the federal government, local governments also moved against the Mormons. The Idaho territorial legislature adopted a law that disenfranchised all Mormons—monogamous and polygamous. The law was upheld by the US Supreme Court. See Davis v. Beason, 133 U.S. 333 (1890). See Edwin B. Firmage, "Free Exercise of Religion in Nineteenth Century America: The Mormon Cases," *Journal of Law and Religion* 7, no. 2 (1989): 281–313 (summarizing the Mormon cases); Orma Linford, "The Mormons and the Law: The Polygamy Cases, Part I," *Utah Law Review* 9, no. 2 (1964): 308–71 (same as previous); Orma Linford, "The Mormons and the Law: The Polygamy Cases, Part II," *Utah Law Review* 9, no. 3 (1965): 543–92 (same as previous).

40. See, e.g., George Ticknor Curtis, *A Plea for Religious Liberty and the Rights of Conscience* (Washington, DC: Gibson Bros, Printers and Bookbinders, 1886);

of their subjective conscience. The challenge to the law's authority did not come from within the subjective self, but rather from allegiance to what Mormons regarded as God's revelations and the community of the Saints. In this sense, the Mormon appeal to conscience, to the extent it existed, was akin to the Catholic recusant approach to confessional solidarity in early modern England, which invoked private conscience to legitimize the illegal practice of Roman religion in the face of hostile government action rather than to elevate personal moral authority vis-à-vis the Catholic magisterium. For example, in an elaborate 1882 letter issued by the First Presidency on how Mormons were to respond to the anti-polygamy Edmunds Act, the word conscience does not appear, although there are appeals to revelation, prophecy, and loyalty to Zion.[41] Alternatively, Mormons argued that religious persecution resulted in unwarranted violence and suffering. Hence, in replying to a defense of the anti-polygamy laws by Vice President Schulyer Colfax, Mormon leader John Taylor likened the federal government's actions to the persecutions of Huguenots, Waldenses, and Albigenses.[42] Tellingly, in rehearsing the stories of Protestant martyrdom, Taylor did not invoke Protestant ideas of conscience but dwelt on the material suffering generated by religious persecution. Mormons also insisted that the authority of the Constitution, properly understood, trumped the decisions of Congress. Revelations published by Joseph Smith during the Mormon turn to secular law insisted that the Constitution was the result of divine inspiration, and in resisting Congressional enactments Mormons could thus insist that they were being true to their religious duty to honor, sustain, and obey the higher law of the Constitution.[43] This infused Mormons' constitutional arguments with a religious significance. For example, when George Q. Cannon, a member of the First Presidency and the political mastermind of Mormon resistance, penned an elaborate response to the Supreme Court's defense

---

Bruce A. Van Orden, *Prisoner for Conscience' Sake: The Life of George Reynolds* (Salt Lake City: Deseret Book Co., 1992).

41. See John Taylor, George Q. Cannon, and Joseph F. Smith, *An Address to the Members of The Church of Jesus Christ of Latter-Day Saints* (Salt Lake City: n.p., 1882).

42. John Taylor and Schulyer Colfax, *The Mormon Question* (Salt Lake City: Deseret News, 1870), 8–9.

43. See D&C 98:5–6; D&C 101:77, 80; D&C 109:54. See also Ashurst-McGee, "Zion in America: The Origins of Mormon Constitutionalism" (discussing the historical background for these additions to Mormon scripture).

of the constitutionality of the Morrill Act, he declared, "[N]ot the least of the considerations which prompt me to this review, is that I desire that all the people of my faith may know that we have not been deceived in our ideas respecting the Constitution and our rights under it."[44] In short, the subjective moral authority of individual conscience played virtually no real role in how Mormons conceptualized their resistance to federal anti-polygamy laws.

The muted role of conscience can be seen in the role of Mormonism in the development of free exercise law during the post-rights revolution era in the United States. The LDS Church's most prominent intervention in those debates came in *Corporation of the Presiding Bishop v. Amos*.[45] In that case the Church successfully defended the exemption of religious institutions from the anti-discrimination rules of Title VII from an Establishment Clause attack, arguing that such an exemption was necessary for religious communities to define their own rules of membership. The Church has successfully defended the same position before the European Court of Human Rights.[46] As scholars have noted, "The connecting thread [in Mormon concerns with religious freedom] is the right of religious organizations to autonomy in their affairs."[47] In this concern can be seen the echoes of the earliest Mormon theology of law, which imagined the creation of Zion as an independent polity with its own laws awaiting the imminent Second Coming. While modern Mormonism has abandoned immediate apocalyptic expectations and any effort to create an independent Mormon commonwealth, Zion remains a potent idea within Mormon thought. Hence the emphasis on the integrity and independence of religious communities. It is a vision of religious challenges to legal authority in which the claims of individual conscience play almost no role. At most, the language of conscience is deployed—as it was by religious dissenters in Tudor and Stuart England—to defend the claims of minority religious communities against the state.

---

44. George Q. Cannon, *A Review of the Decision of the Supreme Court of the United States, in the Case of George Reynolds vs. The United States* (Salt Lake City: Deseret News Printing and Publishing Establishment, 1879), 6.

45. 483 U.S. 327 (1987).

46. See Obst v. Germany, Application No. 425/03 (Dec. 23, 2010) (European Court of Human Rights).

47. Cole Durham and Nathan B. Oman, "A Century of Mormon Theory and Practice in Church-State Relations: Constancy Amidst Change" (November 7, 2006), 28, http://papers.ssrn.com/sol3/papers.cfm?abstract_id=942567.

Conclusion

The idea of conscience developed from scholastic moral philosophy and was honed in the debates of the Protestant Reformation. What emerged were conceptions of conscience that granted enormous epistemic and practical authority to the subjectivity of the self. In its starkest form, conscience suggests that the brute fact of moral conviction can claim a certain kind of moral authority. Mormonism has proven largely hostile to such claims. Its moral epistemology centers on the idea of personal revelation from God, but controls against the antinomian possibilities of such revelation through a robust notion of religious hierarchy and delineated personal stewardships. In this vision, conscience is seen as, at best, a rudimentary form of personal revelation. The result is that there is very little space within Mormonism for the claims of conscience against ecclesiastical authority. For largely historical reasons rooted in their experience as an often-persecuted religious minority, Mormons have developed a theological discourse that tends to emphasize a religious requirement of obedience to secular law. However, Mormon history is replete with examples of Mormon challenges to legal authority. Latter-day Saints have generally not rooted the legitimacy of such challenges in the subjective authority of the individual conscience. Rather, Mormonism has tended to emphasize the claims of communal solidarity and independence when challenging legal authority, a stance that is rooted in some of the earliest and most basic structures of Mormon thought. Mormonism has only blessed resistance to the law when the integrity of Zion—conceptualized as the institutional Church and the Mormon community—have demanded it, and Mormon efforts to limit the reach of the law, such as constitutional litigation and lobbying, have tended to focus on the claims of religious institutions and communities rather than the claims of subjective conscience.

CHAPTER 6

Doux Commerce in the City of God: Trade and the Mormon Ideal of Zion

Introduction

Zion must be at the center of any Mormon account of a good society. Accordingly, any claim that a social or economic practice is contrary to the order of Zion must be taken seriously by a thoughtful and committed Latter-day Saint. Hugh Nibley has argued, albeit in an unsystematic way, that commerce is essentially inconsistent with Zion. Trade, he claims, tends to corrupt the soul, focusing us on selfish and materialistic desires. It involves the oppression of the poor and the vulnerable. Finally, it leads to inequalities that cannot be reconciled with the vision of a righteous city in which there is "no poor among them" (Moses 7:18). This chapter examines Nibley's morally pessimistic assessment of commerce. Ultimately, I find his critique unpersuasive. Drawing on eighteenth-century writers in the *doux commerce* tradition, I argue that trade has the capacity to instill moral habits that can support Zion and help to alleviate the material want that is at the heart of the problem of poverty.

While my assessment of commerce is considerably more positive than Nibley's, my object is not to offer an apologia for modern capitalism or insulate current economic practices from theological critique. There are many aspects of our economic life that are evil, and any interpretation of Zion that renders the ideal of the city of God entirely compatible with our current economic circumstances would diminish the power and usefulness of these doctrines. Nor am I arguing that markets are sufficient as a set of social institutions for bringing us closer to the ideal of Zion. Rather, my goal is more limited. By drawing attention to the features of commerce that make it potentially morally valuable, I hope to do two things. First, an appreciation of the benefits of commerce allows us to reconsider the failure of nineteenth-century Zion-building in terms other than selfishness or shirking. Instead, it reveals the important role of institutions in economic organization, including the organization of Zion. Second, identifying the good of commerce lays the foundation for a critique of modern economic conditions that avoids a blanket condemnation of social practices that can contribute toward the building of Zion.

Zion in Mormon Thought

In 1831, shortly after organizing the Church of Christ, Joseph Smith began an "inspired translation" of the Bible, going through the text of the King James Version and adding additional materials as moved by the Holy Spirit.[1] His revision of the book of Genesis begins with a long framing narrative that recounts a confrontation between Moses and Satan on Mount Sinai, followed by a divine vision of the history of creation. Within this vision, Moses sees the prophet Enoch. The book of Genesis devotes a bare four verses to Enoch (see Gen. 5:21–24), declaring, "And Enoch walked with God: and he was not; for God took him" (Gen. 5:24). In Joseph Smith's book of Moses, however, Enoch becomes a major character. Strikingly, Enoch's ascension to heaven is transformed from an individual experience into a communal one. Enoch preaches God's message to a wicked world. A few people heed his words, and they form a city. "And the Lord called his people Zion, because they were of one heart and one mind, and dwelt in righteousness; and there was no poor among them" (Moses 7:18). In contrast to the Enoch narrative in Genesis, however, it is the entire City of Zion that ascends to heaven. "And it came to pass that the Lord showed unto Enoch all the inhabitants of the earth; and he beheld, and lo, Zion, in process of time, was taken up into heaven. And the Lord said unto Enoch: Behold mine abode forever" (Moses 7:21).

It would be difficult to overestimate the importance of the City of Enoch for Mormon thought. In the book of Moses, Zion is identified with heaven—the dwelling place of God. Likewise, in his 1832 vision of the celestial kingdom, Joseph Smith recorded that the highest level of heaven consists of those "who are come unto Mount Zion, and unto the city of the living God, the heavenly place, the holiest of all" (D&C 76:66). The potency of Zion in Mormon thought comes from the way that it simultaneously functions as an eschatological ideal and a concrete goal of human effort. "Now, as you have asked, behold, I say unto you, keep my commandments, and seek to bring forth and establish the cause of Zion," (D&C 6:6) declares the Lord in an 1829 revelation. For the first two generations of Mormons, this injunction was taken literally. Zion was an actual community that the Mormons were going to build, located first in Jackson County, Missouri, and later—as the vicissitudes of anti-Mormon

1. For a discussion of the historical context for the book of Moses, see Richard Lyman Bushman, *Joseph Smith: Rough Stone Rolling* (New York: Alfred A. Knopf, 2005), 130–43.

violence required frequent relocations—in the Mormon commonwealth established in the Great Basin.[2]

In the book of Moses, Zion is broadly defined in what we might call political and economic terms. In the City of Enoch, "they dwelt in righteousness"—implying particular kinds of interpersonal and communal relationships—and "there was no poor among them"—implying a particular economic order (see Moses 7:18). In Joseph Smith's canonized revelations, it is the economic aspect of this vision that receives the greatest attention.[3] Those revelations articulate a system of voluntary property pooling and redistribution, and an increasingly complicated set of procedures and ecclesiastical institutions to manage the system of consecrations (donations) and stewardships (distributions) (see D&C 42). During the lifetime of Joseph Smith, the Law of Consecration and Stewardship was never fully or successfully implemented. After Joseph's death and the exodus of the Saints to Utah, Brigham Young sought to realize Joseph's goal through a system of cooperative enterprises called United Orders, which were largely aimed at establishing the Mormon commonwealth as economically self-sufficient. These United Orders also ultimately failed because of internal problems, outside competition, and the federal government's legal crusade against the Mormons' polygamy after the Civil War. By the first decade of the twentieth century, Mormons had abandoned the effort to realize Zion in concrete utopian communities.

The retreat from the literal realization of the Law of Consecration and Stewardship after 1900 does not mean that Zion has ceased to be important for Latter-day Saints or has been consigned entirely to a millennial future. The nineteenth-century plan for Zion continues to be held up as an ideal, one that has claims of some kind on the concrete economic be-

---

2. The standard scholarly treatments of the various Mormon efforts to realize Zion in the nineteenth century are Leonard Arrington, *Great Basin Kingdom: An Economic History of the Latter-Day Saints, 1830–1900* (Cambridge: Harvard University Press, 1958); Leonard J. Arrington, Feramorz Y. Fox, and Dean L. May, *Building the City of God: Community and Cooperation Among the Mormons*, 2nd ed. (Urbana: University of Illinois Press, 1992).

3. Toward the end of his life, Joseph Smith also articulated a largely esoteric set of teachings about the political structure of Zion. See generally Bushman, *Rough Stone Rolling*, 519–25; Klaus J. Hansen, *Quest for Empire: The Political Kingdom of God and the Council of Fifty in Mormon History* (Lincoln: University of Nebraska Press, 1974); Patrick Q. Mason, "God and the People: Theodemocracy in Nineteenth-Century Mormonism," *Journal of Church and State* 55, no. 3 (Summer 2013): 349–75.

havior of Latter-day Saints. This can be seen in both institutional and rhetorical terms. For example, the creation of the Church welfare system in the 1930s, which involves a pooling of donations and providing economic relief to distressed Latter-day Saints, was articulated in terms of building Zion. The same is true of the Church's more recent and outwardly directed humanitarian efforts. For example, in a 1991 sermon, Gordon B. Hinckley, who later became president of the Church, spoke of personal and social redemption in terms of Zion. After invoking those "all about us . . . who are in need of help and who are deserving of rescue," giving the example of those mired in addiction or suffering domestic abuse, he quoted the book of Moses and said:

> If we are to build that Zion of which the prophets have spoken and of which the Lord has given mighty promise, we must set aside our consuming selfishness. We must rise above our love for comfort and ease, and in the very process of effort and struggle, even in our extremity, we shall become better acquainted with our God.[4]

The continuing vitality of Zion and its role in contemporary Latter-day Saint thought can be seen in the grammar of the word itself. In Mormon scripture, Zion is always a proper noun. It can refer to concrete individual communities—such as the City of Enoch or the failed attempt to build the city of God in Jackson County, Missouri—or it can be used generally to refer to an ideal righteous community. In contemporary Mormon language, Zion continues to be a noun, but it can also be an adjective. Hence, a Latter-day Saint might speak of a Zion community, a Zion family, a Zion congregation, and so on. Implicit in this usage is the conviction that one can extract a set of morally and spiritually potent teachings from the mass of scriptural and historical stories of Zion and apply them to human lives in the here and now.

Are trade and commerce compatible with the ideal of Zion? This is not a question that Latter-day Saints frequently ask themselves. Most Mormons are content to let their inquiry into the religious legitimacy of trade begin and end with the observation that contemporary Church leaders have not been notable in denouncing the evils of commerce.[5] The question, however, is worth asking. Given the way in which Brigham Young exalted autarky as a primary goal of the United Orders, going so

---

4. Gordon B. Hinckley, "Our Mission of Saving," *Ensign*, November 1991.

5. E.g., Phillip J. Bryson, "In Defense of Capitalism: Church Leaders on Property, Wealth, and the Economic Order," *Brigham Young University Studies* 38, no. 3 (1999): 89–107.

far as to organize boycotts of non-Mormon businesses through Zion's Cooperative Mercantile Institution (ZCMI), it's by no means self-evident that commerce is entirely consistent with Zion, at least as it has been conceptualized by Latter-day Saints in the past.[6] Likewise, Mormon scripture sometimes takes a less than celebratory stance toward trade. In the Book of Mormon, for example, trade is associated with wealth, but that wealth is tied to moral decline:

> And thus the Lamanites began to increase in riches, and began to trade one with another and wax great, and began to be a cunning and a wise people, as to the wisdom of the world, yea, a very cunning people, delighting in all manner of wickedness and plunder, except it were among their own brethren. (Mosiah 24:7)

All of this suggests that Latter-day Saints committed to using the idea of Zion as a guide for their economic thinking should at least entertain the possibility that trade is inherently tainted. In considering this question, Hugh Nibley's writings on Zion provide a useful starting place.

Hugh Nibley's Critique of Trade

Hugh Nibley offers what amounts to a three-part attack on commerce for being inconsistent with the ideal of Zion.[7] To be sure, Nibley does not explicitly attack trade per se, and his approach is discursive and exegetical, which means that it can be difficult to reconstruct his thinking in a set of clear claims. Nevertheless, Nibley is critical of markets in his writings, and his interpretation of Zion drives his criticism. Furthermore, he offers a vision of Zion that suggests that commerce is largely unnecessary, and thus its pernicious consequences need not be tolerated. Broadly speaking, Nibley's indictment of the market has three parts. First, he attacks what he

---

6. For a discussion of the role of ZCMI in boycotting Gentile businesses, see Arrington, *Great Basin Kingdom*, 297–307. For a summary of Mormon hostility to "foreign" trade in the nineteenth century, see Russell W. Belk, "Battling Worldliness in the New Zion: Mercantilism versus Homespun in Nineteenth-Century Utah," *Journal of Macromarketing* (Spring 1994): 9–20.

7. Hugh Nibley's social criticism is contained mainly in two books: Hugh Nibley, *Approaching Zion*, ed. Don E. Norton (Salt Lake City: Deseret Book Co, 1989); Hugh Nibley, *Brother Brigham Challenges the Saints*, ed. Don E. Norton (Salt Lake City: Deseret Book Co., 1994). The arguments addressed in this chapter are set forth most fully in his "Work We Must, But the Lunch is Free," contained in Nibley, *Approaching Zion*, 202–51.

calls "the Work Ethic," a set of perverse moral habits and beliefs reinforced by market exchange. Second, he denounces the inequality created by trade and commerce. Finally, he argues that market exchange rests on the harm and exploitation of the weak and the innocent.

Nibley repeatedly denounces "the Work Ethic."[8] He never clearly states what he means by this term, but he seems to identify it with a set of moral habits growing out of the social Darwinism of nineteenth-century economic liberalism. He writes:

> Darwin gave the blessing of science to men who had been hoping and praying for holy sanction to an otherwise immoral way of life. Malthus had shown that there will never be enough lunch for everybody, and therefore people would have to fight for it; and Ricardo had shown by his Iron Law of Wages that those left behind and gobbled up in the struggle for lunch had no just cause for complaint. Darwin showed that this was an inexorable *law* of nature by which the race was actually *improved*; Mill and Spencer made it the cornerstone of the gospel of Free Enterprise—the weaker must fall by the way if the stock is to be improved.[9]

For Nibley, the Work Ethic consists of a self-centered striving for riches and status that inculcates a sense of entitlement to earned wealth and justifies indifference to the plight of others. This is the moral orientation required by a market economy, and it results in a literally Satanic view of the world, one in which the powerful are able to get anything they desire for money, at the expense of the poor.

At the heart of the Work Ethic, according to Nibley, is a mistaken view of property. On this view, the owner of property deserves his wealth because he has earned it, and he may legitimately withhold property from those in need. Nibley playfully takes the phrase "There is no free lunch" as the embodiment of this mistaken stance. The quintessential example of the Work Ethic in action is the cruel nineteenth-century industrialist. "The mill-owner who threatened to withhold lunch from the workers could always get them to work on his terms, claiming their lunches as his private property to dispose of as he chose."[10] The problem with this stance is two fold. First, it excludes God from the picture of property, denying the reality that the entirety of creation is the property of the Lord, and any wealth that we enjoy and control is only as a gift from God. By failing to acknowledge God's hand in all things, the Work Ethic alienates its

8. E.g., Nibley, *Approaching Zion*, 227, 231, 243–45.
9. Nibley, 206.
10. Nibley, 221.

adherents from the Lord. Second, it can be used to justify cruelty and selfishness. Nibley cites Ayn Rand for the Work-Ethic-inspired view that "altruism . . . is the greatest weakness in our society and the greatest obstacle to the unhindered operation of free enterprise."[11] The result is a damnable unwillingness to succor those in need. "[A]nyone who can argue that it is permissible to deny food to the hungry when we have food 'shall with the wicked lift up his eyes in hell.'"[12]

Nibley also denounces the inequality that results from the operation of market economies. If everything is ultimately a gift from God, then no one can claim to deserve more than anyone else. Commenting on King Benjamin's speech in the book of Mosiah, Nibley writes:

> He is setting the keynote, which is absolute equality. And that follows naturally from the proposition that we owe everything to God, to whom we are perpetually and inescapably in debt beyond our means of repayment.[13]

The evil of inequality is two-fold. First, it consists in one person taking more of the gifts of the Lord than another. "Malthus was wrong,"[14] argues Nibley as he cites the Doctrine and Covenants' statement that "the earth is full, and there is enough and to spare" (D&C 104:17). In taking what is not rightfully his, the man claiming greater wealth can then use this power to oppress the poor. "Brigham Young . . . noted . . . that if the wealth were equally distributed one fine day, it would not be long before it would be unequal as ever, the lion's share going to the most dedicated and competent seekers for it."[15] The rich man may then, Nibley writes sarcastically, "generously offer . . . [the poor] the chance to work for him and get their lunches back—but they must work all day, just for him and just for lunch."[16]

All of this leads to the oppression of the vulnerable. The market transaction that captures Nibley's imagination is the labor contract. Quoting Brigham Young, he writes, "workers [in Victorian Britain] knew that their employers would make them work for nothing, and then compel them to live on roots and grass if their physical organization could endure it, therefore, says the mechanic 'If I can get anything out of you, I will call

11. Nibley, 238.
12. Nibley, 249.
13. Nibley, 225.
14. Nibley, 239.
15. Nibley, 243.
16. Nibley, 243.

it a godsend,' and do what he can to rip off the boss."[17] He dwells at some length on the plight of child laborers suffering in the coal pits of nineteenth-century Scotland, offering it up as the quintessential example of free enterprise. The heartless Victorian industrialist is not an abstract archetype. He writes:

> The story of the mines has been told not to harrow up our souls, but as a gentle reminder that the principles and practices of the nineteenth-century industrialists are still wholly and enthusiastically endorsed by the people of our own society, in proof of which we could cite present-day instances almost if not quite as horrendous as Grandpa's stories of bonny Scotland. The reason things have not changed lies in the basic nature of those principles, of necessity stern and inflexible. A thing is either free or it is not; a free lunch would have to be for everybody, and that would never do in the "real world" in which we live.[18]

Zion, the alternative to the Work Ethic, has three characteristics emphasized by Nibley. The first is the solution of the economic problem. God has taken care for our needs. "[T]he earth is full, and there is enough and to spare" (D&C 104:17). Second, Zion is characterized by an ethic of open-handed sharing, in contrast to the miserly bean-counting of the Work Ethic. Finally, in Zion the higher pursuits of gaining knowledge and building the Kingdom of God replaces a concern for material abundance.

The material needs of human beings in Zion have been satisfied by the abundance of the Lord's gifts. According to Nibley, satisfying such needs is quite simple. The model for the solution to the economic problem in Zion, he says, is the story of manna from heaven in the book of Exodus. The immediate needs of the children of Israel were satisfied, but they were unable to use the divine gift to accumulate wealth. The manna rotted if not eaten immediately. He writes:

> [T]here should be no serious economic problem at the human level: after all, mice, cockroaches, elephants, butterflies, and dolphins have all solved the economic problem—their mere existence on earth after thousands of years of vicissitudes is adequate proof that they have found the secret to survival.[19]

According to Nibley, the solution to the economic problem lies in the limiting of human desires. "The limitation on wants," he writes, "is important, since one often wants what one should not have; a want is 'justi-

17. Nibley, 207.
18. Nibley, 247.
19. Nibley, 235–36.

fied' only when it is a true need, and . . . our real needs are few—'food and raiment,' mansions and yachts not included."[20]

Because the limited legitimate material desires of human beings can be met from the abundance of the Lord's gifts, human interactions in Zion should be characterized by an attitude of open-handed generosity. Nibley here draws extensively on the sermon of King Benjamin and the book of Deuteronomy. King Benjamin teaches that everything we have is an unmerited gift from the Lord, and we are accordingly expected to share it with others. "The extra food on the rich man's table does not belong to him, says King Benjamin, but to God, and *he* wants the poor man to have it (Mosiah 4:22)."[21] From Deuteronomy, Nibley points to property rules that prohibit owners from extracting the last ounce of economic benefit from the harvest, requiring that they leave food for the hungry, poor, and even animals. He also lauds the Jubilee year, which involved a general forgiveness of debts, as well as the injunction to treat strangers with compassion and hospitality.

Finally, Nibley argues that in Zion, material concerns will be decisively subordinated to a focus on higher things. Indeed, Nibley suggests that the only legitimate form of economic activity is agriculture. "Study, the worked of the kingdom, and the cultivating of the soil were Adam's calling for almost a millennium—and he never got bored."[22] Tellingly, Nibley praises the rules in Deuteronomy that make agricultural land inalienable. The implication is that agriculture is a virtuous form of economic activity precisely because it can be separated from trade and the corrupting influence of the Work Ethic. Nibley repeatedly responds to the criticism that life in Zion would be dull and monotonous because of its simplicity. He argues that this need not worry us because, on one hand, our desire for diversity rests on a self-centered illusion that we are special, while on the other hand, we will always have available "the endless reaches of the mind, expanding forever in all directions."[23] There, an "infinite variety invites us, with endless space for all so that none need be jealous of another."[24]

---

20. Nibley, 239–40.

21. Nibley, 241–42 (emphasis in original).

22. Nibley, 208. In support of this proposition, Nibley cites D&C 26:1: "Behold, I say unto you that you shall let your time be devoted to [1] the studying of the scriptures, and [2] to preaching, and to confirming the church, . . . and [3] to performing your labors on the land."

23. Nibley, 242.

24. Nibley, 242.

Some Criticisms of Nibley

Nibley presents himself as describing eternal truths about the nature of economic life drawn from the revealed word of God. At key points in his argument, however, his analysis relies less on Mormon theology than on ideas borrowed from nineteenth- and twentieth-century ideologies, often without attribution.[25] This is important because the economic circumstances he describes, rather than reflecting an unchanging economic truth, may rest on historically contingent conditions. Tellingly, most of his examples of trade involve Victorian labor arrangements. For example, he does not discuss trade in goods, except insofar as he discusses the exchange of labor for food and other necessities. His understanding of labor contracts, in turn, rests on the familiar model of wage slavery, although he does not use the term. David Ricardo, whom Nibley references, argued in 1817 that "[t]he natural price of labour is that price which is necessary to enable the labourers, one with another, to subsist and to perpetuate their race, without either increase or diminution."[26] The implication is that all laborers live on the edge of destitution, with the employer wielding the constant threat of starvation to demand labor in return for a pittance. On this point, however, Ricardo has been proven wrong. Over the course of the nineteenth century, real wages for laborers in Victorian Britain and elsewhere rose, as did their standard of living.[27] Contra Nibley's claim, it simply isn't true that most workers lack sufficient bargaining power with their employers to demand a wage in excess of subsistence. Indeed, contemporary research on famines suggests that

25. To be sure, Mormon theology and scripture is itself at times preoccupied with nineteenth-century concerns, just as much of the Old Testament is preoccupied with the social and political concerns of pre-exilic and immediately post-exilic Israel, or just as much of the New Testament addresses itself to the social problems of first-century Judea and the early Christian communities of the Roman Empire.

26. David Ricardo, *The Principles of Political Economy and Taxation* (Mineola: Dover Publications, 2004), 52.

27. See Gregory Clark, "The Condition of the Working Class in England, 1209–2004," *Journal of Political Economy* 113 (2005): 1307–40; Peter H. Lindert and Jeffery G. Williamson, "English Workers' Living Standard During the Industrial Revolution: A New Look," *Economic History Review* 36 (1983): 1–25.

most instances of starvation are caused by ethnic hatred and political conflict rather than extortionate bosses.[28]

The claim that the economic problem has been solved was also a truism of mid-twentieth-century policy thinking in the United States and Europe after World War II. As early as 1930, John Maynard Keynes argued that the Great Depression was simply the result of social and economic adjustments to technological change, but that "in the long run . . . *mankind is solving its economic problem.*"[29] Nibley supports his claim regarding material abundance—or at any rate sufficiency— by citing the Sermon on the Mount, but the idea that wealth is an exogenous fact and that the primary question is its proper distribution was a key assumption of such mid-twentieth century works as John Kenneth Galbraith's *The Affluent Society* or John Rawls' *A Theory of Justice*.[30] This economic optimism was at the heart of mid-twentieth-century progressive policies such as the social welfare states of Western Europe and the Great Society of Lyndon Johnson in the United States. These political movements dominated Nibley's adult life, and their traces can be seen in the economic assumptions underlying his thought. Even on the political left, however, faith that the economic problem had finally been solved was faltering by the 1970s as stagflation and fiscal crisis wracked the developed world. Globally, the persistence of poverty in the face of successive waves of expert advice directed at its abolition suggests the extreme difficulty of meeting mankind's economic needs.[31] Far from being solved, the economic problem is one of the central moral and practical issues facing humanity.

---

28. See Amartya Sen, *Poverty and Famines: An Essay on Entitlement and Deprivation* (Oxford: Oxford University Press, 1990).

29. John Maynard Keynes, *Essays in Persuasion* (Basingstoke Palgrave Macmillan, 2010), 325 (emphasis in original).

30. See John Kenneth Galbraith, *The Affluent Society*, 40th anniversary ed. (Boston: Mariner Books, 1998); John Rawls, *A Theory of Justice* (Cambridge: Harvard University Press, 1971).

31. For competing views on the difficulties of development economics, see William Easterly, *The White Man's Burden: Why the West's Efforts to Aid the Rest Have Done So Much Ill and So Little Good* (New York: Penguin Press, 2006); Jeffrey D. Sachs, *The End of Poverty: Economic Possibilities for Our Time* (London: Allen Lane, 2005). Both writers take global poverty to be a problem without a simple solution, although Sachs is optimistic about the ability of Western governments to eliminate extreme poverty with a sufficient commitment of resources. Easterly argues that solutions to poverty will necessarily be local and decentralized, and that it is not possible to eliminate extreme want with top-down programs.

Nibley's vision of Zion also has an anti-materialist and austere inflection. This is odd for a Mormon writer. He castigates both market economies and communist economies for their spiritual and intellectual sterility, blaming it on their materialism. "[I]t is because communism is a 'dialectical *materialism*' that it is the drabbest show of all, though our rival establishment is not far behind."[32] When he rhapsodizes about the infinite pleasures of thought and contemplation as the final reward in Zion, he sounds rather more like Plato than Parley P. Pratt. Latter-day Saint thinkers have long acknowledged that Mormonism is itself a kind of materialism.[33] The Doctrine and Covenants, for example, teaches that "[t] he Father has a body of flesh and bones as tangible as man's; the Son also," (D&C 130:22) and elsewhere that "[a]ll spirit is matter" (D&C 131:7). These doctrines suggest that the material is not inferior to the intellectual or the spiritual. Rather, Mormonism embraces what Terryl Givens has called "the collapse of sacred distance,"[34] including the distance between the material and spiritual. Indeed, Mormon theology suggests, "there is a kind of nihilism in the universal," and that attempts to transcend the material result, in Orson Pratt's phrase, with a God that "exists *Nowhere*."[35] Nibley's prioritization of the intellectual over the material as the true source of human happiness thus trades on a dichotomy that Mormon theology has largely rejected.

In economic terms, Nibley's anti-materialism shows up in an ascetic attitude toward material abundance.[36] This asceticism is foreign, however,

---

32. Nibley, *Approaching Zion*, 242.

33. See, e.g., Sterling M. McMurrin, *The Theological Foundations of the Mormon Religion*, reprint edition (Salt Lake City: Signature Books, 1965).

34. Terryl L. Givens, *People of Paradox: A History of Mormon Culture* (New York: Oxford University Press, 2007), 37–51; see also Marc Alain Bohn and James C. Olsen, "Terryl Givens and the Shape of Mormon Studies," *Dialogue: A Journal of Mormon Thought* 43, no. 4 (2010): 212.

35. Nathan B. Oman, "A Local Faith," *Brigham Young University Studies* 49, no. 2 (2010): 171.

36. Truman Madsen recounted conversations with Nibley making a similar point:

> I keep telling him, "Your grandfather gave the Church \$500,000. Do you think it would have been better if he hadn't?" Hugh almost talks like a Franciscan. It would be better if we were all poor. Then we wouldn't be tempted to think God gave it to us and we can use it the way we want. God didn't give it to us; and if he did—honorably—we'd better use it for Him and not for feathering our own nest. Boy, he's tough on that.

to the Mormon tradition. In contrast to the Christian hermits of late Antiquity or the monastic movements of the Middle Ages, there is no Mormon tradition of seeking poverty as a means of achieving greater spirituality. Poverty confers no special spiritual merit in Mormon theology.[37] Rather, it is seen as an evil to be alleviated through material abundance. To be sure, Brigham Young and his compatriots regarded wealth as spiritually dangerous. Speaking of the Saints in 1853, Young said, "They are on the highway to wealth; *and there is danger in it*."[38] He continued:

> This people are gathering much substance around them, which is a principle of heaven—a principle of Zion, but there is fear within us lest it cause us to forget our God and our religion. Whether we have much or little, let it be on the altar for it is all the Lord's, whether this people know it or not.[39]

Nevertheless, in nineteenth-century Mormon sermons, the term "prosperity" virtually always has a positive meaning when applied to Zion.[40] A typical example occurred at one of early Mormonism's holiest moments, the cornerstone laying ceremony of the Salt Lake Temple. In that context Bishop Edward Hunter said, "When we look around us, what do we behold? We see the most unmistakable tokens of prosperity, peace, and plenty; the self-evident fruits of high heaven's protecting care, industry, sobriety, and faith."[41] Similar statements could be easily multiplied.

It is not that the Latter-day Saints took wealth as evidence of righteousness; Brigham Young delighted in denouncing the wickedness of the wealthy.

Quoted in Boyd Jay Petersen, *Hugh Nibley: A Consecrated Life* (Salt Lake City: Greg Kofford Books, 2002), 382.

37. One possible counterexample would be the case of the poor among the Zoramites in the Book of Mormon. In Alma 32, Alma beholds "with great joy" the poverty of the rejected Zoramites because "their afflictions had truly humbled them, and that they were in preparation to hear the word" (Alma 32:6).

38. Brigham Young, September 11, 1853, *Journal of Discourses*, 26 vols. (London and Liverpool: LDS Booksellers Depot, 1854 86), 1:75 (emphasis in original).

39. Young, 1:75.

40. Lorenzo Snow's remarks in an 1867 sermon are typical:

> I am pleased, indeed, to see the prosperity of Zion. I feel a spirit of solemnity upon me while standing here gazing upon this multitude of Saints. Seeing the difficulties through which we have passed, our present prosperity is astonishing to ourselves and equally so to the world. I feel to thank God for the prosperity of Zion as it presents itself at this time.

Lorenzo Snow, October 9, 1867, *Journal of Discourses*, 12:147.

41. Edward Hunter, April 6, 1853, *Journal of Discourses*, 2:37.

Nor did they see poverty necessarily as a sign of divine disfavor. Rather, it is that following on Joseph Smith's denial of a sharp distinction between the material and the spiritual, they regarded material bounty as another of God's blessings. Living in a physical world was not a travail to be suffered through on the way to a higher and immaterial spiritual enlightenment. Rather, material abundance could be—should be—enjoyed with proper gratitude to the Lord. "We like enjoyment here," said John Taylor. "That is right. God designs that we should enjoy ourselves. I do not believe in a religion that makes people gloomy, melancholy, miserable and ascetic."[42] Whatever the merits of Nibley's criticism of conspicuous consumption, his monastic attitude toward material goods—poverty and study as a higher way—breaks with the teachings of Brigham Young and other latter-day prophets.

A Defense of Trade in Zion

Each of Nibley's criticisms of commerce is similarly questionable. Trade depends on and can inculcate a set of moral habits that support the Zion envisioned by the scriptures. While the effects of trade are not universally positive, it can provide a powerful engine for alleviating poverty. Material abundance is a precondition for a society in which there is no poor among us, and commerce can generate that abundance. Finally, while the scriptures denounce poverty, taking advantage of the weak, and societies marked by economic inequalities, the apparently anti-commercial passages relied on by Nibley, when read in context, cannot be taken as providing a blanket condemnation of commercial life.

In 1930, John Maynard Keynes envisioned an imminent future in which the economic problem would be solved. He wrote:

> When the accumulation of wealth is no longer of high social importance, there will be a great change in the code of morals. We shall be able to rid ourselves of many of the pseudo-moral principles which have hag-ridden us for two hundred years, by which we have exalted some of the most distasteful of human qualities into the position of the highest virtues. We shall be able to afford to dare to assess the money-motive at its true value. The love of money as a possession—as distinguished from the love of money as a means to the enjoyments and realities of life—will be recognized for what it is, a somewhat disgusting morbidity, one of those semi-criminal, semi-pathological propensities which one hands over with a shudder to the specialists in mental disease.[43]

---

42. John Taylor, January 5, 1873, *Journal of Discourses*, 15:270.
43. Keynes, *Essays in Persuasion*, 369.

Keynes, of course, was most definitely not a religious idealist,[44] but the libertine economist shares with the ascetic Nibley a similar assessment of the moral habits of the merchant. At the heart of this vision is the assumption that the man or woman of commerce is essentially self-centered and acquisitive, focused on material possessions for their own sake and devoid of concern for other human values. Ultimately it is the morality of Josiah Bounderby in Charles Dickens' novel *Hard Times*, the callous profiteer with a penchant for fraud and sharp dealing.[45]

While it is surely true that some merchants are dishonest misers and some manipulative people enter commerce, it is not true that trade thrives on selfishness and dishonesty. Economists have long recognized that one of the central problems facing commerce is ex post opportunism by trading partners. A story from the classics illustrates the problem. After waging a successful war against a series of Roman generals, the slave army led by Spartacus found itself at the bottom of the Italian boot, seeking escape from the circling legions. Spartacus contracted with a fleet of pirates to carry the escaped slaves to safety, but Plutarch records that "after the pirates had struck a bargain with him, and received his earnest they deceived him and sailed away."[46] It's the kind of predatory dishonesty against those at the bottom of the social ladder—slaves—that Nibley takes as the quintessential example of mercantile morality. Get what you can from the poor, regardless of the cost to them. Spartacus, the entirety of his army, and their families were all crucified by the Romans. What is striking about the story, however, is that it represents a commercial failure. If all traders were pirates, commerce would soon end.

Trade requires trust. Exchange over time requires investment in a transaction in the expectation of future performance by one's counterparty. The vulnerability inherent in commercial relationships is part of what has made it difficult to generate widespread and healthy markets in human history. Law provides one possible solution to this problem. Even if everyone is a self-seeking opportunist, the threat of legal sanctions for breach of contract or fraud will deter misbehavior and generate sufficient trust to

---

44. Keynes was a member of esthete Apostles club at Cambridge and for a time was one of the leading lights of the sexually and culturally precocious Bloomsbury set. See Robert Skidelsky, *John Maynard Keynes, 1883–1946: Economist, Philosopher, Statesman* (New York: Penguin Books, 2005), 145.

45. Charles Dickens, *Hard Times* (New York: Penguin, 2003).

46. Plutarch, "Crassus," in *Plutarch's Lives*, ed. Arthur Hugh Clough, trans. John Dryden and James Atlas, vol. 1 (New York: Modern Library, 2001), 731.

make commerce run. Legal scholars, however, have long recognized that law is far too blunt an instrument to sustain commercial trust, whatever its virtues in mitigating egregious misbehavior.[47] Something beyond law is needed. Commerce, for example, has frequently thrived amid tightly knit ethnic and religious communities—so-called trade diasporas—precisely because the cooperation and solidarity within such communities generates the trust necessary for trade.[48]

Ultimately, successful markets require that traders have a strong internal sense of morality. The most difficult problem facing commerce is opportunism that cannot be detected, even ex post. Economists have called these chances to engage in such undetectable advantage-taking "golden opportunities" and argue that they represent one of the major impediments to successful commerce. Unless people forego the ubiquitous opportunity to engage in small and invisible acts of shirking and fraud, large-scale commerce collapses under the accumulated drag of opportunism and corruption. The only solution to the problem is an internal sense of moral integrity that refuses to engage in opportunism even in the absence of sanctions.[49] In other words, a world of dishonest hucksters, far from being the sine qua non of the market, actually represents a context in which commerce cannot thrive.

The nineteenth-century economic theorists, in whose shadow Nibley implicitly writes, emphasized the importance of competition in economic life. There is, however, an earlier eighteenth-century school of thought

---

47. See Stewart Macaulay, "Non-Contractual Relations in Business: A Preliminary Study," *American Sociological Review* 28 (1963): 55–67; Karl N. Llewellyn, "What Price Contract? An Essay in Perspective," *Yale Law Journal* 40 (1931): 704–51; Oliver E. Williamson, *The Economic Institutions of Capitalism* (New York: Free Press, 1985), 1–14.

48. For a discussion of Chinese trade diasporas in southeast Asia, see Darryl Crawford, "Chinese Capitalism: Cultures, the Southeast Asian Region and Economic Globalisation," *Third World Quarterly* 21, no. 1 (2000): 69–86. For a similar story about Jewish trading networks in early modern Europe see generally "The Magic of Diasporas: Immigrant Networks Are a Rare Bright Spark in the World Economy. Rich Countries Should Welcome Them," *The Economist*, November 19, 2011, http://www.economist.com/node/21538742; Adam Sutcliffe, "Jewish History in an Age of Atlanticism," in *Atlantic Diasporas: Jews, Conversos, and Crypto-Jews in the Age of Mercantilism, 1500–1800*, ed. Richard L. Kagan and Philip D. Morgan (Baltimore: Johns Hopkins University Press, 2009), 18–30.

49. This argument is fully fleshed out in David C. Rose, *The Moral Foundation of Economic Behavior* (New York: Oxford University Press, 2011).

that recognized the tremendous cooperative potential inherent in trade. For all of the violence of their metaphors, the nineteenth-century thinkers that Nibley cites—particularly English writers such as Herbert Spencer—lived in a period of remarkable peace. From 1815 to 1914, there was no general Great Power war in Europe. Conflict was tightly confined, as in the Crimean War, or exported overseas as imperial expansion. Eighteenth-century Europe, in contrast, experienced chronic Great Power conflict with a general European war once or twice a generation. Against the background of this harsher geopolitical environment, thinkers such as Montesquieu saw in commerce a hope for a more peaceful and productive way of life. Strikingly, it was precisely in the effects of commerce on moral habits that he took hope. "Commerce cures destructive prejudices and it is an almost general rule that everywhere there are gentle mores, there is commerce and that everywhere there is commerce, there are gentle mores,"[50] he wrote. "The natural effect of commerce is peace."[51] Trade created the hope for an alternative to a world in which tyrants reign with blood and horror.[52]

There is experimental evidence suggesting that Montesquieu was onto something. Social scientists have developed a series of "games" that they use to model human behavior under various conditions. The most famous of these is the Prisoner's Dilemma, but there are others. One is known as the Ultimatum Game, and it consists of two players. One is given some money. He divides it into two sums, one of which he keeps and one of which he offers to the other player. That player can choose to keep the offered money, in which case both players keep their respective sums. Alternatively, the offeree can refuse to accept the cash, in which case

---

50. Charles de Secondat Montesquieu, *The Spirit of the Laws*, ed. Anne Myers Cohler, Basia Carolyn Miller, and Harold Samuel Stone, *Cambridge Texts in the History of Political Thought* (Cambridge: Cambridge University Press, 1989), 338.

51. Montesquieu, 338.

52. Adam Smith put the point thus:

> Commerce and manufactures gradually introduce order and good government, and with them, the liberty and security of individuals, among the inhabitants of the country, who had before lived almost in continual state of war with their neighbors and of servile dependency upon their superiors. This, although it has been the least observed, is by far the most important of their effects.

Quoted in Debra Satz, *Why Some Things Should Not Be for Sale: The Moral Limits of Markets* (New York: Oxford University Press, 2010), 41.

neither player gets to keep any of the money. Entirely selfish maximizers ought to offer a pittance, while the offeree ought to accept any amount greater than zero. Hence, if player one is given one dollar, he ought to offer player two one cent, and player two ought to accept the offer. Different choices by either party would suggest non-maximizing behavior.

Subjects around the world have been asked to play the Ultimatum Game. These experiments have suggestive results. Purely profit-maximizing strategies are virtually never observed in fact.[53] Nobody divides the dollar into a one-cent pile and a ninety-nine-cent pile. When the first party does offer a severely lopsided division, the second party will reject the distribution, even though doing so results in a loss to both parties. In short, most people seem to have some notion of fair dealing that trumps their economic self-interest. What of the effects of trade? Perhaps people in tightly knit agrarian communities exhibit a preference for fair play, but the heedless profiteering of commerce undermines these moral habits. Researchers observe the opposite tendency.[54] Those engaged in subsistence agriculture are the least likely to make an equitable initial distribution in the Ultimatum Game and the most likely to accept an uneven offer. The more deeply commerce and trade penetrate a society, the more likely its inhabits are to offer equitable initial divisions and refuse inequitable offers.[55] Even within the same society, farmers that produce crops for trade exhibit a greater propensity for fair dealing than subsistence farmers.[56] It is the inhabitants of the agrarian acadias in Nibley's imagination that behave the most like the profit maximizers of classical economics. The more trade there is in a society, the more likely its denizens are to have a strong sense of fair dealing. Such a sense seems to be a moral trait exercised and strengthened by commerce.

---

53. See Eython Weg and Vernon Smith, "On the Failure to Induce Meager Offers in Ultimatum Games," *Journal of Economic Psychology* 14, no. 1 (2003): 17–18; Joseph Henrich, "Does Culture Matter in Economic Behavior? Ultimatum Game Bargaining among the Machiguenga of the Peruvian Amazon," *American Economic Review* 90, no. 4 (2000): 973–79.

54. See Joseph Henrich et al., "In Search of Homo Economicus: Behavioral Experiments in 15 Small-Scale Societies," *American Economic Review* 91, no. 2 (2001): 73–78; Joseph Henrich et al., "'Economic Man' in Cross-Cultural Perspective: Behavioral Experiments in 15 Small-Scale Societies," *Behavioral and Brain Science* 28, no. 6 (2005): 795–815.

55. See Henrich et al., "In Search of Homo Economicus," 73; Henrich et al., "'Economic Man' in Cross-Cultural Perspective," 795.

56. See Henrich et al., "'Economic Man' in Cross-Cultural Perspective," 810.

One of the barriers to establishing Zion is xenophobia, the fear and hatred of those beyond our tribe and family. "Love ye therefore the stranger," commands the Lord in Deuteronomy, "for ye were strangers in the land of Egypt" (Deut. 10:19). Joseph Smith captured this idea when he taught, "Friendship is one of the grand fundamental principles of 'Mormonism'; [it is designed] to revolutionize and civilize the world, and cause wars and contentions to cease and men to become friends and brothers."[57] Likewise, the New Testament urges that within the city of God "ye are no more strangers and foreigners but fellow citizens with the saints, and of the household of God" (Eph. 2:19). Trade has historically been one of the main mechanisms by which people interact with strangers. Commerce provides both a motive and a context for peaceful interactions across tribal boundaries. In the eighteen century, Voltaire observed:

> Take a view of the Royal Exchange in London, a place more venerable than many courts of justice, where the representatives of all nations meet for the benefit of mankind. There the Jew, the Mahometan, and the Christian transact together, as though they all professed the same religion, and give the name of infidel to none but bankrupts. There the Presbyterian confides in the Anabaptist, and the Churchman depends on the Quaker's word. At the breaking up of this pacific and free assembly, some withdraw to the synagogue, and others to take a glass.[58]

To be sure, the commerce Voltaire describes is not Zion.[59] It is not even friendship.[60] It is simply mutual toleration and cooperation. Given the human propensity for conflict and violence, however, this is no mean

57. Joseph Fielding Smith, ed., *Teachings of the Prophet Joseph Smith* (Salt Lake City: Deseret Book Co., 1967), 361.

58. Voltaire, *Philosophical Letters* (Mineola: Dover Publications, 2011), 26.

59. Indeed, Voltaire contrasts the happy interactions on the Exchange for "the benefit of mankind" with the senseless and somewhat comic religious rituals that men engage in after they leave the market.

> This man goes and is baptized in a great tub, in the name of the Father, Son, and Holy Ghost: that man has his son's foreskin cut off, whilst a set of Hebrew words (quite unintelligible to him) are mumbled over his child. Others retire to their churches, and there wait for the inspiration of heaven with their hats on, and all are satisfied.

Voltaire, 26. His breezy contempt for religious faith and ritual would not commend itself to the inhabitants of the City of Enoch.

60. John Finnis, for example, differentiates between cooperative efforts of business and friendship thus:

achievement and is instead a precondition for the deeper bonds of a community in which all are "of one heart and one mind" (Moses 7:18). As the Catholic philosopher John Finnis has observed, "many relationships initiated merely for business and private need or advantage . . . ripen into relationships of more or less intense friendship."[61]

Nineteenth-century Mormon efforts at Zion-building illustrate the dangers of demonizing trade. After decades of violence and dispossession in the eastern United States, the Mormons arrived in the Great Basin extremely suspicious of outsiders and frequently hostile to strangers and non-Mormons, whom they called Gentiles. During the Utah War of 1857, Mormon xenophobia reached a fever pitch, resulting most tragically in the Mountain Meadows Massacre, where fear of outsiders led Latter-day Saints to murder an entire wagon train of men, women, and children.[62] Anti-Gentile sermons by Brigham Young and other Church leaders bear part of the blame for creating the context that ultimately triggered the massacre. Tellingly, Brigham Young denounced outside merchants in Utah, leading zealots in Salt Lake City to break open Gentile-owned stores and steal lead, clothing, and other items.[63] While he rebuked these Mormon thieves and took steps to safeguard the physical safety of Gentile merchants, Brigham Young consistently denounced trade with the outside world. Speaking ten years after the Utah War, he said:

> To return to the subjects of merchandizing and merchants. I know, and knew sixteen years ago as well as I do today, that from the very first the merchants who came here were laying the foundation for the uprooting of this people unless we had exceeding great faith; that every dollar that was given them was given to ruin you and me, and to destroy the kingdom of God on the earth.[64]

> [T]he good that is common between friends is not simply the good of successful collaboration or co-ordination, nor is it simply the good of two successfully achieved coinciding projects or objectives; it is the common good of mutual self-constitution, self-fufillment, self-realization.

John Finnis, *Natural Law and Natural Rights* (New York: Oxford University Press, 1980), 141.

61. Finnis, 142.

62. See generally Ronald Walker, Richard E. Turley, and Glen M. Leonard, *Massacre at Mountain Meadows* (New York: Oxford University Press, 2008).

63. Walker, Turley, and Leonard, 99.

64. Brigham Young, February 3, 1867, *Journal of Discourses*, 11:298.

Accordingly, he organized boycotts of Gentile merchants and tried to cartelize the sale of commodities by Mormons to outsiders.[65] Whatever its other merits, the attempts to limit Latter-day Saint trade with outsiders contributed to nineteenth-century Mormon xenophobia and helped to poison the already troubled relationships between Mormons and Gentiles in Utah, and between Utah and the rest of the nation.

Poverty is an ambiguous moral concept. For some religious thinkers such as Francis of Assisi, poverty is a positive good. Material possessions distract one from God, and we ought to abandon them in order to achieve a higher spiritual state. Alternatively, one might regard poverty as a moral evil because it results from injustice. The poor are poor because they have been victimized by the rich, who have taken their substance. This is the stance of Isaiah when he condemns those that "grind the faces of the poor" (Isa. 3:15; see also 2 Ne. 26:20). Finally, poverty might be condemned simply because of the pain it inflicts on the poor and the limits it places on their lives.[66] Hence, those living in poverty are more likely to be malnourished, sick, uneducated, and socially powerless. They are also more likely to be forced into lives of drudgery. For example, in 1886 Franklin D. Richards lamented the condition of the poor day laborer or the piece worker, saying:

> There was comparatively no room for the exercise of enterprise, of skill, of native wit, and those qualities which God has placed in their nature, and which He designed they should practice and thus become wise and skilled by their own ingenuity.[67]

In doing so, he echoed a criticism of the factory system made over a century earlier by Adam Smith. "The man whose whole life is spent performing a few simple operations of which the effects too are perhaps always the

---

65. For an account of the Mormon boycotts organized through ZCMI, see Arrington, *Great Basin Kingdom*, 297–307. Brigham Young discussed his unsuccessful attempts to cartelize Mormon grain sales to surrounding territories in the 1867 sermon quoted above. See Young, February 3, 1867, *Journal of Discourses*, 11:301–2.

66. Among modern thinkers, this criticism of poverty has been most fully developed by Amartya Sen and Martha Nussbaum. See Martha C. Nussbaum, *Creating Capabilities: The Human Development Approach* (Cambridge: Belknap Press, 2011); Amartya Sen, *Development as Freedom*, reprint edition (New York: Anchor, 2000).

67. Franklin D. Richards, April 6, 1885, *Journal of Discourses*, 26:254.

same . . . generally becomes as stupid and ignorant as it is possible for a human creature to become."[68]

As noted above, the ascetic celebration of poverty is foreign to Mormonism, but both of the other concerns are central to Zion's vision of a city where there are no poor among them. The question is whether trade can alleviate the suffering of poverty, without "grinding the faces of the poor." One response would be to reject trade, as opposed to production, as economically sterile. There is a tradition of economic criticism that attacks merchants as parasitic middlemen between producers and consumers. For example, if one subscribes to a labor theory of value in which economic surplus is generated by workers, then farmers or manufacturers can be lauded as productive, but middlemen add no value as they increase costs. In condemning Gentile merchants in Utah, nineteenth-century Mormon leaders often invoked this idea. What it fails to appreciate, however, is the role of merchants in overcoming problems of information and distribution. Material abundance does not necessarily result from labor. Rather, it results from satisfying the material needs and desires of human beings. We generate material prosperity by rearranging productive assets in ways that allow for more human wants to be satisfied. Knowing which configuration will best advance this goal requires a massive amount of information about the distribution of needs and desires within society—information that no single decision-maker can possess. The only way of solving this information problem is through a system of markets, in which individual choices place pressure on prices that then provide signals to producers as to how to use their resources. This process, however, requires commerce. Traders are vital in this process because through the process of arbitrage, they create the prices that can allocate resources to their best uses.[69]

---

68. Quoted in Satz, *Why Some Things Should Not Be for Sale*, 45.

69. See F. A. Hayek, "The Use of Knowledge in Society," *American Economic Review* 35, no. 4 (1945): 519–30. There are very serious limitations to this argument. The first is that prices do not respond to needs and desires in the abstract. Rather, they respond to the demand for goods and services in the form of buyers with the resources to bid up prices. They are thus likely to undervalue the alternative use of resources to serve the needs of the poor. Second, prices take human desires as exogenous. They do not judge the ultimate moral worth of any particular use of a resource. Thus, the price mechanism is indifferent between the desire to build a temple and the desire to consume pornography. Finally, the ubiquitous problem of externalities means that in order for the price mechanism to function effectively, it must be nested in a system of properly constructed institutions that limit the ability of agents to impose costs on others

The Mormon experience illustrates the virtues of the price system and the limits of alternative allocation procedures. During Joseph Smith's lifetime, the Saints were eager to differentiate the Law of Consecration and Stewardship from utopian communities, such as the Shakers, that held everything in common. Hence, the Mormons of Jackson County sought to create a system in which private property and the price mechanism continued to function.[70] Once in Utah, Brigham Young and his successors, in their push for Mormon autarky, tried to centralize capital allocation within the Latter-day Saint economy through economically oriented Church missions (such as Cedar City's Iron Mission or St. George's Cotton Mission), ZCMI, and Zion's Board of Trade. Generally, these efforts were economic failures. The attempt to introduce silk culture into Utah is a good example.[71] Enormous effort and considerable resources were put into growing mulberry trees in the harsh climate of the Great Basin, importing silkworms, and harvesting silk. In the end, very little silk was produced. It is almost certainly true that the resources put into silk culture could have been more productively employed elsewhere in Utah's economy and that the project contributed to poverty rather than alleviating it.[72]

Our understanding of nineteenth-century Mormon Zion-building has been decisively influenced by the herculean work of Leonard Arrington and his students in documenting this period. Arrington, however, received his academic training at a time—the height of the New Deal—when it was assumed that centrally planned institutions, either in the form of government bureaucracies or massive industrial corporations, were the most effective way of organizing economic activity. Given this intellectual background, it was easy for Arrington and his disciples to see in the centrally planned autarky of nineteenth-century Deseret a harbinger of the

---

or extract resources from them without their consent. Such limitations do not, however, provide reasons for rejecting the price system unless one can show that rival systems run by agents facing the same information constraints are superior. Showing the superiority of an alternative stuffed by omniscient and infinitely beneficent decision-makers proves nothing.

70. Arrington, Fox, and May, *Building the City of God*, 17.

71. See Chris Rigby Arrington, "The Finest Fabrics: Mormon Women and the Silk Industry in Early Utah," *Utah Historical Quarterly* 46 (Fall 1978): 376–96.

72. The fact that Brigham Young felt inspired to foster silk production in Zion is itself striking. Silk is perhaps the quintessential example of a luxury good. Silk is certainly inconsistent with a world in which material enjoyments are to be scorned in pursuit of the higher life of the mind.

enlightened efforts of economic planning that reached their fruition in the Progressive Era and with the New Deal.[73] As a result, Mormon historians have tended to uncritically accept the basic plausibility of centrally directed economic organization, placing blame for the failure of Mormon economic institutions on the moral shortcomings of their participants. Since that time, however, we have gained a greater appreciation for the information problems inherent in hierarchically organized economic endeavors.[74] This suggests that the origins of economic failure in nineteenth-century Utah lie less in the morality and motives of those involved, and more in the informational constraints that Brigham Young and other leaders necessarily operated under. Even if people are fully committed altruists, displacing the decentralized process of price creation and allocation with centrally planned mechanisms will create information problems that become larger the more ambitious the plans become. In the end one must have trade because one must have prices in order to allocate resources effectively.[75]

---

73. On Arrington's intellectual background, see Gary Topping, *Leonard J. Arrington: A Historian's Life* (Norman: Arthur H. Clark Co., 2008), 45–57; Nathan B. Oman, "Mordred Had a Good Point," *Dialogue: A Journal of Mormon Thought* 43, no. 1 (Spring 2010): 201–4; Christopher J. Garrett, "The Defense of Deseret: An Examination of LDS Church Trade Politics and Development Efforts in the American West," *Utah Historical Quarterly* 73, no. 4 (Fall 2005): 366–67.

74. See generally Ronald Coase, *The Firm, the Market, and the Law*, paperback ed. (Chicago: The University of Chicago Press, 1990); Williamson, *The Economic Institutions of Capitalism*; Thomas Sowell, *Knowledge And Decisions* (New York: Basic Books, 1996). Some of the basic insights of transaction cost and information economics arose from the so-called socialist calculation debate that was raging among some economists at the time when Arrington was receiving his training. While the debate never seems to have registered in Arrington's thinking, it posed the basic question of whether a centrally planned economy in the absence of a price mechanism was possible. See Bruce Caldwell, "Hayek and Socialism," *Journal of Economic Literature* 35, no. 4 (December 1, 1997): 1856–90.

75. This argument can be taken further. Hayek claimed that any sustained attempt at centralized economic planning would eventually either abandon centralized planning or fall into tyranny. This is because the central planner would have to resort to coercion to control and mitigate the economic problems created by displacing the price mechanism. See F. A. Hayek, *The Road to Serfdom: Fiftieth Anniversary Edition* (Chicago: University of Chicago Press, 1994). I think that Hayek overstated his case, but I do think he is correct that the rejection of the price system has often been accompanied by increased levels of coercion.

Even if one accepts that trade generates abundance, it might still involve injustice toward the poor. Nibley relies on various scriptural passages to imply that trade virtually always involves oppression of the vulnerable. In the New Testament, he points out that Christ insists that God and mammon—an Aramaic term meaning "money" and generally referring to finance of any kind—are always inconsistent with one another. He also examines the rules in Deuteronomy involving debt and servants, suggesting that these rules establish the basic immorality of labor and debt contracts. Nibley, however, over-reads these passages. One cannot understand biblical discussions of finance and servants without acknowledging the ubiquity of debt slavery in the ancient world. Debt was a mechanism by which the powerful would gain literal ownership of a debtor or the debtor's children. In a modern economy, debt is often used as investment capital to start productive new enterprises. In contrast, in economies dominated by subsistence agriculture—like that described in the Old Testament—debt is generally a response to natural misfortunes like a flood or a bad harvest. Thus, rather than facilitating commerce, the creditor in the biblical world used debt as a mechanism for literally enslaving the unfortunate. Likewise, in the Roman world of the New Testament, much of finance revolved around loans made by and to tax farmers. These publicanii, in turn, were licensed by the authorities to engage in violent extortion. Advanced market economies are beset with various pathologies, but one simply cannot assume that the economic practices of the ancient world condemned in Deuteronomy or the Gospels are closely analogous to modern finance or employment relationships. Social and institutional context matter.

Nibley, for example, argues that the New Testament division between God and mammon encompasses any financial transaction. Brigham Young, however, showed a far more practical and nuanced attitude. Speaking to wealthy Latter-day Saints in pioneer Utah, he is one of the few religious leaders to have ever condemned the rich for refusing to engage in usury.[76] He taught:

> The Lord puts wealth into our hands, and we suffer it to waste, instead of laying it out to usury, and I have often said to the Latter-day Saints: let us see to it, how we use the mercies of the Lord, lest he should give us cursings, instead of blessings. God bless you Amen.[77]

---

76. Compare John Thomas Noonan, *The Scholastic Analysis of Usury* (Cambridge: Harvard University Press, 1957).

77. Brigham Young, November 6, 1864, *Journal of Discourses*, 10:363.

His teaching here was not meant to be metaphorical. His concern was quite literal and practical. He was concerned that the wealth of the Latter-day Saints was being hoarded rather than invested, inhibiting the prosperity of the community. Likewise, in an 1852 sermon, Heber C. Kimball encouraged the Saints to either put their money out at usury or give it to the trustee-in-trust (i.e. Brigham Young) to invest.[78] In effect, the Church was compensating for the primitive state of financial institutions in pioneer Utah by acting as an intermediary between savers and entrepreneurs. The point of citing these passages is not to offer them as proof-texts for modern finance. (They are not.) Rather it is to illustrate that the wickedness or righteousness of financial activity depends on historical and institutional context. It also suggests that the basic financial function of intermediation was not seen as evil by Brigham Young and other early Zion builders.

Adam Smith suggested in *The Wealth of Nations* that markets arise spontaneously from mankind's natural propensity to "truck and barter."[79] Peaceful commerce, however, is not a natural condition. Rather, it is a social achievement, one that depends on institutions and habits that are historically contingent.[80] Indeed, for much of human history economic relationships have been governed mainly by systems of status—lord and serf, peasant and landlord, priest and worshiper, and the like—rather than contract.[81] Hence, one might have an economy in which most production is for subsistence consumption and any surplus is violently expropriated by elites rather than distributed voluntarily through trade. Critical theorists have long pointed out that market exchange depends on various government institutions, such as enforcement of property rights, and thus cannot be sharply differentiated from more violent forms of economic

78. Heber C. Kimball, November 14, 1852, *Journal of Discourses*, 1:357.

79. Adam Smith, *The Wealth of Nations*, ed. C. J. Bullock (New York: Barnes & Noble, 2004), 62.

80. Karl Polanyi persuasively makes this point, although I do not necessarily subscribe to all of the particulars of the historical narrative he offers about the rise of modern markets. See generally Karl Polanyi, *The Great Transformation: The Political and Economic Origins of Our Time*, 2nd edition (Boston: Beacon Press, 2001).

81. In the famous formulation of Henry Sumner Maine, "the movement of the progressive societies has hitherto been a movement *from Status to Contract*." Henry Sumner Maine, *Ancient Law*, ed. Frederick Pollock and Raymond Firth (Boston: Beacon Press, 1963), 165.

organization. On this view, the famous distinction between status and contract is largely illusory.[82] While it is true that the wholly spontaneous and voluntary markets of libertarian theory are largely fictitious, it does not follow that markets exist only at the command of the state and cannot be differentiated from the systems of violent expropriation of the poor condemned by the scriptures. Many markets exist in the absence of legal property and contract rights. Likewise, to suggest that the willingness of the state to violently protect the farmer's property rights makes his trade with the baker as violent and exploitive as the protection racket enforced by the mafia against the baker is to miss a qualitative difference so vast that it amounts to a meaningful distinction of kind. It is true that markets are not purely natural or spontaneous. Normatively, however, far less turns on this fact than critical theorists have assumed.

Understanding the contingency of human commerce allows us to foreground the role of institutions in structuring trade. Not all markets are the same, and their shape depends decisively on the various conventions—legal and social—that give them structure. Accordingly, it is impossible to answer the question "Does trade involve grinding the faces of the poor?" in the abstract. Rather, the question can only be answered in particular historical and institutional contexts. Its answer is ultimately a matter of empirical observation and understanding, rather than scriptural hermeneutic, theological speculation, or philosophical argument. Not all employment relationships take the form of debt slavery or child labor in the coalmines of Victorian Scotland. Every sale of bread is not an abusive extraction of the last ounce of wealth from an impoverished and starving man. These examples are useful not because they reveal what trade is in its true essence, but because they reveal what it can be in its most pathological inflections. There are those that earn a living from rewarding and valuable jobs. There are people that purchase their food in a fair and open market. Creating an institutional context in which such trade is possible will require an enormous number of contingent and controversial empirical judgments. By and large, however, making these judgments will require the tools of the economist, the sociologist, the merchant, and the lawyer, rather than those of the prophet or the theologian.

---

82. This claim comes in a measured and responsible form, and a somewhat wild-eyed and irresponsible form. For an example of the former, see Cass R. Sunstein, *Free Markets and Social Justice* (New York: Oxford University Press, 1997). For an example of the latter, see David Graeber, *Debt: The First 5,000 Years* (London: Melville House, 2012).

There remains the question of commerce and inequality. The scriptures teach, "If ye are not equal in earthly things, ye cannot be equal in obtaining heavenly things" (D&C 78:6). How exactly we are to understand the equality of earthly things is left unclear in these passages. Does it mean equality of material resources, equality of individual welfare, equality of capabilities, equality of opportunities, or something else?[83] I offer no answer to these questions here. Rather, I make the more modest observation that however one defines equality, trade will likely lead to inequality. To be sure, sometimes critics of markets make rather exaggerated claims about the extent to which trade promotes inequality.[84] But one needn't believe that commerce leads inevitably to monopoly and the concentration of the lion's share of wealth in a small group of individuals to appreciate that trade, standing alone, will not produce the egalitarian society envisioned in the scriptures as Zion.

This does not mean that trade is evil. It means that trade is insufficient to bring about the Zion toward which the prophets point. Anarcho-capitalism or other ideologies positing that markets, unaided by other practices and institutions, can achieve a just society are mistaken. The poor are always among us, and their needs have claim on our substance. Likewise, a society riven by divisions between opulence and poverty cannot ultimately hope to achieve the heavenly city where they are of "one heart and one mind." The kind of equality demanded by such a heavenly city and the best way of achieving it are complex philosophical and practical questions that I do not purport to answer. I wish only to suggest that an answer that includes trade and commerce as a central aspect of economic organization and social life should not be rejected. Indeed, far from impeding Zion, commerce can be one of her handmaidens.

This is what the scriptures suggest. In an 1831 revelation, the Lord commanded that trade be established in the Zion of Jackson County:

---

83. Among egalitarian political philosophers there is a huge debate as to what exactly it is that should be equalized and how one is to know when equality has been achieved. Compare for example Ronald Dworkin, *Sovereign Virtue: The Theory and Practice of Equality* (Cambridge: Harvard University Press, 2002) (offering a complex argument in favor of equality of resources); Nussbaum, *Creating Capabilities* (arguing for an equality in the exercise of basic capabilities); and John Tomasi, *Free Market Fairness* (Princeton: Princeton University Press, 2012) (arguing for equality of opportunity).

84. See, e.g., Thomas Piketty, *Capital in the Twenty-First Century*, trans. Arthur Goldhammer (Cambridge: Belknap Press, 2014).

> And again, verily I say unto you, let my servant Sidney Gilbert plant himself in this place, and establish a store, that he may sell goods without fraud, that he may obtain money to buy lands for the good of the saints, that he may obtain whatsoever things the disciples may need to plant them in their inheritance. (D&C 57:8)

In this verse we are given a vision of the role of commerce in Zion. Gilbert is to sell "goods without fraud," dealing honestly and fairly with his customers. The result will be material abundance, "money," and "whatsoever things the disciples may need." Elsewhere, the Lord commended Newel K. Whitney to keep his store (see D&C 63:42) and counseled in favor of decentralized decision-making. "Nevertheless, let him impart all the money which he can impart, to be sent up unto the land of Zion. Behold, these things are in his own hands, let him do according to wisdom" (D&C 63:43–44). Likewise, in Nauvoo, the Lord set up a commercial enterprise to reach out to the world, commanding that a "boarding house . . . for the boarding of strangers . . . be built in my name" (D&C 124:56). Commerce is not Zion, but it is a means by which the Lord can bring about his purposes to create a city where peace reigns, "there [are] no poor among them," (Moses 7:18) and "the stranger that dwelleth with you shall be unto you as one born among you, and thou shalt love him as thyself" (Lev. 19:34).

CHAPTER 7

My Essay on Same-Sex Marriage

I wrote this essay in 2013, as Perry v. Hollingsworth, *the case holding Proposition 8 unconstitutional, was making its final way through the federal courts. The US Supreme Court ultimately declined to take the case, although it did declare a national constitutional right to same-sex marriage two years later in* Obergefell v. Hodges. *This essay was my effort at the time to articulate the reasons that led me, as a believing Latter-day Saint, to reject the Church's position and embrace same-sex marriage. I also wanted to articulate the reasons for my anxieties with how the debates over same-sex marriage had played out. I have made minor stylistic edits, but otherwise the essay is unchanged from 2013.*

Same-sex marriage is going to become a legal and social reality in the United States. As I write this essay, the United States Supreme Court is considering whether a right to same-sex marriage lurks within the Constitution, but ultimately the Court's decision will only impact the timing and method of same-sex marriage's recognition. The reality is that among young Americans, support for same-sex marriage runs at about 70 percent. Among seniors, support is in the 30 to 40 percent range. With each passing day, there are fewer seniors opposed to same-sex marriage and more young people moving into the prime of their voting lives. It may be that as they age, younger Americans' opinions on same-sex marriage will shift. But I doubt it. Laws supported by 70 percent of the population are eventually going to be enacted regardless of what the justices say. Hence, I write of same-sex marriage as a soon to be established fact. The purpose of this essay is to explore my reactions to this new reality. I'm neither entirely joyful about same-sex marriage nor entirely pessimistic. Rather, I am worried. I think that same-sex marriage has the potential to be a positive social phenomenon, but it also has the potential to be destructive. I don't purport to know what its ultimate effects will be, and I suspect that they will be mixed.

I.

I begin with what I think marriage ought to do. There is no single answer to this question. Marriage has a couple of functions, functions that are related to one another but not in any tight or logically necessary way. First, it bonds couples together. Too often, this bonding is identified with romantic love, an intense desire and attachment. The bonding of marriage, however, cannot be reduced to a surge of romantic emotion. Indeed, much of the value of marriage lies in how it ties couples together when they do not feel such emotional surges. We want people to get stuck with one another. To be sure, in some cases they ought to unstick themselves. But marriage is a social institution rather than an external expression of subjective emotion. It is not "a reflection of our love" or at least not only, or even primarily a reflection of our love. Rather, it makes spouses responsible for one another. When I get sick, my wife should take care of me. As she ages, I take care of her. Our financial lives should be intertwined with one another to provide mutual support against life's vicissitudes, and so on. This is love, but it is not love as conceptualized by romance. Indeed, it is a love that manifests itself most powerfully in committed action when the euphoria of psychological attachment wanes. If marriage as a social institution reflects love, this is the love that it reflects. Society benefits from holding married couples to their commitment to one another through the informal force of social pressure and the far blunter instrument of the law. People embedded in such relationships are on average more resilient and productive than their single counterparts. And so on.

Second, marriage legitimates and controls sexual activity. In a post-sexual revolution world, its actual social power in this area has waned dramatically. For most people in the United States, marriage is no longer a necessary condition for legitimate sexual activity. (More on this anon.) Historically, however, one of the main functions of marriage is to differentiate licit from illicit sexuality. Naturally, the way in which it has accomplished this has evolved over time. What is or is not sexually licit within marriage has shifted over time. Furthermore, marriage as a legitimator of sexuality has often coexisted with a great deal of hypocrisy, especially male hypocrisy that has insisted on marital fidelity for women without placing similar restrictions on men. Still, there are good reasons for preferring marital sexuality to its alternatives. Confining sexuality to marriage manages the inherent emotional, physical, and social risks of sex by placing it in the context of committed relationships bolstered by social sanctions against exit. Also, a norm that confines sex to marriage strengthens the socially sanctioned dyad by creating a powerful incentive for entry and a disincentive to exit. Most people want to have sex. Confining sex to marriage makes them want marriage more.

Third, marriage provides a context for childrearing. Ideally, children are born to parents who are committed to one another. That commitment translates into mutual support, which creates a more economically, socially, and emotionally stable environment for children. Children are inherently vulnerable, and their caregivers are also vulnerable. Marriage shields that vulnerability. It provides children with a model of how adults relate to their mates, inculcating the skills necessary for married life when the child becomes an adult. Ideally, it gives them a uniquely strong relationship with an adult of each gender, providing them with tools for making sense of gender identities as they grow. It usually connects children with the individuals who evolutionarily have the greatest incentive to invest in their survival and prosperity. And so on.

Obviously, marriage performs all of these tasks imperfectly. It is both over- and under-inclusive. There are married couples who despise and undermine one another. There are married couples without children. There are many people who see no link between marriage and legitimate sexual activity. Furthermore, I realize that at different points in history, marriage has performed different functions. Therefore, the three I offer here are not a distillation of marriage's historical essence. They are not even offered as a definition of what marriage truly is in some cosmic sense. They are, however, worthy tasks that marriage can and often does perform. They provide a normative basis for a set of social practices and legal rules supporting marriage.

Much has been made in the debates over same-sex marriage of the over- and under-inclusiveness of heterosexual marriage. The most salient arguments have revolved around the link between marriage and childrearing. Proponents of same-sex marriage point out that many marriages are childless but are still regarded as marriages. Furthermore, the sexual revolution has already sundered the social expectation linking childrearing to marriage, and medical technology has even severed the connection between heterosexual intercourse and pregnancy, at least for those who can afford such technology. Accordingly, the biological sterility of homosexual couples cannot be a good reason for excluding them from the institution of marriage, since sterility does not exclude heterosexual couples.

For reasons I will explain below, I don't think that the biological sterility of same-sex couples is a good reason for refusing to provide legal recognition for same-sex marriage. However, I don't think that the over- and under-inclusiveness of traditional marriage means that it is irrational or that its functions cannot ultimately be understood by reference to children. This argument is, I believe, mistaken in a way that reveals a worrying misunderstanding of how marriage works. Laws are often over- and under-inclusive not because they are the result of irrational animus, but because we have reasons to place side constraints on the activity of the state in ways that keep us from creating a more closely tailored legal regime.

Most same-sex marriage advocates, for example, would be comfortable asserting that marriage is a reflection of the love of a gay couple and their desire to form a lifelong union. Notice, however, that if this is the purpose underlying marriage, then the law of same-sex marriage in a state like Massachusetts is under- and over-inclusive. In order to become married, a gay couple need not prove to the state that they love one another, nor do they need to prove to the state that they intend to form a lifelong union. Indeed, if the official tasked with issuing marriage licenses discovers that the couple does not love each other, this does not allow him to withhold the license. This is as it should be. We don't want a world in which government officials inquire into whether couples really love one another. There are two reasons for this. First, it is extremely intrusive, inviting the state to scrutinize the emotions and highly personal decisions of its citizens. We have good reasons to suppose that the state is not institutionally well-equipped to gather the information necessary to make such decisions. And in any case, it makes good sense to not grant the government the power to make such inquiries. Notice, however, that this concern for the intrusiveness of the state does not flow from the irrelevance of love to marriage. It is just that we think the state ought not to make this inquiry. The second reason not to allow the state to determine if prospective spouses really love one another is that such an inquiry is unnecessary. Society has other, informal mechanisms for policing the boundaries of marriage. Even if the state will not disallow a marriage because it determines that love is absent, those that marry without love would quite rightly be subject to the pity and—depending on the precise circumstances—the scorn of their neighbors. This kind of informal pressure can be enormously powerful, and it provides a more nuanced and less dangerous way of policing the boundaries of legitimate marriage than does the ham-fisted actions of the state.

We can apply a similar logic to the relationship between childrearing and marriage. It is true that the state does not refuse to recognize childless marriages, nor does it inquire into the intentions of couples regarding children when the couples get married. This is as it should be. We have good reasons to be suspicious of the state, and we ought not to give it the power to closely interrogate its citizens about such matters. The risk of abuse and error is high, and government officials are very poorly placed to make such judgments. However, this doesn't imply that it is somehow irrational or nefarious to conceptualize a central purpose of the legal institution of marriage as providing a preferred context for childrearing. It just means that the legal institution is embedded in a set of social practices that can rush in where we rightly fear to let the state tread. Hence, we ought to rely on informal social pressures to link marriage and childrearing. We should regard single childrearing as an inferior option from the point of view of children, even if in many cases we might not regard the single parent as morally culpable for this harm. We ought to regard marriages with children as more fully realized and more socially valuable than childless marriages. The childless couple may be the victim of tragedy in being unable to have children. They may have made a choice not to have children, thus rendering a portion of the social concern lavished on their marriage redundant. These, however, are situations in which we do not want the heavy hand of the state to intervene, even though they are central to what marriage ought to be about.

I raised this point not, as I stated, because I regard the biological sterility of gay and lesbian couples as a good reason for opposing same-sex marriage, but because the arguments about the over- and under-inclusiveness of the law of marriage implicitly rest on a divorce of that law from a much richer social context in which non-legal sanctions place pressure on behavior around marriage. As I will discuss below, I think that the maintenance of such pressure is central to the health of marriage, and accordingly I am worried by a prominent public discussion that systematically renders this broader context invisible, focusing only on that small fraction of marriage constituted by legal rules and then speaking as though these legal rules are its entirety or at least the entirety that was up for public discussion.

II.

Let me turn now to what I see as the most powerful arguments in favor of same-sex marriage. For me, they are not ultimately arguments based on freedom or equality. First, I do not think that the law undergirding traditional marriage is a significant imposition on the freedom of gay and lesbian couples. In liberal Mormon circles, at least, the prohibition on same-sex marriage is often analogized to the prohibition on plural marriage. Anti-polygamy laws, however, are not a good analogy to the law undergirding heterosexual marriage. Something like the Morrill Anti-Bigamy Act or the Edmunds-Tucker Act were significant limitations on personal liberty because they criminalized plural marriage and conduct related to plural marriage. Those that violated these laws were prosecuted and sent to prison in their hundreds. Something like Proposition 8, however, does not send anyone to prison or punish gay couples in the same way that the criminal prohibitions on polygamy did. Instead, we are arguing over the rather less fraught question of whether the state should formally recognize as marriages unions that already exist as a matter of fact without legal prohibition and are often recognized under the civil union statutes of various states.

I do not find the equality argument compelling because I do not think that marriage is primarily about equality. I do not think that it is a special status conferred on heterosexuals as a reward for being heterosexual, one from which gays and lesbians are excluded in order to convey a message of social inferiority. Rather, I think that it is an institution that does certain things, serves certain functions. To be sure, legal exclusion from marriage can be a way in which society marks its contempt for a particular group, as in the case of anti-miscegenation laws. On the other hand, I don't think that there is any reason to suppose that mixed-race marriages cannot perform all of the functions that I laid out above. Furthermore, we know that the origin of anti-miscegenation statutes lay in the racism of Jim Crow, and their social meaning as an expression of that system of domination was clear. Finally, it is worth pointing out that at times they were of relatively recent vintage. While laws against sexual mixing between whites and blacks are as old as slavery in the Americas, the formal anti-miscegenation statutes struck down in *Loving v. Virginia* were often a product of the post–Civil War era. Indeed, some of them were not passed until the early twentieth century. Hence, the social message of disdain inherent in such laws is impossible to disclaim. On the other hand, the link between heterosexual unions and marriage has been virtually universal across time and space, and I know of no compelling evidence that its origins lie in hostility to gays and lesbians.

That said, I think that there are some very compelling arguments to be made in favor of same-sex marriage. First, as in heterosexual marriage, I think that society is better off if people are in long-term unions with their sexual partners. Gays and lesbians who are married can reap the same benefits of social stability, economic and emotional support, and the like that accrue to the spouses in traditional marriages. Society is certainly better off if its gay and lesbian citizens are paired in enduring marriages rather than living alone or navigating the shoals of less stable romantic arrangements. Such couples are likely to be more productive and more resilient in the face of life shocks.

I think that there are also powerful childrearing arguments to be made in favor of same-sex marriage. I believe in some version of gender complementarity. Hence, I think that, all things being equal, it is better for children to be raised in a stable home with both a father and a mother. The reality, of course, is that all other things are never equal. The gender of a child's caregivers is not the only, or even the most important, fact about them. Wealthy and well-educated parents tend to provide good outcomes for their children. Not surprisingly, the social outcomes for the children of wealthy and well-educated gay parents tend to be better than the social outcomes for the children of poor and uneducated heterosexual parents. Likewise, the individual childrearing approaches of parents are hugely important. The child of loving gay parents who invest a great deal of time in childrearing will have a better life than the child of abusive and neglectful heterosexual parents.

One might object that the legalization of same-sex marriage will increase the number of children raised by gay and lesbian parents, a situation that, all things being equal, I do not regard as optimal. I doubt that this will be the case. Notwithstanding the biological sterility of same-sex couples, gay and lesbian couples may already become parents through a variety of means. Many are parents as a result of heterosexual relationships, including failed heterosexual marriages. Medical technology, coupled with the availability of mechanisms such as surrogacy contracts, place biological offspring within the reach of at least affluent gay and lesbian couples. As yet, technology requires genetic material from at least one person of the opposite sex, but de facto markets in such genetic material exist.[1] Finally, the law of adoption is conceptually distinct from the law of marriage.

1. Many gays and lesbians become parents through heterosexual relationships, frequently while they're closeted. If we assume that homosexuality is distributed more or less evenly throughout the population, and we assume that gays and lesbians in lower income and educational brackets are more firmly in the closet, then parenthood via heterosexual intercourse would tend to skew among gays and lesbians towards the bottom of the socioeconomic scale. As social acceptance of homosexuality increases and gays and lesbians emerge earlier in their lives from the closet, we would expect to see fewer gays and lesbians become parents via heterosexual intercourse. The other alternative routes into parenthood—adoption and reproductive technology—however, are both relatively expensive. We would thus expect them to be more heavily concentrated among affluent gays and lesbians. As a result, I expect that in the future, same-sex parenthood will increasingly become a middle- and upper-middle-class phenomenon. Accordingly, I would not be surprised if the average outcomes for children of same-sex parents tend to be better than the average outcomes of children of heterosexual parents because the children of gays and lesbians are simply more likely to have affluent parents. Just a speculation.

Marriage is neither a necessary nor sufficient condition for a person to become a legal parent. Hence, even in jurisdictions where same-sex couples cannot marry, they may be able to adopt children. Interestingly, there is no conceptual difficulty in a jurisdiction that recognizes same-sex marriage also prohibiting the adoption by gay couples, although I know of no jurisdiction that does this. Some jurisdictions, however, do have laws that prohibit certain classes of persons from adopting, even if they are married.

One might believe that all the various avenues by which gay and lesbian people may become parents should be shut down. Such a belief strikes me as both mistaken and unrealistic. It is mistaken because I believe many gay and lesbian people are good parents, and it would be barbaric and harmful to sever their children from them. It is also mistaken because it would require a massive invasion of state into parenthood. It is unrealistic for a number of reasons. First, there's no hope of generating the political support for such laws. Second, as an administrative matter, I think it unlikely that the state has the capacity to suppress same-sex parenthood without a massive commitment of resources. Third, the medical and legal technologies that support at least some forms of same-sex parenthood are widely available and could not be realistically confined to heterosexual couples without suppressing them in their entirety, something that simply isn't realistic.

The debate over same-sex marriage and parenthood is thus not really a choice between children growing up in a stable home with a father and a mother versus children growing up in a stable same-sex marriage with two fathers or two mothers. Rather, the debate is over whether we want the children of same-sex parents growing up in stable unions bolstered by the law of marriage, or in same-sex environments that lack the benefit of the stability that such law is supposed to provide. I confess that I am somewhat terrified by the brave new world of family structures created in the aftermath of sexual revolution and medical innovation. I am not convinced that large-scale social experiments in radically new models of parenting are a good idea. For example, I think that widespread divorce has been a tragedy for children. It may well have been an improvement in the lives of adults who are spared confinement in miserable marriages. The many defenders of divorce, however, argue that children on the whole are better off with divorced but happy parents rather than married but miserable parents. In some cases, this is no doubt true. But on the whole, I think it has proven to be an adult-centric fairy tale. Its main function is to help grown-ups avoid facing the negative consequences of their decisions for their children. Now, it may be that the adult misery avoided by divorce is sufficiently serious to justify the misery that divorce inflicts on children. In some cases, this is clearly true. We have not, however, been particularly honest as a society about these questions. I think that similar stories can be told about modern adoption, an experiment in childrearing where the costs to adoptees and to birth parents have not been honestly faced. Hence, there is a part of me that is deeply concerned about embarking on new experiments in same-sex parenting. I think that we should be doing less experimenting on our children.

It is this final intuition that strikes me as one of the most powerful arguments for same-sex marriage. Same-sex marriage is potentially most powerful as a conservative retrenchment and effort to impose a more traditional model on the unruly riot of family structures that already dominate the lives of many children. By recognizing a model of gay and lesbian family life structured around commitment and stability, same-sex marriage has the potential to discourage same-sex parenting marked by more transient romantic attachments as new partners move in and out of children's lives. As a childrearing institution, one of the central functions of marriage is to subordinate potentially anarchic adult desires to the needs of children by celebrating stability and providing ways of deterring adult exit. Marriage does this far less aggressively today than it once did. But to the extent that it can do so for both homosexual and heterosexual unions, it seems to me that the children of those unions will be better off.

Finally, I think that one of the greatest potential benefits of same-sex marriage is that it makes gay and lesbian chastity possible. This is no doubt my most Quixotic argument, but personally it is one that I find compelling. It is Quixotic because chastity has largely ceased to be a virtue in our society. The idea that marriage is a necessary condition for licit sexual activity has collapsed before the onslaught of the pill, secularization, and the declining social stigma attached to unwed parenthood. Among religious conservatives, for whom chastity remains an organizing principle of sexual morality, biblical condemnations of homosexual sex make the idea of gay and lesbian chastity seem incoherent. Nevertheless, I think that chastity is a virtue worthy of cherishing, and gay and lesbian chastity is, frankly, an idea that I find appealing. Chastity is not the same thing as prudery, abstinence, or celibacy. Rather, chastity is the idea that sexuality is one of the central goods of human life but one that must be subject to tight limits if it is not to be socially and spiritually destructive. I do not regard sex as dirty or evil. I do not believe that celibacy represents a higher ideal.

Obviously, I know very little about homosexual sex, but it seems to me that it functions in many of the same ways as heterosexual sex. It creates pleasure. It has the potential to bond people together. From what I gather, it involves the same cocktail of dopamine, oxytocin, and other neurotransmitters that make heterosexual activity so emotionally potent. It is biologically sterile and therefore cannot be part of the unity of love, pleasure, and procreation that can endow heterosexual union with much of its meaning and power. In this sense, I believe in heteronormativity. I believe that there is something uniquely good and powerful about the fecundity of heterosexual union. On the other hand, I also believe that homosexual attraction is more or less fixed. To be sure, I think that our current ideas of sexual identity have been constructed on the basis of an analogy to a pre-critical concept of race, an analogy that exists largely for political purposes. Hence, I think that our current discourse creates neat categories and binaries where I suspect that reality often includes a continuum of sexual proclivities. That said, I think there are a substantial number of people for whom meaningful heterosexual activity is a biological and emotional impossibility. For these people, I think that the best system of sexual morality is a system of chastity, one that embeds licit sexual activity within the context of formal commitment and family formation. In my own all-things-considered judgment, I don't think that celibacy makes good sense for gays and lesbians because I don't ultimately think that celibacy is a good form of human life. Gay and lesbian chastity, however, requires same-sex marriage.

There are two objections to my hope for same-sex chastity. On one hand are those who would insist that chastity is either an anachronistic virtue or one that ought to be relegated firmly to some private realm of personal morality in which it can have no bearing on the legitimacy of a public institution such as marriage. My response to such an objection is that while chastity is partly a matter of conscience and living within a revealed religious order, it can never be a wholly private ideal. Sex and how we order our lives in relation to it is too potent a force in our society for each of us to claim that our sexual morality is ever purely private. Marriage itself, which in large part is an effort to create a public institution that orders sexual conduct, is a testament to this truth. Hence, one might regard my belief in chastity as substantively mistaken. But one cannot place too much hope in the public-private distinction as a means of excluding sexual morality from the realm of public reasons.

The second objection is, frankly, religious. Part of why chastity is important to me is precisely because I am not my own. I've been bought with a price and given gifts from God, gifts that are to be exercised within the bounds that He has set. Hence, for me, religious authority cannot be irrelevant to my consideration of sexual ethics, and I'm not the religious authority on such matters. As a Latter-day Saint, I feel I must acquiesce to the authority of prophets and apostles on such fundamental questions as the basic structure of chastity. However, much as I value my own all-things-considered judgments with regard to sexual morality, I value my religious covenants far more. All I can say is that chastity strikes me as both distinct from and superior to celibacy. I can hope for a movement from religious authority towards a sexual ethic for gays and lesbians that I find more attractive. Same-sex marriage would allow for the realization of such an ethic in a manner that is not achievable in its absence.

III.

Given what I have written thus far, why does same-sex marriage worry me? I worry about basically three things. First, I worry I may be wrong. Second, I worry about the effect of same-sex marriage on the institution of marriage generally. Third, I worry about the effect of same-sex marriage on other institutions. These last two worries depend decisively on the way in which the public meaning of same-sex marriage ultimately gets cashed out in our society. Hence, the way in which same-sex marriage is defended and justified is as important as the reality of same-sex marriages themselves. It is this last point in particular that makes me worried, as I think that many of the arguments that have been used in support of same-sex marriage are potentially troublesome. I worry about the extent to which they will become embedded in our social understanding of marriage.

My first worry is the least interesting. As noted above, I think there are good arguments in favor of same-sex marriage. I find these arguments persuasive. On the other hand, I could well be wrong. I generally describe myself as politically libertarian or libertarian-leaning. This is because I'm skeptical of the state, including in its conservatively celebrated roles of law enforcer and military defender, and I am enthusiastically celebratory of markets. I'm not a libertarian, however, in the sense of placing an exceptionally high moral premium on individualism or personal liberty. I don't want the state to push and bully people, but I think that ultimately Aristotle had it right. We are social animals whose identity is constructed within the thick and opaque web of community and tradition. I am also a social conservative, but not in the sense of believing that the state should aggressively pursue a bundle of neo-puritan policies to recreate some imaginary golden age. Rather, I believe that society is well-served by a healthy dose of stability and that we are far more indebted to the organically grown prejudices of our past than liberals are willing to admit. Hence, despite the arguments I have made in favor of same-sex marriage, there is part of me that screams, "You may be wrong!" Any massive shift in a basic social institution worries me, and no social institution is as basic as the structure of the family. Societies are fiendishly complicated things, and the difficulty of predicting the final consequences of big shifts has made a fool of wiser men and women than me. For a liberal, the appeal to such ignorance about ultimate results seems like a kind of mindless obscurantism at best and a smokescreen for darker motives at worst. We ought to forge ahead with change so long as we know that justice is on our side. Even when I might agree, however, I hear the voices of Cromwell and Hamlet: "I beseech you in the bowels of Christ, think it possible you may be mistaken." "There are more things in heaven and earth, Horatio, than are dreamt of in your philosophy."

My second worry is that same-sex marriage will weaken the institution of marriage itself. For most proponents of same-sex marriage, this worry is self-evidently absurd. They point to my healthy marriage or their healthy marriage and say, "How on earth could gay people getting married have any effect on your marriage. My own marriage will be affected not one whit if lesbians are allowed to marry." Their response is true, but beside the point. It is true because same-sex marriage has no effect on healthy heterosexual marriages, particularly the stable, successful marriages, of the kind of well-educated, middle-class intellectuals who like to debate same-sex marriage. Marriage among such people is actually doing well, and compared to a number of years ago, is enjoying a modest renaissance. Divorce rates are down slightly, and there are other good signs. Straight men and women who love their spouses and are committed to marriage will not be affected by same-sex marriages.

This response to my worry, however, misunderstands how social institutions succeed and how they fail. Think of the social institution of marriage as the set of people who are married or who might become married. The more people who get married and stay married, the more society's sexual and family life is structured by marriage and the healthier marriage is as an institution. The fewer people get married, the fewer people stay married, the less that marriage structures sexual and family life, the weaker the institution of marriage becomes. The institution is thus strengthened or weakened not at its core among people who are happily married but at its margins, among people who might choose marriage or might choose one of the many other family and sexual structures that our society has on offer. If one stops looking at the affluent, the well-educated, and the already married, then the state of marriage in America is far more perilous. Particularly among those toward the bottom of the income distribution, marriage is not in good shape. Indeed, the main problem is not so much divorce as the disappearance of marriage altogether from the lives of many people. In its place, we see a spectrum of transient romantic and sexual relationships, longer-lasting relationships involving various levels of cohabitation, and a universe in which the resulting children live in often-chaotic family structures.

One pat response to marriage's ill health is to insist that it is entirely a matter of economics. In a more prosperous and egalitarian society, such things would not be a problem. We can solve the problems of marriage through the tax code by transferring a greater share of society's wealth to the poor. While I do not doubt that economic strain can be an enormous burden on marriage, this answer is rather too glib in relieving our culture of any culpability in the decline of marriage. It is possible for poor people to form happy and stable marriages. It is possible for poor people to provide their children with stable family structures. Furthermore, the economic and social resources provided by education and money tend to shield people, especially children, from the darker side of alternative family structures. Perversely, in our society, marriage works best for those that need it least, while it is those at the bottom of the economic distribution for whom marriage would be the most valuable.

I think that the waning of marriage is in large part a result of the sexual revolution, which decisively decoupled licit sexuality from marriage. In this world, marriage has become less a social imperative than one among a menu of possible choices about how to order one's romantic and sexual life. In a world where the future is sharply discounted in value vis-à-vis the present, marriage is not always a particularly attractive option given the apparently high sexual opportunity costs and the difficulty of exit. Less formal and enduring structures seem to promise the benefits of affection, companionship, and intimacy held out by marriage without the attendant costs. What is needed in such a world are strong, informal social pressures that push people toward matrimony and discourage alternative forms of sexuality.

This is where my first worry about the way that same-sex marriage has been defended emerges. As already noted, a large part of the attack on the exclusivity of heterosexual marriage has insisted on decoupling the purposes of marriage from childbearing and childrearing, focusing on the over- and under-inclusiveness of the legal structures of marriage. My concern with this argument is its focus on the operation of the law, divorced from the way that law interacts with informal social pressures. Indeed, the argument rests decisively on the idea that we should not consider such pressures when understanding what marriage means as a public institution. Yet it is the lack of vitality in such informal social pressures that I find most worrying. Pushing over and over again the idea that marriage is a legal construct, one unconcerned with children, that can be considered without paying attention to the social pressures that sustain it, strikes me as a dangerous way of talking about marriage. It undermines the vitality of precisely those battered social norms and taboos that marriage requires. This, however, is not my main worry.

Same-sex marriage is the ironic child of the sexual revolution. The emergence of homosexuality from the closet over the last generation is indubitably a result, at least in part, of the decoupling of legitimate sexual activity from marriage. It has employed two not entirely consistent arguments drawn from the sexual revolution. The first is that homosexual acts occur between consenting adults and are therefore beyond the scope of social disapprobation. The second is that sexuality represents an irreducible part of a person's identity, one that cannot be suppressed without violence to one's authenticity and integrity. I find the second class of arguments in defense of homosexuality's emergence from the closet more compelling than the first. It is important to notice, however, that this second class of arguments has its origins in a critique of chastity and marriage, which proponents of sexual revolution stigmatized as sexually repressive and destructive of a straight person's authenticity and integrity.

The irony comes from the fact that the push for same-sex marriage is not entirely—and in some quarters not even primarily—about facilitating and strengthening same-sex marriages. Rather, it is part of the broader normalization of homosexuality. Marriage has historically been the great social legitimator of sexuality. In recent generations, its claim to this role has weakened. Indeed, it was precisely this weakening that allowed homosexuality to emerge from the closet. Yet marriage still has a strong enough hold on the moral imagination of our society that it is the last citadel of heteronormativity that must be stormed in order for homosexuality to claim its final arrival at a place of social legitimacy.

My concern here is not that same-sex marriage will increase the legitimacy of homosexuality. I do not think that this is a problem. I think that by and large homosexuality is biologically determined. This means that I believe both that homosexual desires should be regarded as largely immutable and of very limited appeal to those who are not already predisposed to them. I think that gays and lesbians are entitled to live happy and fulfilling lives, and I suspect, generally speaking, that life is not to be found in the closet. It also means that I don't regard gays and lesbians as socially or sexually predatory. Homosexuality has very little appeal for heterosexuals.[2] It isn't something that is going to spread. Hence my concern with the relationship between same-sex marriage and the sexual revolution does not stem from a hostility towards the social acceptance of homosexuality. I am, however, deeply concerned about the relationship between the arguments of the sexual revolution and the institution of marriage.

I noted at the beginning of this essay that among the young, support for same-sex marriage runs at about 70 percent. Why is it so high? Many would say that if two people love one another, then they ought to be able to get married. We shouldn't judge the love of some as more worthy than the love of others. Notice that this reaction depends on an assumption that marriage as a social institution should not draw distinctions between different family structures or romantic relationships. It's a moral intuition entirely consistent with the ethical stance that emerged from the sexual revolution, namely that love and choice are sacred and that they legitimate themselves. Marriage, however, has never been about treating love as equal. It is about making judgments, marking out limits, and stating that certain forms of love and sexuality are to be preferred to others. Conceptualizing same-sex marriage as an attack on discrimination reaffirms the idea that society ought not to judge the forms in which sexual identity expresses itself. Equally destructive, in my view, is the libertarian argument that sees in same-sex marriage the expression of a choice that justifies itself by virtue of being free. The focus on freedom deprives us of mechanisms by which to make judgments about the substantive content of sexual choices absent harm to others. The harm principle, however, provides us with no guidance on how to live a good life, which is in large part what marriage is

2. I have two caveats here. First, as mentioned above, I think that there are people who fall on a spectrum between hetero- and homosexuality and are therefore more plastic in their sexual identities. Second, I suspect that much of my thinking here implicitly privileges a male perspective. My impression is that female sexuality is somewhat more malleable.

about. From the libertarian view, once we have established that the choice was freely made, barring direct third-party harms, our moral interest in the choice should be at an end.

If the health of marriage is determined at the margin, then I believe that none of these messages are healthy. Imagine the person without a strong commitment to the idea of marriage, but who might be persuaded to marry. This is not the person who is happily married or for whom marriage is a central life goal. Rather, it is the person for whom marriage competes as an option against other romantic and family structures ranging from cohabitation to promiscuity. In a society where marriage is healthy or where we are making serious efforts to revive marriage, we would want to give this person as many powerful messages as possible that marriage is preferable to other structures. It is not simply one choice among others. It is not validated by love and choice. After all, cohabitation or even promiscuity can be validated by loving choice. We might even want to invoke darker emotions such as shame and guilt to encourage this person to organize his or her life around marriage. The most powerful public messages about same-sex marriage, however, center on equality and choice, the very ideas that undermine marriage at the margins. Presenting marriage as a choice or a badge of equality gives our marginal person no reason to get married. Such narratives say nothing about the superiority of marriage. Indeed, these arguments inculcate hostility to the very idea of a hierarchy of family configurations. Furthermore, by embedding same-sex marriage in a narrative of liberal progress in which the irrational prejudices of the past are discarded by the onward march of history, we stigmatize precisely the kinds of social forces—prejudice, disapproval, informal pressure—that shore up marriage at the margins.

In the end, I do not find same-sex marriages threatening to the institution of marriage. I think that same-sex marriages are preferable to their alternatives and that we ought to be actively pressuring gays and lesbians to marry. Also, because I believe that the number of gays and lesbians is biologically determined and quite small, in practice same-sex-marriage will have very little social salience outside of a few areas. What I worry about is the social salience of arguments that have generated the political support for same-sex marriage. To be sure, there are advocates of same-sex marriage that have been focused on the need for gay and lesbian marriages and the way that same-sex marriage would serve the needs of spouses and children. These advocates are to be commended, and in the end, I find their arguments largely persuasive. They are, however, a marginal voice in the larger debate. The larger debate is driven by a set of ideas and social trends that I do not find encouraging. Indeed, one of the few benefits I can see to the Supreme Court resolving the issue is that it would end the constant reiteration of a set of rhetorical tropes about marriage that I do not find encouraging. The downside would be fixing in our nation's oeuvre a new canonical text linking marriage to freedom and equality while condemning the traditions and prejudices surrounding it.

I also worry about the effect of same-sex marriage on other institutions. Here I freely confessed that my main concern is with the Mormon Church. It would be difficult to imagine worse timing and positioning for the Church than Proposition 8. If I am correct in my future prediction, then the Church will have put itself in the position of being the final and most visible advocate of the losing position. Furthermore, in a public debate that has focused decisively on freedom and equality—as opposed to the goods provided by marriage and the way that same-sex marriage may or may not provide those goods—public discourse will label the Church as bigoted and evil in one of the few ways that our public discourse can still robustly articulate an idea of evil. This is mainly a problem of the Church's own creation. The focus on all-out victory in Proposition 8 put the Church in front of other members of the coalition in favor of the proposition and made Latter-day Saints a lightning rod for the backlash. This was entirely avoidable. The Church could still have voiced its position without making itself so publicly salient. Furthermore, its very prominence in Proposition 8 makes it difficult for the Church to modify its stance to accommodate itself to a new reality. From my point of view, the Church's involvement in Proposition 8 was almost wholly destructive, even if one believes that same-sex marriage is a mistake (which I do not). It generated massive public hostility. It produced no discernible legal or political benefits for the Church that I can see. It generated large-scale—precisely how large I do not know—internal turmoil within the Church, particularly among the young. It positioned the Church very badly for a new, post-same-sex marriage reality. I worry about the diminishment of the Church's moral authority among nonmembers and members who will, I suspect, find ways of accommodating themselves to a new social reality. I worry about the effect of residual hostility on the ability of the Church to engage in missionary work. I worry about legal attacks on its tax-exempt status, its freedom of speech, and its freedom of religion. By and large, American constitutional law has tended to provide relatively robust protections for these last two, even for those that American society labels as political pariahs. On the other hand, the record on religious freedom is somewhat patchy, and increasingly I think that the libertarian tradition in American free speech law is coming under pressure from other models that are considerably more comfortable with restrictions on "hate speech." I admit these legal concerns are attenuated, but they are not so attenuated that I don't worry about them.

Finally, major liberal victories make me worry in general about civil society. I worry about the totalizing and universalizing claims of freedom and equality. The victory of such claims, it seems to me, always undermines society's tolerance for tradition, hierarchy, heterogeneity, and the institutions defined by such things. This doesn't worry me a great deal, but in moments of reflection I can manage a little bit of uneasiness. I prefer a society in which not every institution is ordered by liberal principles, and we are capable of understanding the potential goodness of other ways of seeing the moral universe. Indeed, marriage is not a particularly liberal institution. The whole point is that I have greater affection for my wife and children than my fellow citizens. No equal entitlement to my concern here. Love and sexual desire, which are integral to marriage, are also not especially liberal. At the very least, the gender of the beloved matters as well as a host of characteristics that are irrelevant in the liberal public sphere. Likewise, parenthood is illiberal, resting on the authority of mothers and fathers over children and the need for children's lives to be structured not by their own choices but by the choices of those who know better. Religion is not particularly liberal, with its claims to special authority and the construction of communities based on the claims of that authority. These are all forms of human relation that strike me as extremely valuable, but they can't be conceptualized particularly well within the structures of liberal moral thinking. To the extent that liberalism dominates all modes of public discussion to the exclusion of other ways of talking about social goods, these valuable forms of human relation get undermined, even if only incrementally. I try to avoid giving in to my inner Russell Kirk. But I admit at times he's there, and he makes me worry.

IV.

So where does that leave me? To gays and lesbians who are now going to get married, I say congratulations. I hope that you have a happy and fulfilling lives. I hope that your marriages are strong, and I hope that they become an example that will discipline and orient the lives of others. To the advocates of same-sex marriage, I hope that you will stop talking so much about freedom and equality and will start talking about marriage, about how it should organize people's sexual lives and give structure to their families. I hope that your newfound enthusiasm for marriage translates into the revival of some of the informal social pressures and expectations that signal to everyone that marriage is not simply a choice or a right but a preferred way of life. It's probably too much to hope for, but I would love to see a revival of chastity as a widespread ideal, one that can now become possible for gays and lesbians.

To social conservatives, I say that same-sex marriage is an ambiguous defeat, one that bears within itself powerful conservative arguments. Homosexuality is ultimately a peripheral issue to the health of marriage as a social institution. The same-sex marriage enthusiasts have often been heedless in how they have talked about marriage, but same-sex marriage itself needn't be hostile to the purposes of marriage. It depends, in part, on whether marriage catches on among gays and lesbians and even more on the ultimate public meaning attached to the legal recognition of same-sex marriage. Was this another victory of liberty and equality against the barbaric forces of tradition? If so, then marriage as a social institution will have been harmed in some measure. On the other hand, if same-sex marriage is about a renaissance of sexual discipline, long-term commitment, and a focus on the needs of children, then marriage may be strengthened as a social institution. I don't expect the language of liberty and equality around same-sex marriage to recede from the public stage. But having lost the political battle on same-sex marriage, social conservatives should embrace the rhetorical and social possibilities it provides for talking about the good of marriage as opposed to its alternatives. A focus on same-sex marriage as a superior structure for gay and lesbian families, rather than on same-sex marriage as a marker of social equality, strikes me as the best road going forward.

In the end, I don't know what will happen. I think that marriage will be good for gay and lesbian families. I'm less sanguine about the effects of the same-sex marriage debate on our shared public understanding of marriage. I fear that it has reinforced ideas that are destructive to marriage at the margins. The good news is that I may be wrong, which would make me very happy.

CHAPTER 8

"A Welding Link of Some Kind": A Minimalist Theology of Same-Sex Marriage Sealings

The purpose of this chapter is to explore the theological possibility of same-sex marriage sealings in a way that requires minimal theological change and maintains maximum continuity with Church practices. By focusing on the limitations of our knowledge and the history of sealing practices, one can see a place for same-sex marriage sealings that is true to the ongoing work of the Restoration. I will not rehearse the tortured history of the Church with homosexuality and same-sex marriage.[1] Suffice it to say that the pain and anxiety around these issues is having a corrosive effect on Latter-day Saint families and on the ability of the Church to retain members and gain converts. In part this comes from increasing tensions between Church teachings and a culture in the developed world that has become more welcoming of gay and lesbian relationships. It would be a mistake, however, to think of this issue in terms of great and spacious buildings and fingers of scorn (cf. 1 Ne. 8:26–28). Moral tension between the Church and society is inevitable and often healthy. The Church's moral teachings on chastity were increasingly out of step with social norms in the second half of the twentieth century, but this was an era of unprecedented Church growth and high youth retention rates. Rather, conflict around same-sex marriage has proven corrosive because of the internal tensions within our theology.[2] The Church teaches that married family life

1. I will also not address the public policy questions presented by same-sex marriage or the moral questions presented by homosexual relations. I have written about such issues elsewhere. Suffice it to say that I do not find the claim that same-sex marriage poses a threat to the flourishing of earthly families or the vitality of marriage as an institution persuasive, and I believe that homosexual acts within the context of an ethic of chastity organized around marriage are moral.

2. In many ways the current situation mirrors the situation before the 1978 revelation on the priesthood. This comparison is often made in an unhelpful way, particularly by those who glibly equate the Church's teachings on marriage with vicious homophobic animus. However, at several points the underlying structure of the situations is similar. An increasing awareness of the evils of racism in the United States created enormous tension between the Church and the broader

is the best kind of life to live and that gays and lesbians must be excluded from that life. However, homosexual orientation is unchosen, immutable, and more or less evenly distributed through the population. Hence, gay and lesbian Latter-day Saints, their families, and their friends continually crash against this basic conflict in Church teachings.[3]

The Doctrine and Covenants teaches that a "stupor of thought" can be a prelude to revelation (D&C 9:9). I believe this describes the present position of the Church. The same revelation teaches that the way forward is to study a question out in one's mind and then ask the Lord if the answer arrived at is correct (see D&C 9:8). This chapter is an exercise in such studying it out. Asking the Lord if the answers offered here—or something like them—are correct lies with those who have ecclesiastical authority that I lack.

Two Theologies of Homosexuality

The core of the Church's theological opposition to same-sex marriage flows out of the ordinances of the temple and the theology that we use to understand those ordinances. Stated as clearly as possible, here is what I take to be that theology: The process of exaltation consists in following the example of God so as to have the kind of life that He has. God, however, is not alone. Rather, we are the literal spirit children of heavenly parents. Exaltation requires that human beings enter into heterosexual marriages blessed by the sealing authority in the temple. Those who through accidents of birth or circumstances are unable to contract such marriages in mortality are promised that they will be able to contract them in the eternities. Within this understanding, same-sex marriage is impossible because

---

culture. The Church's exclusionary position threatened the viability of the Church, especially in racially diverse societies such as Brazil. Finally, the Church's position created a terrible contradiction between the racist theologies used to justify the ban and the clear scriptural teachings that all of God's children are equal in his sight (2 Ne. 26:33). These three elements are also present in the Church's current position: a shift in moral attitudes, a threat to the continued vitality of the Lord's work, and a wrenching internal contradiction in our theology.

3. Ironically, the Church often presents its teachings on same-sex marriage as part of the Lord's plan of happiness. For most Latter-day Saints directly impacted by these teachings—gay and lesbian members and their families—the teachings create grief and unhappiness. They are sometimes grimly accepted as a test of allegiance to the authority of the Church and its teachings, but I seldom see them joyfully celebrated.

marriage, properly understood, is an imitation of the divine, heterosexual union of heterosexual heavenly parents. A corollary of this theology is that homosexuality—unlike heterosexuality—is an accidental rather than necessary characteristic of one's spiritual identity. Hence, being gay or lesbian is a mortal condition but one that will be corrected in the eternities. There will be no gays and lesbians in the celestial kingdom not because they will be excluded by God but because he will cause them to cease being gays and lesbians. Let's call this the theology of heterosexual exaltation.

I think that the theology of heterosexual exaltation is a fair summary of current Church teachings. However, I know from numerous conversations over the years that many members of the Church are dissatisfied with its stance on same-sex marriage and reject these teachings. Most of this opposition isn't very theologically reflective. It's content to note the destructive consequences of Church teachings in the alienation of gay and lesbian Latter-day Saints and to affirm the love of God. However, "love is love," while a compelling slogan, is not an adequate response to the theology of heterosexual exaltation. Rather, it often amounts to a rejection of any theology more definite than a belief in benevolent theism. This strikes me as too thin of a theological foundation for Church teachings and practices.

There have also been more sustained efforts at articulating a theology of same-sex relationships. The approach I've most often heard is to insist that, contrary to the theology of heterosexual exaltation, homosexual orientation is an eternal characteristic. This approach is intuitively appealing to many gay and lesbian Latter-day Saints. It accords with their own experience of their sexuality, which seems inherent to their identity rather than a temporary condition. Given the constitutive role of sexuality in identity formation, this is unsurprising. As a heterosexual male, I confess that I have difficulty making sense of what it would mean for me to continue to be me but instead be a gay man. It seems that such a person would be someone else, not me. Understandably, many gay and lesbian Latter-day Saints feel the same way about their sexual orientation. Furthermore, for many gay and lesbian Latter-day Saints, the hope of sexual transformation held out in the eternities is not particularly attractive. Again, as a heterosexual man there is nothing especially appealing to me about being transformed after death into a gay man. I understand why a gay man might have a similar reaction to the prospect of post-mortal sexual transformation. If sexual orientation is an eternal characteristic, so goes the argument, then same-sex unions should be sealed in the eternities, and we must re-imagine the imitation of God without any commitment to the unique necessity of heterosexual marriage. Call this the theology of eternal homosexuality.

One of the striking things about these two theologies is their certainty. They both rest on a specific vision of the role of sexual orientation in the eternities. They also go well beyond any teachings that are explicitly contained in the standard works. This is easiest to see in the case of the theology of eternal homosexuality. It reasons theologically from gay and lesbian experience but lacks any clear revelatory warrant. There is simply nothing in the canonized revelations of the Church to suggest that homosexual orientation is eternal. Perhaps less obviously, the theology of heterosexual exaltation rests on a similarly thin foundation in the canon. The idea of heavenly parents is not contained in the scriptures.[4] The sexualized, procreative vision of divine spiritual parenthood is nowhere explicitly set forth. To be sure, references to God as father are ubiquitous, but the theological apparatus of spirit birth and literal eternal parenthood implicit in the theology of heterosexual exaltation isn't to be found.[5] Indeed, Jesus's title of "only begotten son" (e.g. John 3:16) is the one place in scripture where a procreative derivation from God is explicitly stated, and it's exclusive to Christ.[6] Rather, the Doctrine and Covenants speaks of uncreated intelligences with no reference to ideas of spiritual procreation (see D&C 93:29).

Instead of defending one of these positions, I want to explore the implications of saying "We don't know." Both of the theologies sketched above rest on the assumption that we have a fairly clear understanding of what sexuality and relationships in the eternities look like. They assume that this tight vision of the eternities should inform how we think about marriage in mortality and the ordinances that we perform in the temple. I want to suggest that this assumption is mistaken. Rather, what informs our sealing practices is a basic uncertainty about the precise nature of eternal

---

4. For example, there are no references to Heavenly Mother in the standard works.

5. The idea of a "spirit birth" in which human spirits arise through a procreative process analogous to pregnancy involving heterosexual heavenly parents seems to have first been articulated by Brigham Young as part of his Adam-God teachings. It does not appear in the scriptures, was never taught by the Prophet Joseph Smith, and is almost never explicitly articulated in official Church materials. For more on the historical background, see Jonathan A. Stapley, "Brigham Young's Garden Cosmology," *Journal of Mormon History* 47, no. 1 (January 2021): 68–86.

6. Even this is doubtful. "Only begotten" translates the Greek word "monogenes," which does not necessarily have a strong connotation of sexual generation or procreation.

relationships. In the remainder of this chapter, I will argue that this uncertainty lies at the heart of our current sealing practices. I will then argue that when the question of same-sex marriage sealings is seen through the lens of our uncertainty, there is a better way forward for the Church, one that could ameliorate the destructive internal contradictions in our current teachings, give to righteous same-sex couples the blessings of the temple, and integrate their sealings into the great work of Elijah and Malachi.

Kingdom, Lineage, and Family

When asked today to explain the significance of temple sealings, Latter-day Saints will respond by speaking in terms of happy nuclear families. Our greatest joy in this life comes from the love of husbands and wives, parents and children. Through sealing ordinances husbands and wives are bound together for eternity. Likewise, by being born in the covenant or through adoptive sealings, children are connected to their parents in the eternities. Thus, the earthly joys of families are carried forward after death and into exaltation. For all of its hope and truth, this is an incomplete description of how sealing ordinances function, both historically and today. They have never neatly mapped onto a model of the nuclear family. Careful attention to temple practices reveals that over the course of the Restoration, there have, broadly speaking, been three distinct approaches to temple sealings. We can refer to them as kingdom, lineage, and family.[7] While there is considerable overlap between them and no idea is ever fully abandoned, these three approaches follow a roughly chronological order, with kingdom dominating from the 1840s to 1894, lineage dominating from 1894 to about 1955, and family dominating from 1955 to the present. Each era has blessed temple sealings that depart from a model of the nuclear family.

For much of the nineteenth century, sealing ordinances centered on what can be called kingdom theology. The focus was on using the sealing power to knit together post-mortal priesthood kingdoms. The basic idea was that exaltation consists of priesthood kingship, with the goal of connecting everyone back to God as the divine king through a series of nested kingdoms created by networks of sealing ordinances. This can be

7. Elsewhere, I have provided a more comprehensive history of the development of marital sealing rules with accompanying documentation. My summary here is based on that research. Nathan B. Oman, "The Development of Modern Latter-Day Saint Marriage Rules," William & Mary Law School, July 12, 2022, https://papers.ssrn.com/sol3/papers.cfm?abstract_id=4161021.

seen most clearly in two now-abandoned sealing practices: plural marriage and the law of adoption. Contemporary Latter-day Saints tend to assume that nineteenth-century Mormon polygamists shared modern Saints' vision of eternal nuclear families but simply multiplied the families. While some nineteenth-century polygamists spoke in these terms, it is at best an incomplete account of their theological vision. One of the main reasons people performed plural marriage sealings was to secure a place in an exalting priesthood network. This can be seen in the common practice of non-conjugal plural marriage sealings. Thus, women were sealed posthumously to Joseph Smith and other dead Church leaders as plural wives. Some women were sealed polygamously to Joseph or Brigham while remaining married to another man. Finally, some women were sealed polygamously without having any substantial earthly connections to their "husbands." In all of these cases, the sealings were less a matter of forming nuclear families than of becoming part of a royal priesthood network.

The law of adoption had a similar function. Instituted in the Nauvoo Temple shortly after Joseph's martyrdom, this was the practice of sealing non-biologically related adults to Church leaders as adopted sons or daughters. After the abandonment of Nauvoo, no new law of adoption sealings were performed until the dedication of the Saint George Temple in 1877. Thus, while these law of adoption networks operated as important social units during the exodus, for decades the law of adoption was mainly a theological idea for understanding sealing ordinances. Like plural marriage sealings, these adoptive sealings referenced a family relationship, but their purpose was to extend exalting priesthood networks by providing a way of being sealed into the eternal kingdom of a high priesthood leader.

While vestiges of kingdom theology remain in the modern temple, most notably in the language of the endowment ceremony and the words of the sealing ceremony, temple theology underwent a revolution in the 1890s under the direction of President Wilford Woodruff. Most famously, he issued the 1890 Manifesto, which began the process of abandoning the practice of plural marriage. Less well known, but in some ways more significant for temple practice, in the April 1894 general conference, he announced a revelation ending the law of adoption and counseled Latter-day Saints to research their family history and perform sealing ordinances for ancestors along family lines.

The emphasis in this new sealing theology was on lineage rather than kingdoms. The goal, according to President Woodruff, was to "[h]ave children sealed to their parents and run this chain through as far as you can get it."[8] This was a new idea in 1894.[9] The emphasis on the primacy of lineage can be seen in two ways. First, adoptive sealings along non-family lines were abandoned. When requested to do so, President Woodruff went so far as to formally cancel previous law of adoption sealings to allow sealings based on family lineages. Second, while there was an emphasis on intergenerational chains of sealings, there wasn't an effort to ensure that sealing ordinances mirrored the structure of nuclear families. Until well into the twentieth century, for example, the First Presidency did not routinely use its authority to cancel marital sealings in cases of divorce or remarriage after the death of a spouse. Rather, both men and women could be sealed a second time without a cancellation, regardless of gender or of how the earthly marriages ended. The same rule was applied to posthumous temple sealings. The result was numerous situations where men and women were enmeshed in networks of multiple marriage sealings that did not correspond to mortal family structures (including even polygamous households).

In the 1920s and early 1930s, when rules governing multiple marriage sealings were tightened under President Grant, the Church again did not seek to mirror nuclear families. Rather, rules harked back to nineteenth-century kingdom theology, with multiple sealings permitted to widowed or divorced men, but with a newly added requirement that women had to receive a cancellation of sealing after being divorced or widowed before a second temple marriage was possible. The obvious model here was nineteenth-century polygamy, and the resulting networks of sealed relationships did not mirror the structure of monogamous, nuclear families. After 1934, the same rule was applied to proxy sealings. Men were to be sealed to all of the women to whom they had been married while alive, but women were to be sealed only to their first husbands. Thus, throughout the post-1894 period, the emphasis was on intergenerational continuity rather than a tight ritual mirroring of an ideal nuclear family structure in the eternities.

---

8. Brian H. Stuy, ed., *Collected Discourses Delivered by President Wilford Woodruff, His Two Counselors, the Twelve Apostles, and Others* (Woodland Hills: B. H. S. Publishing, 1987), 4:73.

9. Prior to President Woodruff's revelation, the practice was to adoptively seal non-Latter-day Saint ancestors either to a righteous Latter-day Saint descendant or to a high Church leader. Seeking out one's kindred dead was seen in terms of performing proxy baptisms rather than creating eternal connections via sealing ordinances that mirrored family lines.

After World War II, the Church began an ambitious program of international expansion in earnest. At the center of the successful missionary message of the second half of the twentieth century was the nuclear family. The Church placed an increasing emphasis on strong marriages between husbands and wives committed to sacrificing together for the welfare of their children. The temple became central to the message that families could be together forever. This can be seen most dramatically after 1955 when the Church dedicated its first overseas temple in Switzerland. Prior to the 1950s, regular temple attendance was not emphasized as a part of Latter-day Saint devotional life. It was common for a member of the Church to visit the temple only once or twice in his or her lifetime. The international temples of the 1950s signaled an aspiration that regular temple worship be put within the reach of all Latter-day Saints, regardless of where they lived. The emphasis on temple worship went hand-in-hand with an emphasis on eternal nuclear families.

There was an irony, however, in how the new emphasis on temple worship and eternal families impacted sealing practices. When temple worship went from an occasional to a regular feature of devotional life, the Church faced a logistical challenge. Temple work is only possible if the temples have the names of deceased persons for whom patrons can perform ordinances. By the early 1960s, the temples were running out of names. The Church responded with the name extraction program. The problem was that at scale it was impossible to ensure that sealing ordinances followed the 1934 proxy sealing rules. With many of the genealogical records, for example, one cannot know if a woman has previously been widowed or divorced when she married the husband in the record being harvested. In 1969, these pressures led President McKay to change the proxy sealing rules to allow men and women to be sealed to all of the spouses to whom they had been married in life, even though such sealings can create networks of polygynous and polyandrous sealings that do not correspond to mortal family relationships. When faced with a choice between mass temple work and sealings that mirrored some ideal family structure, President McKay chose mass temple work.

The Complexity of Marriage Sealings

What are we to make of the layering of rules and theologies that govern marriage sealings? There are two sources of ambiguity. The first is the brute fact of multiple marriage sealings that seem to imply eternal networks which do not mirror nuclear families. Such multiple sealings are not an exceptional part of temple practice. Millions of such ordinances have been and continued to be performed for the living and the dead. There are a variety of possible responses. Although its popularity has waned since the Manifesto, one might affirm eternal polygamy on a massive scale. This is not theologically attractive to most contemporary Latter-day Saints and has been rejected by many high Church leaders. (President McKay explicitly stated his belief that polygamy was not an eternal principle.) In any case, it leaves unanswered the question of the status of multiple marital sealings by women. The contemporary Church has emphasized three points in answer to these questions. First, God loves his children and will order the hereafter in his infinite wisdom for their happiness. Second, no one will be forced in the eternities into a relationship that they do not desire. Third, despite these uncertainties, performing temple ordinances is vital to the Lord's work. These points, while affirming the love of God and hope for the hereafter, do not provide any clear picture as to the nature of post-mortal relationships. In effect, the answer to the question of what eternal families will look like is "We don't know."

The second source of ambiguity is the diverse theological goals that have been offered for sealing ordinances. Sealings have been used to create non-familial networks of priesthood kingdoms centered on high Church leaders. They have been used to create huge polygamous households. They have been used to connect lines of descendants and ancestors that mirror family—if not always genetic—lineages. Finally, sealing ordinances have been used to continue the happiness of nuclear families on earth into the eternities. To some extent, contemporary sealing rules reflect all of these theologies. None of them standing alone accounts for the totality of sealing practices. It is not clear that these goals are all consistent with one another. At least in the cases of the law of adoption and plural marriage, President Woodruff very publicly announced revelations reversing earlier practices. On a quieter level, President Grant made major changes to sealing rules that were partially reversed by President McKay.

The theology of heterosexual exaltation also does not fit closely with sealing practices. Recall that that theology sees temple marriage as the solely legitimate imitation of a dyad of heterosexual heavenly parents. Right now, we regularly perform sealings in our temples that do not reflect this model of a heavenly dyad. Consider one example: Widowed men can be sealed to multiple spouses while living. Likewise, women can be posthumously sealed to multiple men. Imagine Joe marries Jill in the temple and then Jill dies. In the meantime, Jane marries John in the temple, and John then dies. Jane and Joe then marry, and after their deaths their children seal them together with a proxy ordinance.

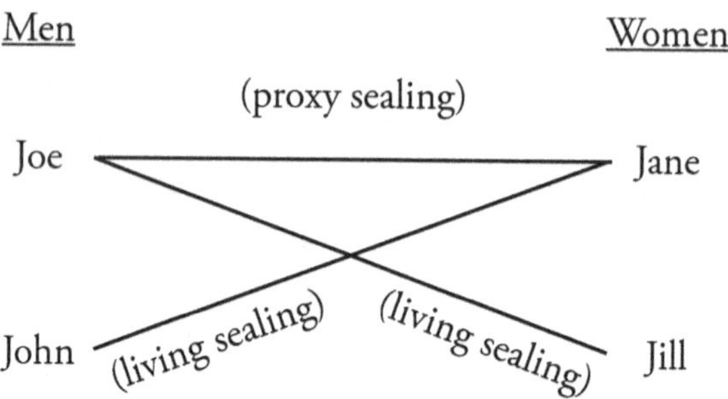

Such a scenario is explicitly allowed under current rules and presumably has happened numerous times.[10] In this example, Joe is sealed to Jane and Jill, who is sealed only to Joe. Jane is sealed to Joe and John, who is sealed only to Jill. All of the sealings are equally valid. Whatever else can be said about such sealings, they do not, taken in their entirety, reflect the dyad envisioned by the theology of heterosexual exaltation. They cannot even be reconciled with such a theory by endorsing post-mortal polygamy because the multiple sealings are symmetrical rather than asymmetrical by gender. At best the theology of heterosexual exaltation can affirm that in some way we do not understand this tangle of sealings will be resolved into heavenly dyads to everyone's satisfaction in the hereafter, although if we assume that all three of these earthly marriages were happy and successful, it's difficult to see precisely how this would happen. We just don't know.

The proponent of the theology of heterosexual exaltation might be tempted at this point to affirm that Church leaders are fallible and reject sealing practices that diverge from that theology. Hence, previous ordinances that diverge from the theory of heterosexual exaltation were simply wrong, as are current sealing rules that result in networks of apparently equally valid sealings rather than a single heterosexual dyad in imitation of heavenly parents. Such an approach would render much of the sealing work of the Restoration invalid. Literally millions of ordinances have been performed under these rules. It would also be radically inconsistent

10. See *General Handbook: Serving in The Church of Jesus Christ of Latter-Day Saints* (Salt Lake City: The Church of Jesus Christ of Latter-day Saints, 2021), 38.4.1.7.

with current sealing policies which are not—and never have been—premised on the requirement that only sealings mirroring a dyad of heavenly parents are permissible. Rather, the Church regularly performs multiple sealings of various kinds that do not conform to a model of heavenly parents and says in effect, "We do not know the precise significance of these ordinances in the hereafter."

"A Welding Link of Some Kind"

If we put both a faith in the necessity and power of sealing ordinances and the humility of "We don't know" at the center of our theology of temple sealings, what might our vision look like? The Restoration began in earnest with the visit of Moroni and the translation of the Book of Mormon. Both emphasized the final verse of Malachi in which the prophet says that the earth will be cursed unless the hearts of the children turn to their fathers and the hearts of the fathers turn to their children (see JS—H 1:39, 3 Ne. 25:6, Mal. 4:6). Toward the end of his life, Joseph Smith interpreted this verse in an epistle to the Church subsequently canonized as section 128 of the Doctrine and Covenants. "It is sufficient to know in this case," he wrote, "that the earth will be smitten with a curse unless there is a welding link of some kind or another between the fathers and the children, upon some subject or another" (D&C 128:18). In the epistle, he went on to associate the needed welding link with baptism for the dead. However, on other occasions, Joseph associated the welding link with the sealing power, and after his death succeeding prophets extended the logic of proxy baptisms to all temple ordinances, which are now available to both the living and the dead. The level of abstraction at which Joseph begins is striking. Notice that in D&C 128, the welding link is singular. Baptisms for the dead are part of the link, but they are not the link in its entirety, a fact emphasized by the later introduction of other proxy temple ordinances. Indeed, the welding link is not a reference to any particular ordinance. Rather "a welding link of some kind" among all of humanity is necessary to the salvation of God's children as a whole, otherwise "the earth will be smitten with a curse" (D&C 128:18).

Latter-day Saints are accustomed to thinking of the sealing power in terms of two distinct ordinances: marriage sealings and adoptive sealings. As we have already seen, however, differing theological meanings have been assigned to these sealings over the history of the Restoration. An adoptive sealing between an adult man and Heber C. Kimball in the

Nauvoo Temple had a very different meaning than the sealing of small children to their recently converted parents in a modern temple. Likewise, my temple marriage to my wife in 1999 had a very different meaning than a mid-nineteenth-century polyandrous sealing of a married woman to Joseph Smith or Brigham Young as a plural wife. The most explicit discussion of the sealing power in the standard works suggests that its scope is far more expansive than our current discourse suggests. The Doctrine and Covenants speaks of "all covenants, contracts, bonds, obligations, oaths, vows, performances, connections, associations, or expectations" as coming within the power to "seal by the Holy Spirit of promise" (D&C 132:7). The revelation goes on to talk about a particular kind of sealing—plural marriage—as an instance of this broader power. Just as sealing practices manifest great diversity within the categories of marriage and adoption, scripture seems to contemplate a multiplicity of different kinds of sealings.

If we think of individual sealings as forging part of the single great welding link of which Joseph wrote, then the sprawling multiplicity of sealing practices becomes less bewildering. Law of adoption sealings, plural marriage sealings, sealings of marriages that end in divorce, multiple modern marriage sealings for the living and the dead; none of these ordinances are wasted. Each becomes another connection in the great link that will weld all of the children of God together and save them from the curse of their alienation and mutual forgetfulness. The answer of "We don't know" ceases to be a dodge that leaves the efficacy and necessity of every sealing hanging. Rather, it becomes an acknowledgement that every sealing contributes to the welding link even if we do not know the precise configuration of post-mortal relationships. Such a view need not imply the abandonment of eternal families and the hope that doctrine holds out, but it does give meaning to the mass of other temple sealings that have been performed over the course of the Restoration. They, too, have a role in forging the welding link. This approach leaves the precise mechanics of salvation less clear than in the theology of heterosexual exaltation, but it has the virtue of better fitting current and past sealing practice and not relying on elaborate extra-scriptural ideas.

Same-Sex Marriage Sealings

This brings us to the question with which we began: same-sex marriage sealings. Against a background of the history of sealing practices, it is not true that one needs a precise account of a sealing's meaning in the hereafter to be able to perform a marriage sealing. We already regularly perform sealings in the temple whose final eternal significance we do not purport to precisely understand. Indeed, the meaning and scope of marriage sealings has changed over the course of the Restoration. We have not had a single model of marriage. Rather, we learn that the sealing authority extends to "[a]ll covenants, contracts, bonds, obligations, oaths, vows, performances, connections, associations, or expectations" (D&C 132:7). The Church has never sealed same-sex marriages in its temples, but such unions could fit under the categories of "covenants," "bonds," "vows," and "connections." As to the precise theological status of sexual identity in the eternities, the Church could say, "We don't know." The Church currently performs marriage sealings where the precise meaning of the union in the eternities is unknown, but we are confident that "the power of godliness" (D&C 84:20) manifested in the ordinance will bless the couple, and the ordinance itself forms a part of the great latter-day work of creating the welding link of which Joseph Smith prophesized.

My hope in presenting these ideas is that they might provide a possible path forward for the Church that resolves the destructive conflict within our current practices and teachings around same-sex marriage. I long for a way in which gay and lesbian Latter-day Saints can live within the kind of faithful, covenanted, and committed companionship that the Church rightly holds out as the good life. Same-sex marriage sealings could enfold such lives into the Church and bless them with the power that comes through temple ordinances. At the same time, I take very seriously the need for continuity and loyalty to the Restoration. The ideas presented here also seek to engage respectfully with the theology of heterosexual exaltation without endorsing the theology of eternal homosexuality. Rather, my goal is to accommodate uncertainty on the precise eternal status of homosexuality. There needn't be consensus on that issue in order to bless same-sex marriage sealings. It is enough to say that all sealings contribute to the great welding link and that we do not know the details of the eternities. This is something that we already do in other contexts.

The change this chapter contemplates could be easily and simply explained. The Church could say:

> For many years we have struggled with how best to minister to gay and lesbian Latter-day Saints while affirming the importance of chastity outside of marriage, fidelity to husbands and wives, the priority of children, and the promises of eternal families made in the temple. After pleading with the Lord, we have received a revelation that same-sex couples may be sealed

> in the temple. Throughout the Restoration changes have been made under prophetic direction in temple ordinances and practices. Today's change is the latest chapter in that continuing story. Like prophets going back to Nephi, we "do not know the meaning of all things" (1 Ne. 11:17), but we know that today's decision will bless the lives of those who live worthy to be sealed in the temple and that all of the ordinances—past, present, and future—performed in the Lord's House contribute to his great plan for the human family. The Church continues to affirm that sexual relations outside of marriage violate God's commandments, and same-sex couples are subject to the same standards of behavior as opposite sex couples.

Whether this is what the Lord wants for his Church is not my question to answer. I believe that the Church's current position creates corrosive contradictions that pose an existential threat to the continued vitality of the Lord's work. In the past, the Lord has blessed dramatic changes in Church practices when the continuation of those practices threatened the future of the Lord's Kingdom. I pray that He will do so again.

CHAPTER 9

"I Will Give Unto You My Law": Section 42 as a Legal Text and the Paradoxes of Divine Law

Divine law occupies an uneasy place in the modern world, thanks to a long history. For thinkers in antiquity, divine law was hypothetical.[1] They did not identify it with the actual rules that operated within a particular society. One might sanctify one's traditions, but neither Solon nor Lycurgus was Moses delivering a legal code claiming divine authorship. In the Middle Ages, however, Muslims, Jews, and Christians sought to turn divine law into a juridical reality. Indeed, what we today call a "religion" was then referred to as a "law." Hence, medievals spoke of the law of Christ, the law of the Jews, or the law of the Saracens rather than of Christianity, Judaism, or Islam. The concrete effort to realize divine law created conflicting jurisdictional claims that resulted in clashes between secular and religious authority, such as the murder of Thomas Becket, Archbishop of Canterbury, by knights of Henry II of England in 1170.

These clashes had their origin in the disintegration of the primal legal unity represented by the idea of divine law.[2] Early canonists at the outset of the medieval era cast the church as an integrated legal system. Later, royal chanceries set up their own legal systems in imitation of the church, which made possible conflicts such as that between Henry II and his "troublesome priest." Still later, as power consolidated in national governments, the relationship between divine and secular law gradually reversed. Law ceased to be primarily a matter of scriptural exegesis and increasingly became something like the common law of England: a set of rules promulgated by a secular political authority. In the contemporary world, we arrive at the Weberian ideal of law as the rationalization of the state's monopoly on legitimate violence. And in such a context, divine law has few places it can take root—other than in the realm of the private, the moral, or the religious.

---

1. See generally Rémi Brague, *The Law of God: The Philosophical History of an Idea*, trans. Lydia G. Cochrane (Chicago: University of Chicago Press, 2007).

2. See generally Harold J. Berman, *Law and Revolution: The Formation of the Western Legal Tradition* (Cambridge: Harvard University Press, 1983).

Section 42 of the Doctrine and Covenants (D&C) represents a Mormon response to the predicament of divine law in modernity. The text, originally presented as the "Laws of the Church of Christ," is a jurisprudential document, one that purports to come from God. It thus presents itself as divine law. A careful reading of the text, however, shows the way in which the idea of divine law at work in section 42 is defined in part through a dialogue with the secular law. Several historians have argued that early Mormons adopted a "theocratic ethic" in which the prophetic commands of revelation were held superior to any demand of secular law.[3] Whatever the merits of this view as a historical interpretation of the ideology of nineteenth-century Mormonism, the text of section 42 reveals a more ambiguous position.[4] On one hand, the text seems to challenge the sovereignty of the state. At the same time, it both retreats from such challenges and molds itself in dialogue with the secular law's treatment of the practices it defines. For its part, the idea of a theocratic ethic presents a relatively simple model of the relationship between divine and human law, in which the demands of the revealed law are always held to be superior to and sovereign over the demands of secular law. But this model does not adequately capture the idea of divine law revealed in section 42. Rather, the revelation provides a way of accommodating divine law to the reality of secular dominance. The approach first seen in section 42 was dramatically repeated in Mormonism's abandonment of polygamy at the end of the nineteenth century.

In this chapter, I explore the idea of divine law that emerges from section 42. First, I show how the revelation operates as a legal text. Such an interpretation makes the best sense of its textual history. I then argue that what the text offers to readers is ultimately a paradox, a divine law that ignores competing sovereignties in its assertion of authority while simultaneously sacralizing its own accommodation to modern legal realities.

---

3. D. Michael Quinn is the author of this interpretation, which has been followed by several other scholars. See D. Michael Quinn, *The Mormon Hierarchy: Origins of Power* (Salt Lake City: Signature Books, in association with Smith Research Associates, 1994); see also Gary James Bergera, *Conflict in the Quorum: Orson Pratt, Brigham Young, and Joseph Smith* (Salt Lake City: Signature Books, 2002).

4. This is not a challenge per se to the interpretation that Quinn and Bergera offer of a particular period in Mormon history. I believe that at times their claims are overstated, but this is a distinct issue from the exegesis of section 42, which is my sole concern in this chapter.

While lacking the simplicity of a theocratic ethic, this approach allows divine law to continue operating in a world where secular legal regimes claim overwhelming practical dominance.

Exegesis of section 42 begins with its textual history. On January 2, 1831, Joseph Smith received a revelation now canonized as section 38. Some months earlier, Mormon missionaries on their way to Missouri to preach to the Lamanites had converted a large group of Campbellites and Baptist primitivists in Kirtland, Ohio. At the time, Joseph Smith was still living in New York. The January revelation commanded that the Saints "should go to the Ohio" (D&C 38:32). It went on to promise, in God's voice, that "there I will give unto you my law" (D&C 38:32). Accordingly, Joseph relocated his family to Kirtland the next month, and beginning on February 9 began receiving the promised law.[5] What would eventually become section 42 was received in three parts on two separate days. The initial version of what was to become Doctrine and Covenants 42:1–69 was first recorded on February 9, 1831.[6] The first part of this text dealt with various missionary callings (see D&C 42:1–10), while the core of what came to be called "the Law" lies behind what is now D&C 42:11–69. Subsequently, on February 23 Joseph met with a group to consider "how the Elders of the church of Christ are to act upon the points of the Law," and recorded the initial version of what eventually became D&C 42:70–93, which provided a gloss on the previously received text.[7] Further, as will be discussed below, the Law was substantially revised before settling into its current form, but from the beginning it was self-consciously presented as "the law which I [the Lord] shall give unto you" (D&C 42:2)—that is, as a legal text. (When John Whitmer transcribed Joseph's revelations into an official notebook kept in Kirtland and later in Missouri, he generally prefaced each new entry with the word "Commandment," written in large

5. For an account of Joseph Smith's move to Kirtland and the circumstances in which what became section 42 was given, see Richard Lyman Bushman, *Joseph Smith: Rough Stone Rolling* (New York: Alfred A. Knopf, 2005), 122–26, 144–55.

6. Grant Underwood, "'Laws of the Church of Christ' (D&C 42): A Textual and Historical Analysis," in *The Doctrine and Covenants: Revelations in Context*, ed. Andrew H. Hedges, Spencer Fluhman, and Alonzo Gaskill (Provo & Salt Lake City, Utah: BYU Religious Studies Center & Deseret Book Co., 2008), 109.

7. See Underwood, 111–12.

text. However, when he recorded the text of what would become D&C 42:1–72, he wrote in large script "The Laws of the Church of Christ.")[8]

It might be surprising that the text of the revelation was altered. But legal texts are practical documents. Their purpose is to give guidance in particular contexts by providing rules. The idea that the text changes to reflect new rules and practices is unobjectionable.[9] Indeed, we expect this of legal texts. And the complex textual history of section 42 suggests that it originally functioned in part as a legal text in this way.[10] The earliest manuscript of section 42 no longer exists, but we do have numerous pre-publication copies made by individual Latter-day Saints, as well as more official compilations kept by Joseph Smith's scribes. Additionally, various versions of the texts that eventually became section 42 were published in *The Evening and the Morning Star*, the 1833 Book of Commandments, and the first edition of the Doctrine and Covenants in 1835. These early versions of section 42 show that the original text was substantially revised prior to its 1835 canonical presentation. The legal character of the text suggests how Latter-day Saints negotiated these changes. According to Orson Pratt, Joseph Smith distinguished between revelations that were published as authorities to the community and revelations that were of merely historical significance—a distinction that suggests a quasi-legal understanding of the revelation's textuality.[11]

---

8. See Robin Scott Jensen, Robert J. Woodford, and Steven C. Harper, eds., *Revelations and Translations: Manuscript Revelation Books* (Salt Lake City: Church Historian's Press, 2009), 86, 92, 104.

9. Or at least mostly unobjectionable. Lon Fuller famously argued that a law that shifted too rapidly threatened the concept of the rule of law, what Fuller called "the internal morality of law." See Lon L. Fuller, *The Morality of Law*, revised edition (New Haven: Yale University Press, 1969).

10. For a detailed discussion of that textual history, see generally Robert J. Woodford, "The Historical Development of the Doctrine and Covenants" (PhD dissertation, Provo, Utah, Brigham Young University, 1974), 525–69. For Joseph Smith's manuscript copies of the revelations that became section 42, see Jensen, Woodford, and Harper, *Revelations and Translations*, 95–105, 107.

11. Orson Pratt wrote, "Joseph, the Prophet, in selecting the revelations from the Manuscripts, and arranging them for publication, did not arrange them according to the order of the date in which they were given, neither did he think it necessary to publish them all in the Book of Doctrine and Covenants, but left them to be published more fully in his History. Hence, paragraphs taken from the revelations of a later date, are, in a few instances, incorporated with those of an earlier date. Indeed, at the time of compilation, the Prophet was inspired

Likewise, the minutes of the Kirtland High Council in 1834, where the decision was made to compile what became the 1835 edition of the Doctrine and Covenants, suggests a similarly ahistorical, legalistic understanding of the text. "The Council then proceeded to appoint a committee to arrange the items of the doctrine of Jesus Christ, for the government of the Church of Latter-Day Saints. . . . These items are to be taken from the Bible, Book of Mormon, and the revelations which have been given to the Church up to this date, or shall be until such arrangements are made."[12] Notice that the Doctrine and Covenants is compiled "for the government of the Church." Envisioning something quite distinct from a mere record of past revelations, the council contemplated a compilation of scriptures from multiple sources that would then serve as an authoritative guide to current practice.[13]

Consider some passages in what appears today as verses 30–37 of section 42. These verses set forth rules governing the consecration of property to the Church and the deeding back to members of individual stewardships. The procedures described in the earliest manuscript copy of the Law are different from those found in the final version. In Joseph Smith's manuscript notebook, for example, the text describes the procedure for administering any residual property remaining in the hands of the Church after stewardships have been doled out to members. It reads, "The Residue shall be kept in my Store house to administer to the poor & needy as shall be appointed by the Elders of the Church & the Bishop."[14] This version

---

in several instances to write additional sentences and paragraphs to the earlier revelations." Orson Pratt, *Millennial Star*, April 25, 1857.

12. "Minutes of the High Council, Kirtland, September 24, 1834," *Millennial Star*, March 19, 1853.

13. It is interesting to compare the structure contemplated by the Kirtland High Council's resolution with the earliest governing document for the Church, the "Articles of the Church of Christ," written in 1829. The Articles were drawn up by Oliver Cowdery in 1829 and were almost immediately replaced by what became section 20 of the Doctrine and Covenants. The Articles are written in the first person by the voice of the Lord, but the substance consists largely of verbatim quotations from the ecclesiological passages in the Book of Mormon, particularly in Moroni, strongly suggesting that Oliver Cowdery simply compiled scriptural passages to create a governing document for the then-contemplated church. See generally Scott H. Faulring, "An Examination of the 1829 'Articles of the Church of Christ' in Relation to Section 20 of the Doctrine and Covenants," *Brigham Young University Studies* 43, no. 4 (Winter 2004): 57–91.

14. Jensen, Woodford, and Harper, *Revelations and Translations*, 99.

of the text was then included in the 1833 Book of Commandments.[15] In the 1835 edition of the Doctrine and Covenants, however, the decision-making body controlling the residue of property was designated as "the high council of the church, and the bishop and his council," reflecting the more elaborate ecclesiastical structure that had been created in the intervening years.[16] Likewise, the earliest version of the text seems to contemplate a single act of consecration upon conversion.[17] In contrast, the 1835 edition introduces a second consecration: "If there shall be properties in the hands of the church, or any individuals of it, more than is necessary for their support" (D&C 43:33).[18] As Grant Underwood points out, all these changes passed without comment at the time, suggesting that early Mormons understood the evolution of the text not as the corruption of a divine original but simply as a juridical updating.[19] Just as the United States Code is only accidentally a record of particular legislative enactments, serving primarily and essentially as a compendium of currently valid law, the text of the 1835 Doctrine and Covenants was less a record of a distinct revelatory event than the product of successive "legislative" amendments. All these exegetical details suggest that the Law of section 42 is to be understood as a law in more than one sense.

Of course, law is a famously slippery concept. All the words common in Western thought that could be rendered as "law"—*nomos, lex, ius, aequitas, Recht, loi, droit,* right, equity, and so forth—have slightly different meanings. Lon Fuller's broad definition of law as the process of subjecting human action to the government of rules, however, is capacious enough for us to refer to section 42 as law without embarrassment.[20] And we have already seen some clear reasons to believe that the revelation should be regarded as a legal text. Still, we can ask in exactly what sense the Laws of

15. Robin Scott Jensen, Richard E. Turley, and Riley M. Lorimer, eds., *Revelations and Translations, Volume 2: Published Revelations,* The Joseph Smith Papers (Salt Lake City: Church Historian's Press, 2009), 104.

16. Jensen, Turley, and Lorimer, 432. The current edition of the Doctrine and Covenants follows the 1835 version of the D&C 42 text.

17. Jensen, Woodford, and Harper, *Revelations and Translations,* 99–100.

18. Compare Jensen, Turley, and Lorimer, *Revelations and Translations, Volume 2,* 99 (setting forth the original procedure).

19. Underwood, "The Laws of the Church of Christ," 114.

20. See Lon L. Fuller, "Law as an Instrument of Social Control and Law as a Facilitation of Human Interaction Essay," *Brigham Young University Law Review* 1975, no. 1 (1975): 95 ("rules can emerge and become effective as law without receiving the imprimatur of any explicitly legislative organ of government").

the Church of Christ is law. Understanding a legal text as the product of successive rounds of legislative amendment provides a way of understanding the revision of the Laws of the Church of Christ between 1831 and 1835. For all of that evolution, however, section 42 also aligns itself with a more cosmic vision of divine law.

Legislation was an idea familiar in the America of the 1830s,[21] but there is another way of thinking about law that is profoundly uncomfortable with the idea of legal change. This approach presents a continuum. At one end is the notion of law as an ancient and sanctified (but nonetheless conventional) tradition, as in the Roman *mos maiorum*.[22] At the other end is the notion of law as a timeless statement of cosmic truth. For example, during the classical period, Muslim theologians argued that the Qur'an—and with it the *sharia*—was an uncreated emanation from God.[23] Section 42 invokes something of this more eternal notion of law, although where it falls between the *mos maiorum* and the uncreated Qur'an is unclear. As noted earlier, the Laws of the Church of Christ proper does not begin until verse 11 in the current edition of the Doctrine and Covenants, verses 1–10 being concerned with individual missionary callings. In verses 18–29, which form a kind of preface to the rapidly evolving material on the law of consecration, the Law recapitulates in effect the second half of the Decalogue (the latter six of the Ten Commandments). It thus simultaneously links itself to the ancient order of things going back to the children of Israel and invokes what nineteenth-century Americans—influenced as they were by Protestant thought—saw as a changeless standard of God's moral

21. For a discussion of the role of legislation during the early nineteenth century, see Kermit Hall, *The Magic Mirror: Law in American History* (New York: Oxford University Press, 1989), 87–105.

22. Ancient Roman jurists thought of law in terms of the *mos maiorum*, the ancient traditions of the city dating back to the Laws of the Twelve Tables. On this view, legislation was seen as suspect innovation at best. At worse, it was—literally, given the religious significance of the *mos maiorum*—a form of sacrilege. See Hans Wolff, *Roman Law: An Historical Introduction* (Norman: University of Oklahoma Press, 1978), 63. Of course, the Romans maintained a distinction between secular law, *ius*, and sacral law, *fas*, but this did not mean that *ius* was bereft of religious significance, just that it didn't necessarily govern cultic practices, which were left to priests and augers.

23. According to these theologians, the Qur'an "endures forever with and through the divine Ipseity and is indivisible from it, with neither beginning nor end in eternity." Henry Corbin, *History of Islamic Philosophy*, trans. Phillip Sherrard (London: Kegan Paul International, 1993), 11.

truth. By recapitulating the scriptural prohibitions against theft, murder, and adultery, the revelation was thus laying claim to being something more than a compendium of current policies regarding consecrated properties.

Moderns, of course, identify law with rules promulgated by the state.[24] Max Weber, as already noted, captured the common sense of modernity when he defined the state as "the form of human community that (successfully) lays claim to the monopoly of legitimate physical violence."[25] Modernity's common sense couples this view with the positivist position that there is a conceptually sharp distinction between law and morals, mere counsel and threats backed by legitimate violence. Tellingly, Grant Underwood discusses section 42's recapitulation of part of the Decalogue as "the Church's moral code" and the "ethical vision of the Ten Commandments."[26] By invoking concepts—moral and ethical—that modern positivism conceptually separates from the legal, Underwood here imposes on the text a set of categories that the text itself does not embrace. On this point, it is striking that the Law explicitly challenges the state's Weberian monopoly on force, declaring, "thou shalt not kill. [H]e that k[i]lleth shall die" (see D&C 42:19).[27]

The way in which section 42 recapitulates the Decalogue underlines its legal and political function. The connection between section 42 and Exodus runs deep. The story of Sinai in Exodus 20, one of the two places in the Bible where the Ten Commandments are given, marks a key moment in the narrative of God's chosen people. The children of Israel have been slaves in Egypt, living under the yoke of Pharaoh. Having escaped his armies through the miraculous parting of the Red Sea, they find themselves for the first time beyond the political sovereignty of Egypt. And it is at *this* moment that God delivers His law to Moses. It is the transmission of the law from God to Moses and from Moses to the people that founds them as a political community. Prior to Exodus 20, the children of Israel are slaves or fugitives, the opposite of an autonomous polity; after the promulgation of God's law at Sinai, they are no longer merely a

24. This idea was just beginning to receive a forcefully philosophical articulation at the time Joseph Smith began publishing his revelations. See John Austin, *The Province of Jurisprudence Determined*, ed. H. L. A. Hart (Indianapolis: Hackett Publishing Company, 1998).

25. Max Weber, *The Vocation Lectures* (Indianapolis: Hackett Publishing Company, 2004), 33.

26. Underwood, "The Laws of the Church of Christ," 117.

27. Jensen, Woodford, and Harper, *Revelations and Translations*, 99.

household—or worse, slaves, adjuncts to the household of Pharaoh—but instead they become a nation. In the language of classical political philosophy, the Decalogue marks the transformation of the people from an *oikos* to a distinct *polis* with its own *nomos*.

All this is strikingly reflected in the historical context of section 42's original reception. In the January 1831 revelation mentioned at the outset of this chapter, the Lord vouchafed the Saints "a land of promise, a land flowing with milk and honey" (D&C 38:18). The revelation went on to link this promised land with the foundation of a new and sovereign community: "But, verily I say unto you that in time ye shall have no king nor ruler, for I will be your king and watch over you. Wherefore, hear my voice and follow me, and you shall be a free people, and ye shall have no laws but my laws when I come, for I am your lawgiver, and what can stay my hand?" (D&C 38:21–22). The revelation then commands Joseph to "go to the Ohio," but Kirtland is not the promised land. That is to be located in Jackson County, Missouri. Rather, Ohio is a stopping place where, the Lord promises, "I will give unto you my law" (D&C 38:32). Joseph's revelations thus explicitly place the coming forth of the Laws of the Church of Christ in the narrative context of the exodus, with Kirtland as a new Mount Sinai, whence he issues a new law that founds a new community set to inherit a new promised land.[28]

The New Testament, however, complicates this reading of section 42. The synoptic Gospels use the same narrative motif to mark the foundation of the Christian community but in a context that never makes of the Decalogue a replacement of rival earthly authorities. In the Sermon on the Mount, Jesus, acting as a new Moses, delivers to his followers a new law on the mountaintop, and it is this new law that then founds them as a community. Indeed, in the famous hypertheses of the sermon—"Ye have heard it said . . . . But I say unto you . . ." (see Matthew 5:21–45)—Jesus recapitulates key portions of the law given to Moses at Sinai. But even as he is presented as the lawgiver, the same Jesus of the synoptic Gospels emphatically declares his willingness to render unto Caesar the things that are Caesar's (see Matthew 22:21), just as Paul was anxious to make clear that Christians should submit themselves to "the powers that be" (see Romans 13:1). We thus have two distinct models for the founding of a community via the Decalogue: the unlimited sovereignty of Israel in

28. I am indebted to Joseph Spencer for pointing out to me the way in which section 38 reinforces the nesting of the Laws of the Church of Christ in the Sinai narrative in Exodus.

the Hebrew scriptures, but also the nonstatist claims of New Testament Christianity. Strikingly, the Zion founded by the partial recapitulation of the Decalogue in section 42 takes an ambivalent, middle position between these two poles.

The tendency toward one of these poles can be witnessed before the revelation that would become section 42 was given. The January 1831 revelation mentioned before (now D&C 38) speaks of the law in relationship to political sovereignty—"ye shall have no king nor ruler" and "ye shall have no laws but my laws when I come" (D&C 38:21, 22)—suggesting the primacy of the Sinai narrative rather than the Sermon on the Mount. This tendency then also appears in section 42. In fact, at least two textual features of the Laws of the Church of Christ point toward the more aggressive position represented by the nation of Israel. First, recall that verses 70–93 in the current version of section 42 were not part of the original law. They were instead added subsequently to instruct "how the Elders of the church of Christ are to act upon the points of the Law."[29] This is important because these verses disclaim the death penalty announced in the original text of the "Laws of the Church of Christ" (again: "He that k[i]lleth shall die"). Instead, the later addition commands that criminal malefactors are to be "delivered up and dealt with according to the laws of the land; . . . and it shall be proved according to the laws of the land" (D&C 42:79). But this clarification—a gloss that provides an alternative procedure for dealing with the reality of a functioning secular law—throws into relief the original law's insistence upon the death penalty for murderers. Tellingly, the initial prohibition is not treated as a justification for the secular legal regime; rather it is treated as an alternative to it.

The second aspect of the revelation that takes a more aggressive stance on sovereignty lies in the specific way the original Laws of the Church of Christ recapitulates the Decalogue. According to one tradition, the commandments contained in the first half of the Decalogue—the prohibitions on polytheism, idolatry, and the like—all relate to matters governing humanity's relationship with God. In contrast, the commandments contained in the so-called second tablet—the commands against coveting, theft, murder, adultery, and so on—all relate to relations between people rather than between people and God.[30] This division tracks a number of

29. Underwood, "The Laws of the Church of Christ," 111–12.

30. See, e.g., John Calvin, *Institutes of the Christian Religion*, ed. John T. McNeill, trans. Ford Lewis Battles (Philadelphia: Westminster John Knox Press, 1960), 376–77 ("God has so divided his law into two parts, which contain the

fault lines that run deep through Western political thought: the first tablet deals with matters of religion, the second with matters of politics; the first tablet deals with sacred matters, the second with profane; the first tablet deals with matters of church, the second with matters of state. This division has even been mapped epistemologically, with the first tablet identifying wrongs known by special revelation, the second identifying wrongs that can be divined by universal natural reason. If one approaches the Laws of the Church of Christ with this traditional understanding of the Decalogue in mind, it is immediately striking that its recapitulation of the Ten Commandments contains no references to the first tablet and names only commandments from the second tablet. The founding law of Zion plants itself firmly on the political, secular, state, and universal side of the Decalogue. This is, again, suggestive of a certain conflict between revealed law and secular law.

There are, however, features of the current text of section 42 that significantly qualify the way in which the Laws of the Church of Christ challenge the sovereignty of the secular law. First, as just noted again, verses 70–93 of the current text were given separately from the original law. They came in response to a very concrete, practical question from the elders assembled in Kirtland. Having been given the law, they wanted to know what to do in concrete practice. Strikingly, this further revelation (received only two weeks after the original) retreats from the more absolute claims made in the original law of February 9. Most dramatically, as already noted, the call for the death penalty is relaxed, with malefactors being given over to the ordinarily constituted legal authorities. Likewise, the implementing verses in this section assume an ecclesiastical jurisdiction independent of the state to try matters such as adultery but with its remedial options clearly limited to excommunication from the ecclesiastical community.

Further, as discussed earlier, later editorial alterations to the text of the original law—especially in connection with procedures involving the consecrations of properties—put on display a revealed law that is in dialogue with the secular legal system. In particular, two changes in the text minimize the confrontation between the law of consecration and stewardship and the common law rules of property. First, after the text has been edited, there is no longer any attempt by the Church to retain a property interest in the stewardships. The earlier regime had assumed that even

---

whole righteousness, as to assigning the first part to those duties of religion which particularly concern the worship of his magesty; the second to the duties of law that have to do with men").

after property was given as part of a stewardship, the bishop would retain the discretion to alter the allotment. Allowing such fractured control over property, however, was anathema to the common law of nineteenth-century America. It smacked of the repudiated doctrine of feudal tenures and seemed inconsistent with the allodial character of American real property.[31] Unsurprisingly, the result of the original law's organization of affairs was litigation against the Church by disaffected members—litigation that generally did not go in the Church's favor.[32] Hence, the text was altered so that property was given "with a covenant and a deed [note the inclusion of the technical, legal term] which cannot be broken" (D&C 42:30). This change in the text marks a retreat from ecclesiastical control over property once it had been given as part of a stewardship. Prior to the change, the Church claimed the right to repossess property given as part of a stewardship; after the change, the recipient of such property owned it free and clear of any ecclesiastical claims.

The fully revised version of the law also emphasizes in various places the fact that consecrations to the Church were for the care of the poor and benefit of Church officers. One of the legal problems with the system of consecration and stewardship was that the deeding of property to the Church, followed by an immediate deed from the Church back to the individual—the procedure generally employed in consecrations—looked like a dummy transaction of the kind the common law has always treated suspiciously.[33] On the other hand, gifts to eleemosynary institutions or for the support of ministers are examples of transactions that the common law has traditionally been enthusiastic about protecting from subsequent legal attack. Hence, the revised text describing the law of consecration and stewardship did so in terms that were more likely to be treated favorably in litigation. This example, combined with those just discussed, suggests that

---

31. For a detailed discussion of how the law of consecration and stewardship clashed with the ideology of common law property rules in the United States, see Nathan B. Oman, "'The Living Oracles': Legal Interpretation and Mormon Thought," *Dialogue: A Journal of Mormon Thought* 42, no. 2 (Spring 2009): 1–19.

32. See Edwin Brown Firmage and Richard Collin Mangrum, *Zion in the Courts: A Legal History of the Church of Jesus Christ of Latter-Day Saints, 1830–1900* (Urbana: University of Illinois Press, 1988).

33. Dummy sales, for example, are a classic way of secreting property from creditors. Likewise, immediate sale and deed-back transactions were frequently used as a device for creating security arrangements that were otherwise deemed fraudulent by the early common law.

what is now section 42 is as comfortable within an amiable relationship to secular law as it is with a stronger rivalry with secular law. The revelation draws on both the Sinai narrative's sense of the sovereignty of divine law and the Gospels' willingness to work within the context of other laws held to be sovereign.

What are we to make of this complex document? In a sense, the textual history of section 42 recapitulates the history of the idea of divine law, moving from the idea that divine law is a juridical reality to the idea of a divine law that exists in the spaces left open by secular law. That history is compressed from the fourteen centuries beginning with the disintegration of the Roman Empire to the fourteen days between February 9 and February 23, 1831. The law of February 9 speaks in an imagined space where no competing sovereignty exists, where Zion can be founded in an empty world through a new law delivered by a new Moses. The Saints have no king nor any law but the law of God (see, again, D&C 38:21–22). By February 23, however, the elders require a gloss, instructions on "how [they] . . . are to act upon the points of the Law." They find themselves living in a world inhabited by a robust secular law, so they need to know how the divine law is to interact with it. The response then and thereafter is a ceding of murder and the protection of property to the law of the land, coupled with the creation of an ecclesiastical structure to deal with moral questions. In effect, the gloss of February 23 transforms Zion from a kingdom into a church and the divine law into a system of morality.

I want to note two things about this process. First, there is a stunning and daring anachronism in the law of February 9. The problematic relationship of divine and secular law had been a matter of dispute since at least the twelfth century, and early nineteenth-century America offered a perfectly workable solution to this problem in the Protestant settlement between church and state. That solution can be found reflected in the Church's statement on government, authored by Oliver Cowdery and canonized as section 134. It comfortably adopts the settlement worked out in the late seventeenth and eighteenth centuries in the wake of the wars of religion. It divides the social universe into the realm of "civil officers and magistrates" (D&C 134:3), who are to protect "the free exercise of conscience, the right and control of property, and the protection of life" (D&C 134:2); and religion, where "men are amenable to [God], and to him only, for the exercise of [conscience], unless their religious opinions prompt them to infringe upon the rights and liberties of others" (D&C 134:4). Cowdery's presentation of matters is all very clean and neat and

Lockean.[34] The Laws of the Church of Christ, however, resolutely refuses to take the easy way out offered by this settlement. Instead the Lord speaks on February 9 as though the whole medieval and early modern confrontation between divine and secular conceptions of law had never happened.

The second thing worth noting is that accommodation to the competing claims of secular sovereignty, presented in the last part of what is now section 42, is itself presented as a revealed law. For Christian and Jewish thinkers, the accommodation of divine law to the new realities of an ascendant secular law required a massive effort of exegesis and reinterpretation. It is a project with which Islamic jurists continue to grapple. This effort occurs in the commentary that surrounds the sacred text. In contrast, in section 42 the solution of retreat and compromise by divine law in the face of secular reality is not left to theologizing that takes place off the scriptural page. Rather, the accommodation and ambivalence is written directly into the divine law itself, as a revealed word. In other words, while it is tempting to read the uncompromising revelation of February 9 as the real or authentic law and the February 23 text as a retreat, it must be recognized that the February 23 text is presented as a revelation speaking in the first-person voice of God. When the deconstructed revelation that emerges from the textual history is reconstructed into the canonized text of section 42, we are left with a double-minded, almost agonistic text. Again, the history from late antiquity to the nineteenth century and from February 9 to February 23 is united in a single authoritative revelation. Both the initial indifference to competing sovereignties *and* the retreat in the face of the demands of secular jurisdictions are presented as part of the same divine law.

This same paradoxical approach to divine law was manifest again—and most dramatically—in the struggle over polygamy. In addition to whatever else it was, the passage of Mormonism from monogamy to po-

---

34. Or nearly so. While verse 5 in the current version offers an account of political legitimacy and the right of revolution that might have been cribbed from *The Second Treatise on Government*, verse 1 does make the un-Lockean claim that "governments were instituted by God" (and therefore apparently not by social contract). For an illuminating exchange on section 134, compare Frederick Mark Gedicks, "The Embarrassing Section 134," *Brigham Young University Law Review* 2003, no. Spring (2003): 959–72 with Rodney K. Smith, "James Madison, John Witherspoon, and Oliver Cowdery: The First Amendment and the 134th Section of the Doctrine and Covenants," *Brigham Young University Law Review* 2003, no. Spring (2003): 891–940.

lygamy and back to monogamy was a legal event.[35] While the exact origins of plural marriage within Mormonism are controversial, as a textual and scriptural matter it makes its appearance in what has become section 132 of the Doctrine and Covenants, a revelation first recorded on July 12, 1843. There, the command to take plural wives is presented as a revealed "law . . . instituted from before the foundation of the world" (D&C 132:5). Here again we see divine law in its most uncompromising and cosmic sense. But this law instituted before the foundation of the world soon found itself in conflict with the laws of the United States. In 1862, Congress passed the Morrill Anti-Bigamy Act, and after the Supreme Court blessed its constitutionality in 1879, the federal government loosed a hail of prosecutions and increasingly punitive legislation against the Latter-day Saints. Over the course of the 1880s, hundreds of Latter-day Saints were incarcerated, Mormon polygamists and all Mormon women were formally disenfranchised (in Idaho Territory all Mormons were deprived of the vote), and the United States began proceedings to confiscate Mormon temples and other Church property.

Faced with institutional annihilation for the Church and the permanent political subjugation of all Latter-day Saints, Wilford Woodruff recorded in his diary on September 25, 1890:

> I have arrived at the point in the History of my life as the President of the Church of Jesus Christ of Latter Day Saints whare I am under the necessity of acting for the Temporal Salvation of the Church. The United State[s] Government has taken a Stand & passed Laws to destroy the Latter day Saints upon the subject of poligamy or Patriarchal order of Marriage. After Praying to the Lord & feeling inspired by his spirit I have issued the [Manifesto announcing the end of plural marriages] which is sustained by My Councillors and the 12 Apostles.[36]

He was later called to defend his actions in a sermon delivered in Logan, Utah, where he insisted, "I should have let all the temples go out of our hands; I should have gone to prison myself, and let every other man go there, had not the God of heaven commanded me to do what I

---

35. The best legal history of the anti-polygamy battles is Sarah Barringer Gordon, *The Mormon Question: Polygamy and Constitutional Conflict in Nineteenth-Century America* (Chapel Hill: University of North Carolina Press, 2002).

36. Wilford Woodruff, *Waiting for World's End: The Diaries of Wilford Woodruff*, ed. Susan Staker (Salt Lake City: Signature Books, 1993), 386–87.

did do."[37] Here, what might appear to be a gesture of accommodation or retreat is again presented as direct revelation. Whatever the complexities of post-Manifesto polygamy, plural marriage's demise in Mormon practice resulted from a claim to revelation rather than exegesis. The divine law both demanded its practice *and* suspended it.

Section 42 does not offer an entirely satisfying vision of divine law. The persistence of Mormon fundamentalism attests to the unwillingness of many to accept a divine law that claims both ultimate legitimacy and God's sanction for retreat in the face of secular opposition. The paradox lies in the fact that both the divine law instituted before the foundations of the world and the pragmatic accommodation to the "powers that be" claim divinity. The self-immolation of martyrdom in loyalty to an original revelation seems more authentic than a revealed law that in the end is willing to retreat—hence the persistence of polygamy in remote corners of the Intermountain West. The paradoxical vision of divine law presented in section 42 and dramatically enacted in the rise and fall of Mormon polygamy, however, has two major virtues. The first is the simple integrity of survival.[38] Collective martyrdom is ultimately an act of disloyalty to the community, to its continued life and existence. Section 42 provides a vision of divine law that need not end every conflict with secular authority in religious war and—given the overwhelming coercive capacity of the secular state—in defeat for the believers. The second virtue of section 42 is the unwillingness of divine law to protect itself by simply underwriting the legitimacy of secular power. By writing retreat into the fabric of divine law itself, section 42 leaves perpetually open the possibility of conflict and critique. The sanctification of survival thus needn't necessarily imply the sanctification of quietism.

Seeing section 42 as a legal text allows us to do two things. First, it gives us a model for understanding its layered textual history. Seeing scripture as law rather than the record of a sacred, revelatory event offers a reconciliation of the text's claim to authority and the way in which the authoritative text has manifestly been altered over the course of its life. Second, and more important, it provides us with a way of thinking about

---

37. "Excerpts from Three Addresses by President Wilford Woodruff Regarding the Manifesto," included in current editions of the Doctrine and Covenants alongside Official Declaration 1.

38. I borrow this phrase from a perceptive essay by Fred Gedicks. See Frederick Mark Gedicks, "The Integrity of Survival: A Mormon Response to Stanley Hauerwas," *DePaul Law Review* 42 (1993): 167.

divine law within Mormonism. Section 42 does not present the theocratic ethic posited by some Mormon historians. Any claim to absolute ecclesiastical sovereignty is negated by the negotiation with secular law revealed in the history of the text and the shift between the February 9 portion of the text and the February 23 portion of the text, as well as the 1835 alterations to the law of consecration in order to take into account secular, legal developments. At the same time, section 42 is structured so as to challenge and reject the neat dichotomies between church and state, secular and sacred, public and private, that run through modern political thought and, one might add, the far more conventional section 134. What we are left with is a divine law that both makes claims to sovereignty and sacralizes the compromise of those claims in the face of modern legal realities. The paradox of such a divine law is precisely what allows it to both survive and claim authority for Latter-day Saints in a modern world dominated by a secular law with overwhelming coercive force.

CHAPTER 10

Nomos, Narrative, and Nephi: Legal Interpretation in the Book of Mormon

I. Introduction

In 1827, a young man named Joseph Smith began reporting to family and friends that an angel had visited him and revealed gold plates buried in a hill not far from his family's farm in Palmyra, New York. Smith later claimed to have recovered the plates, which he said were covered with ancient writing, and he began dictating a "translation" of the text "by the gift and power of God" to a series of amanuenses. By 1830, the oft-interrupted task of dictation was complete. Smith showed the plates, which he had previously refused to show to anyone, to a select group of friends who signed an affidavit stating that "Joseph Smith . . . has shown unto us the plates of which hath been spoken, which hath the appearance of gold; and as many of the leaves as the said Smith has translated we did handle with our hands. . . ."[1] Shortly thereafter, Smith insisted, he returned the plates to the angel from whence they had come. Smith published his dictated text a short time later as the Book of Mormon. By April 1830 Smith had formally organized a church accepting the book as an additional volume of scripture to supplement the Bible, and converts began flocking to the new movement. Nearly two centuries later, The Church of Jesus Christ of Latter-day Saints that Smith and his book founded claims just over 16.5 million official members.[2]

Since even before its publication, the text of the Book of Mormon has been a prisoner to the miraculous and outlandish story of its own origin. For Latter-day Saints, the Book of Mormon is primarily a sign. Until recently, they have been less concerned with the narrative or even the theological content of the Book of Mormon than with its role in the founding myth of their religion.[3] For them, the book is a miraculous link

1. See *The Testimony of the Eight Witnesses*.

2. See The Church of Jesus Christ of Latter-day Saints, "Worldwide Statistics," Newsroom, accessed June 15, 2020, https://newsroom.churchofjesuschrist.org/facts-and-statistics.

3. See generally Noel B. Reynolds, "The Coming Forth of the Book of Mormon in the Twentieth Century," *Brigham Young University Studies* 38, no. 2 (1999):

between ancient prophets and Joseph Smith as the modern prophet of God's latter-day work.[4] For those outside the faith, of course, the stories of golden plates, angelic visitors, and ancient prophets have a very different meaning. Nearly a year before the publication of the Book of Mormon, the *Wayne Sentinel*, one of Palmyra's local papers, insisted that "the whole matter is the result of gross imposition, and a grosser superstition."[5] It is a way of treating the Book of Mormon that has not changed markedly in the almost two succeeding centuries. In a 2006 *Slate* article, Jacob Weisberg adopted the same approach. Discussing why he would not vote for a Latter-day Saint, he wrote:

> I wouldn't vote for someone who truly believed in the founding whoppers of Mormonism. The LDS church holds that Joseph Smith, directed by the angel Moroni, unearthed a book of golden plates buried in a hillside in Western New York in 1827. . . . Smith was able to dictate his "translations" of the Book of Mormon first by looking through diamond-encrusted decoder glasses and then by burying his face in a hat with a brown rock at the bottom of it. He was an obvious con man.[6]

Mirroring Latter-day Saint readings, such dismissive treatments also take the Book of Mormon primarily as a sign rather than a text. The content of

---

7–47 (providing a content study of Mormon sermons and publications showing that prior to the 1980s, the text of the Book of Mormon received relatively little attention among Latter-day Saints).

4. For example, in January 1831, less than a year after the publication of the Book of Mormon, Joseph Smith's mother, Lucy Mack Smith, wrote a letter trying to convert her brother to the new faith:

> By searching the prophecies contained in the old testament we find it there prophesied that God will set his hand the second time to recover his people in the house of Israel. he has now commenced this work. he hath sent forth a revelation in these last days, & this revelation is called the book of Mormon, it contains the fullness of the Gospel to the Gentiles, and is sent forth to show unto the remnant of the house of Israel what great things God hath done for their fathers; that they may know of the covenants of the Lord & that they are not cast off forever, and also of the convincing of both Jew and Gentile that Jesus is the Christ the Eternal God and manifests himself unto all nations.

Lucy Smith to Solomon Mack, Jr., 6 Jan. 1831, reprinted in Dan Vogel, ed., *Early Mormon Documents: Volume 1* (Salt Lake City: Signature Books, 1996), 215.

5. *Wayne Sentinel*, 26 Jun. 1829, reprinted in Dan Vogel, ed., *Early Mormon Documents: Volume 2* (Salt Lake City: Signature Books, 1998), 218–19.

6. Jacob Weisberg, "Romney's Religion: A Mormon President," *Slate*, December 20, 2006.

the book is less important than the conclusions that one draws from the story of its origin.

The gravitational force of the book's origin story has also infected the discussion of the content of the text. Latter-day Saints have tended to treat the Book of Mormon as a trove of theological proof texts. The authority of the text as scripture has vouchsafed the value of these textual snippets for believers. Indeed, because Latter-day Saints ground the value of the text in the miraculous story of its production, they have generally not felt called upon to understand or evaluate the text on its own terms. A similar, if inverted, dynamic arises for non-Mormons. Mark Twain, who seems to have actually read large chunks of the Book of Mormon, insisted that it was "chloroform in print."[7] In his eyes the book consisted of little more than a chaotic pastiche of ideas and themes taken from the Bible, and it lacked any coherent form or message. Modern readers, including those sympathetic to Mormonism, have often come to similar conclusions.[8]

---

7. See Mark Twain, *Roughing It* (Hartford: American Publishing Company, 1886), 127; Richard H. Cracroft, "Distorting Polygamy for Fun and Profit: Artemus Ward and Mark Twain Among the Mormons," *Brigham Young University Studies* 14, no. 2 (1974): 272–88.

8. Literary critic Harold Bloom, despite his admiration for Joseph Smith's religion-making imagination, writes, "What is a contemporary non-Mormon, interested in American religion, to do with the Book of Mormon? I cannot recommend that the book be read either fully or closely, because it scarcely sustains such reading." Harold Bloom, *The American Religion: The Emergence of the Post-Christian Nation* (New York: Simon & Schuster, 1993), 86. See also Bloom, 82. ("Whatever his lapses, Smith was an authentic religious genius, unique in our national history"). Like many other scholars, Bloom concludes that not only is the Book of Mormon not worth reading because of any intrinsic merit or interest that it might hold but that its text is not even particularly important for understanding Mormonism. See Bloom, 85 ("With the Book of Mormon, we arrive at the center of Joseph Smith's prophetic mission, but hardly at any center of Mormonism, because of Smith's extraordinary capacity for speculative development in the fourteen years that remained him after its publication"). Bloom goes on to write, "[The Book of Mormon] has bravura, but beyond question it is wholly tendentious and frequently tedious." Bloom, 86. Bloom here follows the work of Mormon historians who have identified Smith's main period of theological creativity with the so-called Nauvoo period from 1839 to 1844. See generally Thomas G. Alexander, "The Reconstruction of Mormon Doctrine: From Joseph Smith to Progressive Theology," *Sunstone* 5, no. 4 (August 1980): 24–33. More recent work, however, throws into question the claim that Smith's Nauvoo-period theology represented a sharp and discontinuous break with

Even the hit Broadway musical that took its name from the book contains virtually no content from the book itself, even as musical satire.

More recently, however, there has been a scholarly reevaluation of the Book of Mormon. In the multi-volume Oxford History of the United States, Daniel Walker Howe claims:

> The Book of Mormon should rank among the great achievements of American literature, but it has never been accorded the status it deserves, since Mormons deny Joseph Smith's authorship, and non-Mormons, dismissing the work as a fraud, have been more likely to ridicule it than to read it.[9]

A number of treatments of the text's literary structure and content have appeared in scholarly presses for an academic audience.[10] Other works have looked at the complicated reception history of the book.[11] The Book of Mormon has been examined in comparative works looking at other religious and scriptural traditions.[12] Scholarly editions of the text have been produced.[13] Even Mormon theological writings have been marked

---

his earlier teachings. See generally David L. Paulsen, "The Doctrine of Divine Embodiment: Restoration, Judeo-Christian, and Philosophical Perspectives," *Brigham Young University Studies* 35, no. 4 (1995): 6–94 ("My reading of the evidence leads me to reject two propositions: [1] that the doctrine of divine embodiment was articulated for the first time in 1838, and [2] that prior to 1838 Latter-day Saints understood God to be an immaterial being").

9. Daniel Howe, *What Hath God Wrought: The Transformation of America, 1815–1848* (New York: Oxford University Press, 2007), 314.

10. See generally Grant Hardy, *Understanding the Book of Mormon: A Reader's Guide* (New York: Oxford University Press, 2010); Terryl L. Givens, *The Book of Mormon: A Very Short Introduction* (New York: Oxford University Press, 2009).

11. See generally Elizabeth A. Fenton and Jared Hickman, eds., *Americanist Approaches to the Book of Mormon* (New York: Oxford University Press, 2019); Paul C. Gutjahr, *The Book of Mormon: A Biography* (Princeton: Princeton University Press, 2012); Terryl L. Givens, *By the Hand of Mormon: The American Scripture That Launched a New World Religion* (New York: Oxford University Press, 2003).

12. See generally Jad Hatem, *Postponing Heaven: The Three Nephites, the Bodhisattva, and the Mahdi*, trans. Jonathon Penny (Provo: Neal A. Maxwell Institute for Religious Scholarship, 2015).

13. See Royal Skousen, ed., *The Book of Mormon: The Earliest Text*, trans. Joseph Smith (New Haven: Yale University Press, 2009) (an effort to reconstruct as far as possible the earliest, pre-publication version of the Book of Mormon based on Skousen's multi-volume critical edition of the Book of Mormon text); Laurie F. Maffly-Kipp, ed., *The Book of Mormon*, trans. Joseph Smith Jr. (New York: Penguin Classics, 2008) (a Penguin Classics edition of the text prepared

by increasingly sophisticated engagement with the text of the Book of Mormon.[14] All of this work is marked by a turning away from the traditional discussions of the book which is centered on polemics about its origins or its place in the biography of Joseph Smith and the movement he created. Rather, the most recent generation of scholarly work has focused on the Book of Mormon text itself, looking at its meaning, structure, and possible connections with discussions and debates beyond Mormonism.

This chapter contributes to this latest generation of scholarship by offering a close reading of some of the earliest narratives in the book from a legal perspective and bringing them into dialogue with contemporary legal theory.[15] I examine the Book of Mormon as a legal text, arguing that these narratives embody a surprisingly nuanced debate about the nature of legal interpretation. One of the central themes in the opening narratives in the book is the conflict between the character of Nephi and his brothers. Nephi, the narrator in this part of the text, structures his story around a series of confrontations with his older brothers, Laman and Lemuel, and one of his main rhetorical agendas is to justify himself and his father against their attacks. In large part, this conflict is ultimately about what it means to follow the law. From the story emerge two quite

for religious studies students); Grant Hardy, ed., *The Book of Mormon: A Reader's Edition* (Urbana and Chicago: University of Illinois Press, 2003) (an edition of the text designed to be read as a literary creation rather than a devotional volume, including a critical apparatus).

14. See, e.g., Joseph M. Spencer, *An Other Testament: On Typology*, 2nd edition (Provo: Neal A. Maxwell Institute for Religious Scholarship, 2016); Adam S. Miller, *An Experiment on the Word* (Provo: Neal A. Maxwell Institute for Religious Scholarship, 2014); Joseph M. Spencer and Jenny Webb, eds., *Reading Nephi Reading Isaiah: Reading 2 Nephi 26–27* (Salt Lake City: Salt Press LLC, 2011); Adam S. Miller, ed., *A Dream, a Rock, and a Pillar of Fire: Reading 1 Nephi 1* (Provo: Neal A. Maxwell Institute for Religious Scholarship, 2017); Adam S. Miller and Joseph M. Spencer, eds., *Christ and Antichrist: Reading Jacob 7* (Provo: Neal A. Maxwell Institute for Religious Scholarship, 2018); Matthew Bowman and Rosemary Demos, eds., *A Preparatory Redemption: Reading Alma 12–13* (Provo: Neal A. Maxwell Institute for Religious Scholarship, 2018).

15. The earliest appearance of the Book of Mormon in legal scholarship appears to have been in 1898. See James Williams, "The Law of the Book of Mormon," *Law Magazine and Review: A Quarterly Review of Jurisprudence* 24, no. 2 (1898): 138–44. The most comprehensive treatment of legal narratives in the book is John W. Welch, *The Legal Cases in the Book of Mormon* (Provo: Brigham Young University Press, 2011).

different conceptions of the function and meaning of rules. For Laman and Lemuel, following the law is a matter of the formal content of rules and conforming one's conduct to that formal content. In contrast, for Nephi law is embedded within a much broader narrative that provides the law with meaning and importance. To follow the law is less a matter of the formal content of rules than of enacting those narratives in one's own life.

This divide between law as formal rules and law as narrative mirrors the discussion within contemporary legal theory between traditional positivist accounts of law and the jurisgenerative theory of Robert Cover.[16] According to Cover, one of the important functions of law is its role in the creation of the narratives that undergird the normative structures (nomos) of communities. Taking Jewish law as his model, Cover points toward the possibility of a world in which law's connection to violence can be secondary to its role as an engine of social meaning. Within this framework, Nephi is offering a jurisgeneritive vision of law-following. However, the Book of Mormon breaks with Cover's formulation by also gesturing toward the inadequacy of legal interpretation as a nomos-sustaining ac-

16. See Robert M. Cover, "The Supreme Court 1982 Term—Forward: Nomos and Narrative," *Harvard Law Review* 97 (1983): 4–68; Robert M. Cover, "Violence and the Word," *The Yale Law Journal* 95, no. 8 (July 1986): 1601. There is an extensive literature on Cover's thought. See, e.g., Aviam Soifer, "Covered Bridges," *Yale Journal of Law & the Humanities* 17 (2005): 55–80; Samuel J. Levine, "Halacha and Aggada: Translating Roberts Cover's Nomos and Narrative," *Utah Law Review* 1998 (1998): 465–504; Judith Resnik, "Living Their Legal Commitments: Paideic Communities, Courts, and Robert Cover," *Yale Journal of Law & the Humanities* 17 (2005): 17–54; Suzanne Last Stone, "Rabbinic Legal Magic: A New Look at Honi's Circle as the Construction of Law's Space," *Yale Journal of Law & the Humanities* 17 (2005): 97–124; Robert A. Burt, "Robert Cover's Passion," *Yale Journal of Law & the Humanities* 17 (2005): 1–8; Perry Dane, "The Public, the Private, and the Sacred: Variations on a Theme of 'Nomos and Narrative,'" *Cardozo Studies in Law and Literature* 8, no. 1 (1996): 15–64; Robert C. Post, "Who's Afraid of Jurispathic Courts: Violence and Public Reason in Nomos and Narrative," *Yale Journal of Law & the Humanities* 17 (2005): 9–16; Suzanne Last Stone, "In Pursuit of the Counter-Text: The Turn to the Jewish Legal Model in Contemporary American Legal Theory," *Harvard Law Review* 106, no. 4 (1993): 813–94; Suzanne Last Stone, "Judaism and Postmodernism Law and Hermeneutics in Rabbinic Jurisprudence: A Maimonidean Perspective," *Cardozo Law Review* 14 (1993): 1681–1712; Suzanne Last Stone, "Justice, Mercy, and Gender in Rabbinic Thought," *Cardozo Studies in Law and Literature* 8, no. 1 (1996): 139–77.

tivity. In the Book of Mormon narrative, it is only when interpretation is coupled with the imprimatur of supernatural intervention that a new nomos is created. Contemporary legal theories cannot, of course, look to the supernatural in grounding the law as an engine of nomos creation. However, the story of Nephi does point toward the inadequacy of founding the normative power of law purely on its interpretive fecundity. In so doing, my reading of the Book of Mormon offers both an example of Cover's approach and a critique of it.

This chapter proceeds as follows. Part II provides an account of the debate over the nature of following the law in the Book of Mormon, showing through a close reading of the story of Nephi's confrontation with his brothers their contrasting approaches to legal authority. Part III shows how Laman and Lemuel's approach to rule-following fits within one of the main streams of analytic jurisprudence but how, within that framework, Nephi's response to their claims is largely incomprehensible. Part IV shows how Nephi's approach does make sense within Robert Cover's approach to law even as his story challenges Cover's central claim about how interpretation becomes law. Part V concludes.

II. The Debate Over Rule-Following in the Book of Mormon

The Book of Mormon opens with the story of Lehi and his family. Lehi is living in Jerusalem in the decade just before the Babylonians destroy the city in 587 BCE. He has a vision of a pillar of fire in which he learns that the city will be destroyed unless it repents. The people of Jerusalem reject his message, seek his death, and Lehi flees with his family into the desert. For many years they wander in the wilderness, suffering various difficulties, until they arrive at the seashore, a land they name Bountiful. God directs them to build a ship, which they do, and they finally voyage to a new promised land that the Lord has prepared for them. The story's arc of exile, exodus, and arrival, however, is ultimately tragic rather than triumphal. From the beginning, conflict between Lehi's sons divides the family. His younger son, Nephi, believes Lehi, receives his own revelations from God, and embraces the family's exodus and search for a new promised land. In contrast, Nephi's older brothers, Laman and Lemuel, are never fully persuaded of their father's prophetic bona fides. They insist that he has been led astray by "the foolish imaginations of his heart" (1 Ne. 2:11), constantly complaining that they have been forced to leave their comfortable life in Jerusalem for nothing. The conflict between

Nephi and his brothers flares up repeatedly and violently in the desert. Upon arriving in their promised land, the family splits into warring tribes of Nephites and Lamanites.

This opening portion of the Book of Mormon, which follows the biblical convention and is divided into "books" named 1 Nephi and 2 Nephi, is written in the first person. The narrator is Nephi, and we learn that he is composing his record many decades after the fact, with a full knowledge of how conflict with his brothers will mature into permanent enmity and warfare. The narrative is didactic rather than objective, and among the narrator's other agendas, Nephi is at pains to justify himself and his father against the accusations of his brothers. The action of the narrative consists of a series of incidents in which Nephi confronts the complaining and faithless Laman and Lemuel. The tension and violence escalate, reaching a climax when God commands that the family build a ship to travel to their new promised land. Surprisingly, at the heart of the conflict between Nephi and his brothers is what we can fairly characterize as a legal dispute. Their argument is ultimately about what it means to follow the law. From it emerge two quite different conceptions of the function and meaning of rules. To see how this is so, however, requires careful attention to the book's narrative structure and its extensive use of biblical allusion in particular.

A. Strategies of Biblical Allusion in the Book of Mormon

Even the most casual reader of the Book of Mormon will notice its heavy dependence on the Bible. It is written in self-consciously archaic language that deliberately apes the Jacobean idiom of the King James Version. The characters within the narrative are aware of the biblical texts, and at various points they quote large portions of the King James Version nearly verbatim.[17] God, prophecy, prayer, visions, dreams, revelations, exodus, sin, redemption, promised lands, chosen people, holy records, apocalyptic expectations, and a host of other biblical themes and elements appear repeatedly. For many readers the intertextuality between the Book of Mormon and the Bible reveals the former as a clumsy copy

---

17. See generally Joseph M. Spencer, *The Vision of All: Twenty-Five Lectures on Isaiah in Nephi's Record* (Salt Lake City: Greg Kofford Books, 2016) (discussing the use of Isaiah in the Book of Mormon); Spencer and Webb, *Reading Nephi Reading Isaiah* (same as previous).

of the latter.[18] On this view, the Book of Mormon's use of biblical themes represents little more than random copying as Joseph Smith composed the narrative at breakneck speed in 1829. The problem with this approach to the text, however, is that presenting the Book of Mormon as an essentially mindless pastiche of biblical tidbits tends to foreclose the kind of careful attention to the text that reveals the underlying structure, complexity, and subtlety of its narrative.

Readers of the Bible face a similar interpretive choice. Certain narratives in the book clearly copy the basic structure of earlier narratives. Source critics provide us with an appreciation of the complex textual history of the Bible. Such repetitions can thus be seen as simply the narrative seams left by earlier copying and redacting. As modern narrative critics such as Robert Alter and Meir Sternberg have pointed out, however, the danger of source criticism is its tendency to cast the final biblical text as a rather artless jumble of earlier sources.[19] What can be missed is the care and artistry employed by the final redactors. For example, Robert Alter argues that repetitions of certain narrative structures are deliberate allusions by reference to which the reader is supposed let the earlier narrative determine her response to the later narrative.[20] By making deliberate choices about how to structure the similarities and differences in the narratives, the author of the final biblical text adds layers of meaning and commentary through the Bible's own self-allusions.

A similar approach can be taken to the intertextuality of the Bible and the Book of Mormon. Rather than seeing the latter's reliance on the former as evidence of plagiarism, it is more fruitful to examine quotations and the borrowing of biblical themes and narrative structures as a part of a strategy of allusion by Book of Mormon narrators that serves complex

18. As one early nineteenth-century critic of the Latter-day Saints put it, "this book is bespangled from beginning to end not only with thoughts of sacred writers, but with copious verbal extracts from King James' translation." Grant Hardy, "The Book of Mormon and the Bible," in *Americanist Approaches to the Book of Mormon*, ed. Elizabeth A. Fenton and Jared Hickman (New York: Oxford University Press, 2019), 115 (quoting Jonathan Turner, *Mormonism in All Ages: Or, the Rise, Progress, and Causes of Mormonism with the Biography of Its Author and Founder, Joseph Smith . . .*, 1842).

19. See generally Robert Alter, *The Art of Biblical Narrative*, 2nd edition (New York: Basic Books, 2011); Meir Sternberg, *The Poetics of Biblical Narrative: Ideological Literature and the Drama of Reading*, reprint edition (Indiana University Press, 1987).

20. See Alter, *The Art of Biblical Narrative*, 55–78 (discussing type-scene narratives).

purposes.[21] For example, early on in the Book of Mormon story, Lehi sends his sons back to Jerusalem to obtain sacred records from a wicked man named Laban. When they try to purchase the records, Laban beats Nephi and his brothers, steals their property, and drives them into the desert. Nephi's older brothers, Laman and Lemuel, wish to abandon their quest for the records, and Nephi exhorts them by explicitly invoking the example of the biblical exodus:

> Therefore let us go up; let us be strong like unto Moses; for he truly spake unto the waters of the Red Sea and they divided hither and thither, and our fathers came through out of captivity, on dry ground, and the armies of Pharaoh did follow and were drowned in the waters of the Red Sea. (1 Ne. 4:2)

At this explicit level, Nephi comes across as a cocksure little brother confident that he is going to reenact the exodus story at its dramatic climax, with himself cast as Moses miraculously defeating the armies of Pharaoh.

The narrative structure, however, also contains a darker allusion to Moses, one at odds with the cocksure Nephi's invocation of triumph on the shores of the Red Sea. Nephi returns to Jerusalem and there comes upon the drunken Laban. The story continues, "I was constrained by the Spirit that I should kill Laban; but I said in my heart: Never at any time have I shed the blood of man" (1 Ne. 4:10). In the passage that follows, Nephi argues with the Spirit until he is finally persuaded of the necessity of killing Laban. In contrast to the blithely self-confident character who invokes Moses parting the Red Sea at the beginning of the story, the Nephi who kills Laban is tortured by what he sees as the dreadful necessity of murder.[22]

Nephi's killing of Laban is also a reference to Moses. The narrative marks Nephi's first action in the story. Thus Nephi is introduced, as is Moses in the Bible, with a morally ambiguous homicide. The second chapter of Exodus recounts how Moses killed an Egyptian overseer he

---

21. Readers of the Book of Mormon often miss this point. Devout Latter-day Saints regard the book as an ancient text rather than a production of Joseph Smith. They are thus often uncomfortable directly addressing the text's obvious reliance on the seventeenth-century King James Version. Non-Mormon readers immediately note the text's reliance on the KJV but tend to see that reliance as crude rather than subtle.

22. Others have argued that the murder of Laban is narratively structured in such a way as to highlight Nephi's reconsideration of his original understanding of God's commands in at the opening of the Laban narrative. See Joseph M. Spencer, *1st Nephi: A Brief Theological Introduction* (Provo: Neal A. Maxwell Institute for Religious Scholarship, 2020), 66–81 (discussing the Laban narrative in 1 Nephi).

saw beating an Israelite slave. He hid the body in the sand, but when Pharaoh discovered the killing, Moses was forced to flee into the desert (see Ex. 2:11–15.) Like Nephi's confrontation with Laban, the killing of the overseer marks Moses's first action in the biblical narrative. The murder seems motivated by indignation at the overseer's unjust cruelty toward the Israelite slave, yet still Moses must conceal the killing and flee its consequences (Ex. 2:11–15.) Likewise, Nephi kills Laban, who he says "had sought to take away my own life" (1 Ne. 4:11) and had stolen all Lehi's property. Yet Nephi shrinks from the act, fears that the killing will be discovered, and like Moses, flees into the desert.

The narrative provides an ironic commentary on Nephi's glib call to his brothers to be like Moses. Nephi-as-narrator is in dialogue with the character of Nephi in the narrative. He is like Moses, yes, but not in the way that the character thinks. The irony of Nephi's glib identification with Moses emphasizes the real difficulty and moral anguish involved in actually following the Mosaic example. Far from being a mindless pastiche of biblical elements, the killing of Laban reveals how the Book of Mormon's allusions to the Bible are deliberately structured in ways that deepen the meaning of the book's narrative, adding layers of implicit commentary on the actions recounted by the narrator.

B. The Conflict Between Nephi and His Brothers

Careful attention to the use of explicit and implicit biblical allusion reveals the structure of the legal argument between Nephi and his older brothers. The key conflict comes in what is 1 Nephi chapter 17 in the modern edition of the Book of Mormon. The current structure of chapters and verses, however, is not native to the Book of Mormon text. Rather, it was adopted in an 1879 printing for ease of reference.[23] As a result, the narrative breaks signaled by the original seven chapters of 1 Nephi have

23. This edition was prepared by Orson Pratt, a senior member of the Church's governing Quorum of the Twelve Apostles and an influential Mormon intellectual. He created the system of chapters and verses that continue to be used in modern editions of the Book of Mormon. See Paul C. Gutjahr, "Orson Pratt's Enduring Influence on The Book of Mormon," in *Americanist Approaches to the Book of Mormon*, ed. Elizabeth A. Fenton and Jared Hickman (New York: Oxford University Press, 2019), 83–102 (discussing the structure and lasting influence of the 1879 edition).

been lost.[24] In the 1830 edition of the Book of Mormon, what is today chapter 17 came more or less in the middle of what was Chapter V (see 1 Ne. 16–1 Ne. 19:21).[25] The previous chapters close out the account of events in Jerusalem and its environs. Chapter V in the original text tells of the family's travels in the wilderness to a temporary stopping place at the seashore called Bountiful. From there, they embark on a voyage across the sea to reach the new promised land (see 1 Ne. 16–1 Ne. 19:21). The arc of the original Chapter V thus tells of the exodus of the Lehites from Jerusalem. Admittedly, they went into the wilderness as early as the original Chapter I, but prior to the original Chapter V, the narrative still centers on Jerusalem, with the brothers returning to get the records from Laban and then debating over their significance and the significance of Lehi's resulting prophetic dreams (see 1 Ne. 1–1 Ne. 15).[26] Thus the original Chapter V is the heart of the exodus narrative in 1 Nephi, the story of God's chosen people crossing the wilderness to their new promised land.

Chapter 17 in the current edition begins with the compressed account of eight years of wandering in the wilderness, the entry into the land Bountiful, and God's command to Nephi to build a ship. The text says:

> And it came to pass that after I, Nephi, had been in the land of Bountiful for the space of many days, the voice of the Lord came unto me, saying: Arise, and get thee into the mountain. And it came to pass that I arose and went up into the mountain, and cried unto the Lord. And it came to pass that the

---

24. According to the convention in Book of Mormon scholarship, chapter numbers in the original text are given using Roman numerals and are always capitalized, while chapter numbers in the modern edition are given using Arabic numerals and are not capitalized. The original edition of the Book of Mormon contained no verse numbers. The original chapters of 1 Nephi and their corresponding chapter and verses in the modern edition of the Book of Mormon were: Chapter I (1 Nephi 1–5, telling the story of leaving Jerusalem and recovering the plates of brass); Chapter II (1 Nephi 6–9, telling the story of Lehi's Dream and Nephi's response); Chapter III (1 Nephi 10–14, telling the story of Nephi's Vision); Chapter IV (1 Nephi 15, telling the story of Nephi's argument with his brothers over the meaning of the visions); Chapter V (1 Nephi 16–1 Nephi 19:21, telling the story of traveling in the wilderness, building a ship, and traveling to the new promised land); Chapter VI (1 Nephi 19:22–21:26, containing Nephi's extensive quotations from Isaiah); Chapter VII (1 Nephi 22, containing Nephi's interpretation of the quoted Isaiah passages).

25. The text contained in original Chapter V.

26. The text contained in original Chapter I, Chapter II, Chapter III, and Chapter IV.

> Lord spake unto me, saying: Thou shalt construct a ship, after the manner which I shall show thee, that I may carry thy people across these waters. And I said: Lord, whither shall I go that I may find ore to molten that I may make tools to construct the ship after the manner which thou hast shown unto me? And it came to pass that the Lord told me whither I should go to find ore, that I might make tools. (1 Ne. 17:7–10)

Like Moses in Exodus, God calls Nephi to the top of a mountain where he gives instructions on leading a chosen people to the promised land (cf. Ex. 3). Like Moses, upon hearing God's command, Nephi is incredulous. Moses's response to the Lord on the mountain was "Who am I, that I should go unto Pharaoh, and that I should bring forth the children of Israel out of Egypt?" (Ex. 3:11).[27] Nephi asks, "Whither shall I go that I may find ore to molten?" (1 Ne. 17:10). As with Moses on the mount, God answers his servant's questions, and the servant then sets forth to obey the divine command.

After Nephi begins work on the ship, Laman and Lemuel taunt him, and when Nephi sorrows at the "hardness of their hearts" (1 Ne. 17:19), they say:

> We knew that ye could not construct a ship, for we knew that ye were lacking in judgment; wherefore, thou canst not accomplish so great a work. And thou are like our father, led away by the foolish imaginations of his heart; yea, he hath led us out of the land of Jerusalem, and we have wandered in the wilderness for these many years; and our women have toiled being big with child; and they have born children in the wilderness and suffered all things, save it were death; and it would have been better that they had died before they came out of Jerusalem than to have suffered these afflictions. (1 Ne. 17:19–20)

Tellingly, this passage seems to retell the story with which Nephi-as-narrator began chapter 17 (cf. 1 Nephi 17:1–4). In contrast to their interpretation, however, Nephi presented the journey in the wilderness and the endurance of "our women" in providential terms of God's mercy.[28] In

27. In all quotations from the Bible, I use the King James Version. Whatever its limitations as a translation, it clearly influences the language of the Book of Mormon, whose biblical allusions must be understood against the background of the KJV's language.

28. Grant Hardy has noted the paucity of references to women in the Book of Mormon, arguing that readers should be particularly attentive to situations, such as chapter 17, where the narrator makes repeated references to women. Such references, he argues, are more likely to mark deliberately structured narrative

Laman and Lemuel's interpretation, "it would have been better they had died" (1 Ne. 17:2–3).

The narrator invites the reader to interpret this passage against the background of Exodus. God's chosen people are led by revelation out of a wicked country and travel to the promised land. Their way is blocked, however, by a body of water that they are called to miraculously cross. In Exodus the body of water is the Red Sea, while in Nephi 17 it is "Irreantum, which, being interpreted, is many waters" (1 Ne. 17:5). That being the case, the lament of Nephi's brothers also seems to echo the lament of the Children of Israel on the shores of the Red Sea. The Exodus story reads:

> And they said unto Moses, because there were no graves in Egypt, hast thou taken us away to die in the wilderness? Wherefore hast thou dealt thus with us, to carry us forth out of Egypt? Is not this the word that we did tell thee in Egypt, saying, Let us alone, that we may serve the Egyptians? For it had been better for us to serve the Egyptians, than that we should die in the wilderness. (Ex. 14:11–12)

Both Nephi's brothers and the Children of Israel are enmeshed in a narrative irony. They both believe that they know how the story is going, but both are mistaken.

As Moses explains to the Israelites on the shores of the Red Sea:

> Fear ye not, stand still, and see the salvation of the Lord, which he will shew to you today: for the Egyptians whom ye have seen to day, ye shall see them again no more for ever. The Lord shall fight for you, and ye shall hold your peace. (Ex. 14:13–14)

Likewise, Nephi will offer his own rebuke to his brother's accusations that he is a fool who cannot build a ship or cross the waters.

> And I said unto them: If God had commanded me to do all things I could do them. If he should command me that I should say unto this water, be thou earth, it should be earth; and if I should say it, it would be done. And now if the Lord has such great power, and has wrought so many miracles among the children of men, how is that he cannot instruct me, that I should build a ship? (1 Ne. 17:50–51)

Notice how Nephi's rebuke explicitly harks back to Moses before the Red Sea—"If he should command me that I should say unto this water, be thou earth, it should be earth"—reinforcing the sense that Laman and

---

elements because of their rarity. See Hardy, *Understanding the Book of Mormon: A Reader's Guide*, 18.

Lemuel don't really understand the story that they are inhabiting, the story of Moses and the exodus from Egypt.

Laman and Lemuel offer their own gloss on Moses in verse 22, and in so doing, model a particular type of scriptural and legal interpretation. They say:

> And we know that the people who were in the land of Jerusalem were a righteous people; for they kept the statutes and judgments of the Lord, and all his commandments, according to the law of Moses; wherefore, we know that they are a righteous people; and our father hath judged them, and hath led us away because we would hearken unto his words; yea, and our brother is like him. (1 Ne. 17:22)

There is a great deal going on in this sentence. It begins with an assertion that the people in Jerusalem were righteous. If this is true, of course, the entire journey through the desert has been pointless. The claim is justified by an appeal to Moses, but unlike the narrative references made by Nephi, the appeal is an explicitly "legal" one. The people of Jerusalem were righteous because they "kept the statutes and judgments of the Lord . . . according to the law of Moses" (1 Ne. 17:22).

Whereas Lehi claimed that the people of Jerusalem were unrighteous because of a revelation from a pillar of fire, Laman and Lemuel come to the opposite conclusion on the basis of legal analysis (see 1 Ne. 1:6; cf. Ex. 13:21–22).[29] Their response is rooted in a conclusion based on the formal application of rules. Note also the way that they understand Lehi's rebuke to the people at Jerusalem as a legal act—"he has judged them" (1 Ne. 17:22)—one that he has performed badly. Indeed, whereas in Nephi's narrative, Lehi's preaching is evidence of his divine calling, Laman and Lemuel understand the preaching—"his words"—very differently (cf. 1 Ne. 1).[30] For them the preaching, far from being prophetic or divine, was a purely rhetorical or sophistic exercise. It was an illegitimate way of getting power that is implicitly contrasted to the legitimacy of the "statutes and judgments of the Lord" (1 Ne. 17:22).

Where Nephi locates Moses in the experience of his family's exodus, Laman and Lemuel locate Moses in the correct application of rules. "Statutes and judgments" dominate stories of preaching and fleeing the wrath that is to come. Nephi's response to his brothers directly attacks

---

29. In 1 Nephi, a pillar of fire appears to Lehi; in Exodus, the Children of Israel are guided through the desert by a pillar of cloud by day and a pillar of fire by night.

30. Compare with Nephi's account of his father's preaching.

their understanding of Moses's significance. Where they see Moses as a lawgiver whose "statutes and judgments" provide a determinate and juridical criterion of righteousness, Nephi insists on the primacy of Moses as the hero of a story of exodus and desert redemption.

> And it came to pass that I, Nephi, spake unto them, saying: Do ye believe that our fathers, who were children of Israel, would have been led away out of the hands of the Egyptians if they had not hearkened unto the words of the Lord? (1 Ne. 17:23)

Notice the way in which Nephi directly attacks his brother's criticism of Lehi's words as a means to illegitimate power. It was only by hearkening to the "words of the Lord" (not his "statutes and judgments") that the Children of Israel were redeemed. He then proceeds to recapitulate the story of the original exodus in a way that parallels the journey of the Lehite group out of Jerusalem. First, he says:

> Now ye know that Moses was commanded of the Lord to do that great work; and ye know that by his word the waters of the Red Sea were divided hither and thither, and they passed through on dry ground. (1 Ne. 17:26)

This miraculous crossing of water can be seen as a reference to the situation of Nephi before Irreantum, the great waters that he will pass through the miracle of God's revealed plan to build a ship. Next, Nephi invokes the story of the Children of Israel being fed by manna from heaven and the water that sprang forth when Moses struck the rock (1 Ne. 17:28–29; cf. Ex. 16–17).[31] This also seems to be a reference to the experience of the Lehites. Immediately prior to the story of Nephi's attempts to build the ship, we have the story of how the family was threatened with starvation when Nephi broke his bow, and the miraculous manner in which he was able to find food through the intervention of God (see 1 Nephi 16:18–31).

Nephi ends his recounting of the story of the exodus with the story of the invasion of Canaan.

> And after they had crossed the river Jordan he did make them mighty unto the driving out of the children of the land, yea, unto the scattering them to destruction. And now, do ye suppose that the children of this land, who were in the land of promise, who were driven out by our fathers, do ye suppose that they were righteous? Behold, I say unto you Nay. (1 Ne. 17:32–33)

Notice that here Nephi is offering a counter criterion for judging the righteousness of a people. Where Laman and Lemuel look to the legal

---

31. Exodus 16–17 is the story of God's miraculous care of the children of Israel in the desert.

criteria of keeping "statutes and judgments," Nephi appeals to a violent, historical event. We can read this appeal to the invasion of Canaan against the background of Lehi's prophecies in Jerusalem. Lehi's "words," far from being an attempt to lead people into the desert and get power over them, actually consisted of an effort to save them from imminent military catastrophe. Nephi reads the story of Moses as ultimately judging righteousness in terms of geopolitical events.[32] This reading is reinforced by the fact that Nephi-as-narrator knows that after Lehi and his family left, Jerusalem was—like the Canaanites—destroyed by invaders—in this case the Babylonians—because of its wickedness (see 2 Nephi 1:4).

C. Two Approaches to Legal Interpretation

At its heart, the story in chapter 17 is about two dueling ways of understanding how one follows authoritative texts—how one follows the law. Laman and Lemuel offer a legal reading whereby scriptures provide rules that are then used to judge righteousness. Nephi, on the other hand, constructs his entire narrative around a competing view of scripture. On this view, scripture's normative power comes from the recapitulation of its stories in the lives of those that accept its authority. It orders the lives of those subject to its authority not through a set of juridical rules but through a set of narratives that transform existence from a mere sequence of events into the incarnation of God's working in the world.

Some readers may be skeptical of my claim that Nephi-as-narrator and his brothers are engaged in a legal debate. But the text supports such a legal framing. We are told that the records recovered from Laban which played such a prominent role in the early portion of the narrative contain "the five books of Moses" (1 Ne. 4:11), and when Nephi recounts his internal dialogue justifying the murder of Laban he explicitly conceptual-

---

32. It should go without saying that Nephi's argument here is morally problematic, suggesting as it does that human war and violence reveal God's judgements on human beings as opposed to seeing war and violence as forms of human wickedness. Nephi as narrator is unconcerned with these objections, although later Book of Mormon narrators take a critical stance toward linking military events to judgments of wickedness or righteousness. See Nathan B. Oman, "Standing Betwixt Them and Justice: War and Atonement in the Book of Mormon," in *God Himself Will Come Down: Reading Mosiah 15*, ed. Joseph M. Spencer and Andrew Smith (Seattle: Latter-day Saint Theology Seminar, 2023), 121–32 (discussing war in the Book of Mormon and the idea of discerning God's judgments in geopolitical events).

izes the records as a legal text. "I also thought," he says, "that they [his descendants] could not keep the commandments of the Lord according to the law of Moses, save they should have the law" (1 Ne. 4:15). We thus cannot read Nephi as rejecting the authority of "the law" (tellingly, this is his term for the records), and the accusations of false judgment leveled by Laman and Lemuel in chapter 17 must be answered. If we don't read Nephi as offering a response to the legal claims of his brothers in chapter 17, then their central accusation is left unanswered, which seems an implausible reading given the clear self-justificatory agenda of Nephi-as-narrator. Nephi answers their charges by appropriating the narrative of Moses and exodus for himself and his father. Furthermore, this is presented as a fully adequate response to his brother's accusations of legal malfeasance. Later in the story, Nephi explains that in reading "things . . . which were written in the books of Moses. . . . I did liken all scriptures unto us, that it might be for our profit and learning" (1 Ne. 19:23). In short, recapitulating in his life the story of the scriptures seems to be how Nephi seeks to "keep the commandments of the Lord according to the law of Moses" (1 Ne. 4:15).

There is one final bit of evidence that Nephi is offering a legal hermeneutic. Much later in the Book of Mormon, after Nephi has been replaced as narrator by another character, we are given a glimpse of the law among his descendants:

> Now there was no law against a man's belief; for it was strictly contrary to the commands of God that there should be a law which should bring men on to unequal grounds. For thus saith the scripture: Choose ye this day, whom ye will serve. (Alma 30:7–8)

This is the only place in the Book of Mormon where a legal rule is explicitly derived from a biblical text. The scripture in this case is Joshua 24:15.[33] Strikingly, Joshua 24 is also a legal text. It presents the so-called Shechem Covenant, in which Moses's successor, Joshua, gathers the Children of Israel together at the end of his life and gives them the choice of following God or choosing instead the gods of the Canaanites or the Egyptians.[34]

---

33. The verse reads, "And if it seem evil unto you to serve the Lord, choose you this day whom ye will serve; whether the gods which your fathers served that were on the other side of the flood, or the gods of the Amorites, in whose land ye dwell: but as for me and my house, we will serve the Lord."

34. This is the only passage in the Hebrew Bible where the children of Israel are given such an explicit choice to serve Yahweh or other gods. See Joseph A. Fitzmyer, *New Jerome Biblical Commentary*, 2nd edition (Bloomsbury Academic,

The formal juridical content of Shechem Covenant is given in verses 19–21, where it reads:

> And Joshua said unto the people. Ye cannot serve the Lord: for he is an holy God; he is a jealous God; he will not forgive your transgressions nor your sins. If ye forsake the Lord, and serve strange gods, then he will turn and do you hurt, and consume you, after that he hath done you good. And the people said unto Joshua, Nay; but we will serve the Lord. (Josh. 24:18–19)

It would thus be entirely natural to read the Shechem Covenant as embodying the opposite rule as that given in the Book of Mormon. Far from proclaiming that there is "no law against a man's belief," the Shechem Covenant suggests that those who forsake God will be severely punished. One can, however, derive the Book of Mormon rule from the narrative content of Joshua 24. In effect, the Nephite rule puts the law follower in the position of Joshua and the Children of Israel, faced with the choice that they were given at Shechem, namely the choice to serve the Lord or "the gods which your fathers served that were on the other side of the flood, or the gods of the Amorites" (Josh. 24:15). This is, of course, precisely the interpretive approach taken by Nephi in 1 Nephi 17, but in the later narrative it appears quite explicitly as a legal hermeneutic.

III. Laman, Lemuel, and Legal Positivism

The nature of rules and rule-following has long been at the center of the philosophy of law. John Austin launched the modern debates on the topic by offering an account of rules based on the ideas of threats and punishment.[35] On his theory, a rule of law is a standing threat from a sovereign that under certain conditions he or she will mete out punishments to offenders. Austin's theory launched legal positivism by divorcing the structure of legal rules from moral norms, but it has now been rejected by virtually all positivists. As H. L. A. Hart pointed out, Austin's approach to

---

1990), 130 ("[M]ost remarkably, Israel is given a choice not to worship Yahweh"). This is sufficiently odd that Robert Alter suggests that the choice is meant sarcastically. See Robert Alter, *The Hebrew Bible: A Translation with Commentary*, 1st edition (New York, : W. W. Norton & Company, 2018), 2:75 n.15.

35. See John Austin, *The Province of Jurisprudence Determined*, ed. H. L. A. Hart (Indianapolis: Hackett Publishing Company, 1998), 1–25 ("Lecture I" setting forth Austin's theory on the relationship between rules and threats).

rules faces a number of difficulties.[36] Chief among these is that it fails to account for the law from an internal perspective. The good-faith rule follower makes a distinction between obeying a rule and reacting to the threats of the highwayman. Laws, Hart argued, have a kind of normativity.[37] The normativity cannot be identified with moral obligations, but it also cannot be reduced to the prudential avoidance of threatened sanctions.

The modern discussion of rule-following has blossomed beyond the debate between Hart and Austin. Lon Fuller famously argued that governing through rules imposed certain minimal moral requirements on rulers.[38] One cannot subject human behavior to the governance of rules—Fuller's definition of law—without certain adverbial constraints on official action such as prospectively, generality, and the like.[39] More recently Frederick Schauer has developed a complex theory about the internal structure of rules.[40] Every rule, he argues, contains an implicit claim about the world. Consider the rule "No vehicles in the park." Such a rule rests on the judgment that it is dangerous to have vehicles in the park. In particular cases one might question this judgment. Perhaps driving a moped through the empty park at midnight presents no dangers. However, if one is following the rule, such individual judgments are irrelevant. Rather, one acts in accordance with the rule's empirical judgment as to the dangerousness of vehicles in the park regardless of one's own assessment of the fact of the matter. Schauer calls this process of deference to the implicit judgment embedded in a rule "empirical entrenchment."[41] The purpose of such entrenchment, or at any rate its effect, is to allocate decision-making power between rule authors and rule followers. To obey a rule is to renounce personal judgments in favor of the authority of the rule.

Schauer's model of rules and obedience to them roughly captures Laman and Lemuel's approach to following the law. They see the righ-

---

36. See H. L. A. Hart, *The Concept of Law*, 2nd ed. (Oxford: Clarendon Press, 1994), 18–26 (setting forth Hart's criticism of Austin).

37. See Hart, 89–91 (discussing the internal point of view of the law).

38. See generally Lon L. Fuller, *The Morality of Law*, revised edition (New Haven: Yale University Press, 1969).

39. See Fuller, 34–94 (setting out "The Morality That Makes Law Possible").

40. See generally Frederick Schauer, *Playing by the Rules: A Philosophical Examination of Rule-Based Decision-Making in Law and in Life* (New York: Oxford University Press, 1991).

41. See Schauer, 47–53 (arguing the rules should be understood as entrenched generalizations).

teousness of the people of Jerusalem in terms of rule-following, of keeping the "statutes and judgments of the Lord." Notice that in identifying rules with God they emphasize the self-abdication involved in their allegiance to the rules. In contrast, they claim that Lehi—rather than God—has judged the people, putting Lehi's agency in the foreground. The primary function of the "statutes and judgments of the Lord" is to allocate power vertically. The emphasis is on control. The rule controls the rule follower by prohibiting certain acts. To use Schauer's language, it also controls rule appliers through the exclusionary force of empirical entrenchment. It is tempting to read Nephi's approach as condemning this rules-based condemnation as mistaken. Yet in the opening chapter of the Book of Mormon, Lehi condemns the people of Jerusalem for their "abominations" (1 Ne. 1:13) and he "testified [note the legal term] of their wickedness and their abominations" (1 Ne. 1:19). In other words, taken on its own terms, Laman and Lemuel's legal claim is false. The people of Jerusalem were not a "a righteous people" and they had not "kept the statutes and judgments of the Lord" (1 Ne. 17:22). Tellingly, Nephi's narrative makes this abundantly clear.

However, Nephi's broader approach to following the law is largely incomprehensible within this framework of rules and rule-following. When Nephi structures his narrative so as to draw comparisons to the story of Exodus with him and his father cast as Moses, he is making a point about following the law of Moses. He is providing a response to the accusations of unfaithfulness to the law leveled by his brothers. However, this response, with its emphasis on narrative and recapitulation, cannot fit within the framework of rule-following that has developed from the contemporary debates in legal positivism and analytic jurisprudence. His approach to following the law requires a broader framework to be comprehensible.

IV. Nephi's Nomos and the Limits of Narrative

The legal theory of Robert Cover provides such a framework. Cover's approach to law places the meaning-making power of narrative at the center of our conception of law. In contrast to the dominant strains of contemporary legal philosophy, Cover relegates the process of formally applying and enforcing rules to a secondary and disfavored position in legal thought. His theory thus makes sense of the move that Nephi makes of placing the intertwining of life and narrative at the center of his response to his brothers' legal polemic. However, where Cover sees the subjective commitment to narrative at the center of law's authority, Nephi's story suggests commitment cannot ground law, which is always experienced as something in excess of subjective commitment, something that partakes of the structure of transcendence.

A. Robert Cover's Theory of Law

In his celebrated *Harvard Law Review* article,"Nomos and Narrative," Robert Cover offered a jurisprudence that placed the creation of shared meaning at the center of his conception of law.[42] According to Cover, "We inhabit a *nomos*—a normative universe. We constantly create and maintain a world of right and wrong, of lawful and unlawful, of valid and void."[43] For Cover a nomos arises out of narrative. He imagines a process of decentralized mythmaking within largely autonomous communities pursuing a constant process of internal story telling.

> The intelligibility of normative behavior inheres in the communal character of the narratives that provide the context of that behavior. Any person who lived an entirely idiosyncratic normative life would be quite mad. The part that you or I choose to play may be singular, but the fact that we can locate it in a common "script" renders it "sane"—a warrant that we share the same *nomos*.[44]

This process creates and maintains a normative universe independent of the official machinery of the state. In the face of legal positivism, which Austin has since identified law with the state, Cover insists that the nomos created by this decentralized extra-judicial narrative-making is law. He calls the process of nomos creation jurisgenesis.

The dominant model for jurisgenesis within Cover's theory is Jewish law.[45] The appeal of halakhah for Cover lies in its interpretive fecundity. The sages of the Talmud and the rabbis who have debated, expanded, and interpreted them over the intervening centuries were all engaged in a self-consciously legal project, one that operates without the support of a state and frequently in spite of it. In the halakhah, Cover saw a model for law in which the creation of meaning was prioritized over the needs of brute social control. Rather, it provided a model of what he called the "paideic" use of law, namely as a resource for the creation of a nomos. Building on the insight of the sixteenth-century rabbi Joseph Caro, Cover writes:

---

42. See generally Cover, "Nomos and Narrative."
43. Cover, 4.
44. Cover, 10.
45. See Cover, 12.

> Caro's commentary and the pahorisms that are its subject suggest two corresponding ideal-typical patterns for commingling corpus, discourse, and interpersonal commitment to form a *nomos*. The first such pattern, which according to Caro is world-creating, I shall call "paideic," because the term suggests: (1) a common body of precept and narrative, (2) a common and personal way of being educated into this corpus, and (3) a sense of direction or growth that is constituted as the individual and his community work out the implications of their law.[46]

The second "ideal-typical pattern" that Cover identifies for the law is what he calls "the imperial mode."[47] In its imperial mode, law does not create a new nomos but rather seeks to maintain an already existing normative world through the process of cutting back new "paideic" uses of law. It was an ideal that led Cover to an almost unrelentingly negative view of contemporary legal interpretation and adjudication. Indeed, in Cover's theory, the activity of government courts is almost wholly destructive. Cover famously claimed:

> Judges are people of violence. Because of the violence they command, judges characteristically do not create law, but kill it. Theirs is the jurispathic office. Confronting the luxuriant growth of a hundred legal traditions, they assert that this one is law and destroy or try to destroy the rest.[48]

For Cover, adjudication is destructive in two ways. First, adjudication always involves choosing between rival legal interpretations. The judge faces litigants with a dispute. She must decide the case and in deciding the case, one or both of the litigants' interpretations of the law will be declared wrong, in effect killed and banished from the official legal community. Second, the decisions of judges are always tied to the violence of the state. As Cover evocatively wrote, "Legal interpretation takes place on a field of pain and death."[49] The law always contemplates violently ripping into someone's life and redirecting it in a way to which that person objects and does not choose or desire. This may be justified, but it is, in Cover's opinion, always violent and destructive in some way.

The final key concept in Cover's theory of law is commitment. There must be something that differentiates mere storytelling and interpretation from law. This is important because Cover is making the strong claim that world-creating mythmaking is an important element of the law.

---

46. Cover, 12–13.
47. Cover, 14.
48. Cover, 53.
49. Cover, "Violence and the Word," 1601.

> To live in a legal world requires that one know not only the precepts, but also their connections to possible and plausible states of affairs. It requires that one integrate not only the "is" and the "ought," but the "is," the "ought," and the "what might be." Narrative so integrates these domains. Narratives are models through which we study and experience transformations that result when a given simplified state of affairs is made to pace through the force field of a similarly simplified set of norms.[50]

However, for these narratives to have the dignity of law they must do more than speculate about some possible utopian future. "[L]egal interpretation cannot be valid if no one is prepared to live by it."[51] He goes on to write, "The transformation of interpretation into legal meaning begins when someone accepts the demands of interpretation and, through the personal act of commitment, affirms the position taken."[52] Cover thus offers a vision of the law that is centered on the power of narrative coupled with personal commitment to create a normative world that gives rules their meaning and power. The formal process of enforcement, which has been at the center of our thinking about law since at least Austin, is given the secondary and potentially destructive role of merely maintaining the nomos created by law in its paideic guise.

Nephi's approach to legal interpretation bears a striking resemblance to Cover's theory of jurisgenesis. Given what is ultimately their common origin in the reading of the Bible, this is unsurprising. Laman and Lemuel ostensibly seek to follow the law—the "statutes and judgments of God." They see those judgments only in terms of control and ultimately, to use Cover's term, as jurispathic. In effect, they wish to invoke legal rules in order to negate the new systems of meaning promulgated by Lehi and Nephi, systems of meaning that have upended the family's life. Nephi's approach to legal interpretation, in contrast, gives rise to a new nomos. By recapitulating the story of Exodus, Lehi and his family are following "the law of Moses," but in doing so they literally create a new nation in a new promised land. The Book of Mormon is thus faithful to Cover's injunction that "we ought to stop circumscribing the *nomos*; we ought to invite new worlds."[53] Nephi offers up a model of following the law of Moses that is far more open to new worlds than that which was proposed by Laman and Lemuel. Where they reduce the law to the narrow question

---

50. Cover, "Nomos and Narrative," 10.
51. Cover, 44.
52. Cover, 45.
53. Cover, 68.

of whether Lehi has correctly judged the people of Jerusalem according to "the statutes and judgments of the Lord," Nephi's narrative recapitulation of the story of the law creates a new chosen people, a new exodus, and a new promised land. This seems to be precisely the kind of nomos-creating interpretive fecundity that Cover celebrates.

In Cover's theory, Nephi's narrative would rise to the level of law because he "accepts the demands of interpretation" through "the personal act of commitment." Indeed, Nephi literally inscribes his new interpretation of the law on his life and the life of his family. He is not spinning merely discursive narratives and interpretations. Rather, the story of his family is written, to use the words of the colophon with which he introduces his narrative, in "their sufferings and afflictions in the wilderness" (see 1 Nephi 1:1).[54] Legal interpretation for Nephi also takes place on a field of pain and death, but it is not the pain and death meted out by the bureaucratized violence of the state lamented by Cover. Rather it is the pain and death of a story written on one's life, a life that cannot be recovered once it has been wagered on an interpretation of God's law. However, while Nephi's story fits within Cover's approach to law, it also challenges the primacy Cover accords to commitment as the mechanism by which interpretation becomes law.

B. Law Beyond Narrative

What seems to be missing from Cover's account of nomos is any role for the transcendent, for something beyond ourselves that presses in and makes demands. On his account of jurisgenesis, it is the process of narrative coupled with commitment that transforms interpretation into legal meaning. This is ultimately a highly subjective notion of how a nomos is founded. On his account the only outside force that interrupts the process of narrative and commitment is the imperial force of adjudication and violence. Cover's invocation of commitment—with its echoes of a

54. The text of chapters and verses in 1 Nephi is preceded by a lengthy colophon summarizing the content of the book. Unlike the chapter headings in the current edition of the Book of Mormon, which were added in 1981 as a reference aid, this colophon is part of the original Book of Mormon text. See generally Thomas W. Mackay, "Mormon as Editor: A Study of Colophons, Headers, and Source Indicators," *Journal of Book of Mormon Studies* 2, no. 2 (1993): 90–109; John A. Tvedtnes, "Colophons in the Book of Mormon," in *Reexploring the Book of Mormon: A Decade of New Research*, ed. John W. Welch (Salt Lake City and Provo, UT: Deseret Book Co. and FARMS, 1992), 13–16.

self-creating existentialist morality, albeit one embedded within a communal discourse—is striking precisely because the examples of jurisgenesis on which he draws involve mainly insular religious communities.[55] These communities see themselves as called by God rather as founding themselves through narrative and commitment.

Consider the famous Talmudic story of the Oven of Akhnai, a narrative that would seem to provide the quintessential example of Cover's ideal of jurisgenesis. The story begins with a dispute between Rabbi Eliezer and the other rabbis over the ritual status of a certain kind of stove.[56] Rabbi Eliezer defends the purity of the stove, but the other rabbis are unpersuaded. He then appeals to a series of miracles in favor of his interpretation. At his word, a tree uproots itself and moves across the land. "A carob tree is no argument,"[57] respond the rabbis. The water of a brook then reverses direction. "A stream is no argument,"[58] they respond. Rabbi Eliezer says, "If the law accords with my opinion, let the walls of this House of Study demonstrate it!"[59] and the walls begin to bend. Rabbi Joshua, however, rebukes the building. "If the Sages debate among themselves on a point of halakha, what has this to do with you?"[60] he says. Finally, Rabbi Eliezer appeals to heaven, and a voice cries out from above, "Why do you challenge Rabbi Eliezer, for the halakha accords with him in all matters!"[61] Rabbi Joshua, however, remains unmoved. "It [i.e. the Torah] is not in Heaven,"[62] he says. We then learn that God laughs and says, "My children have outvoted Me, my children have outvoted Me!"[63] The story is fascinating, suggesting as it does the primacy of individual interpretation and judgment over even the claims of divine authority. Cover's theory of law offers up something like this hope. He seems to imagine the halakhic tradition detached from claims to divine authority, a model in which a pluralistic process of jurisgenesis can proceed ad infinitum.

---

55. See Cover, "Nomos and Narrative," 26–35.

56. The story is contained in the Babylonian Talmud in the Second Tractate Bava Metzi'a 59a. See Norman Solomon, trans., *The Talmud: A Selection* (New York: Penguin Classics, 2009), 469–72.

57. Solomon, 469.

58. Solomon, 469.

59. Solomon, 469.

60. Solomon, 470.

61. Solomon, 470.

62. Solomon, 470.

63. Solomon, 470.

Whatever the attractions of such a vision, however, it is doubtful that the Oven of Akhnai points toward such a process. The Oven of Akhnai responds to the condition of Jewish law in the generations after the destruction of the Second Temple.[64] Having lost the centralizing authority that existed prior to the Diaspora, the rabbis were looking for a mechanism to keep Judaism from fragmenting into the chaos of sectarian interpretive communities. The solution was not to embrace the joy of anarchic interpretation. Rather, it was to adopt a juridical rule in which the majority interpretation of the rabbis on a point of law was granted authority against contrary interpretations.[65] This is what happened between Rabbi Eliezer and the rival rabbis in the Oven of Akhnai story. Rabbi Eliezer was trying to justify his minority interpretation in the face of the majority. The Talmud ends the story by saying, "On that day they brought all the things Rabbi Eliezer had declared pure and burnt them, then voted to place him under ban."[66] Far from celebrating individual interpretation or hermeneutic pluralism, the Oven of Akhnai is about subjecting interpretation to a non-interpretive rule of social control. To be sure, the story acknowledges the costs of this approach. After his excommunication, the grief of Rabbi Eliezer is titanic.[67] On Cover's view, one would be forced to see the ban against Rabbi Eliezer as a simple exercise of the jurispathic function by the other rabbis. However, something else is going on here as well.

In a sensitive essay on Cover's jurisprudence, Suzanne Last Stone argues that ultimately, Jewish law cannot provide the counter narrative to modern jurisprudence for which Cover was searching.[68] He wished to frame law as independent of the violence of authority or the teleological

---

64. See Menachem Elon, *Jewish Law: History, Sources, Principles*, reprint edition (Philadelphia: The Jewish Publication Society, 2003), 1:41–46 (discussing the periodization of Jewish legal history).

65. See Elon, 1:245–247 (discussing how halakhic authority serves to limit sectarian schism). See also Elon, 260–64 (discussing the Oven of Ahknai and halakhic authority).

66. Solomon, *The Talmud*, 470.

67. The Babylonian Talmud says upon hearing of the ban:

> Thereupon Eliezer himself rent his garments, removed his shoes, slipped from his seat and sat upon the ground. His eyes filled with tears, and as they did so the world suffered; olives, wheat and barley all lost a third, and some say that even the dough that women were kneading spoiled.

Solomon, 471.

68. See generally Stone, "In Pursuit of the Counter-Text."

search for some objective truth of the matter regarding legal texts. In its place, he hoped for a world in which legal interpretation—and especially constitutional interpretation—was an endlessly open system of plural meanings. The halakha, Stone argues, is far more teleological than Cover's relentless prioritizing of jurisgenesis requires. She insists that:

> [Cover and his disciples] should be cautious not to derive too many lessons from the counter-text of Jewish law. For, in the final analysis, Jewish law is not only a legal system; it is the life work of a religious community. The Constitution, on the other hand, is a political document. It may even be a nomos, in the Maimonidean sense of the term. But it will not be Torah.[69]

There are similar limits on the model of jurisgenesis in the Book of Mormon. Nephi offers up a way of following the Law of Moses that is far more open to new worlds than that which was proposed by Laman and Lemuel. Where they reduce the law to the narrow question of whether Lehi has correctly judged the people of Jerusalem according to "the statutes and judgments of the Lord," Nephi's narrative recapitulation of the story of the law creates a new chosen people, a new exodus, and a new promised land. This seems to be precisely the kind of nomos-creating interpretive fecundity that Cover celebrates. However, Nephi's confrontation with his brothers ultimately presents the Oven of Akhnai in reverse. He does not seek to refute Laman and Lemuel's claim regarding "the statutes and judgments of the Lord" with arguments about the facts of the case, the scope of the rules, or even the spirit that animates them. Rather, the disagreement with his brothers turns violent. Nephi recounts how "they were angry with me, and were desirous to throw me into the depths of the sea" (1 Ne. 17:48). His response to their violence is not an argument but an appeal to the authority of supernatural intervention on his behalf. He says:

> In the name of the Almighty God, I command you that ye touch me not, for I am filled with the power of God, even unto the consuming of my flesh; and whoso shall lay his hands upon me shall wither even as a dried reed; and he shall be as naught before the power of God, for God shall smite him. (1 Ne. 17:48)

It would be unfair to equate the morally serious Rabbi Joshua in the Oven of Akhnai narrative with the murderous Laman and Lemuel in the Book of Mormon. It is striking, however, that the Book of Mormon narrative vouchsafes Nephi's interpretation not through commitment or the juris-

69. Stone, 894.

pathic function of courts but through the literal presence of God's power. The Book of Mormon thus shares with the Oven of Akhnai a teleological concern with the preservation of community and the proliferation of interpretations. Where the aggadah in the Talmud points toward the principle of majority interpretation, the Book of Mormon accepts the authority of miraculously wandering trees, brooks turned upstream, bending walls, voices from heaven, and a younger brother smiting his faithless siblings with the power of God. In the end, Nephi's jurisprudence cultivates the interpretive fecundity of the law, but it also testifies to the inadequacy of mere commitment standing alone to found a community.

The climax of Nephi's story also points towards something more than simply "the imperial mode." It is a claim to law that rests on an eruption into the world of some transcendent authority. When Rabbi Joshua says that the Torah is not in heaven, he is making a similar claim. He is saying that the authority of the rabbi's interpretive project is dependent on the divine blessing placed on their activity when God committed the Torah to their care. In this, his claim is actually quite similar to the claim put forward by Nephi to ground his authority on miraculous power. Both appeal beyond interpretation and subjective commitment.

This claim can be made more precisely. From an "internal point of view," to borrow a phrase from H. L. A. Hart, law is founded on transcendence rather than commitment. As I have written elsewhere:

> Law provides a kind of sacred space for secular societies. It guides and controls actions. It coerces. It may be justified or not justified. But it does more than this. It maintains the constant experience of something pressing in on us from beyond, a claim to authority that displaces our individual judgments. It creates an order, a *nomos* in Cover's terms, but not because it provides a place for our constant self-creation (although it may do this). Rather in claiming authority it points us back to the experience of transcendence, which seems to be a hunger that cannot be satiated even when we vociferously insist that our laws are not Torah and do not come from God.[70]

This is true even in our disenchanted world.[71] Law still functions within practical reasoning as a form of authority. When a lawyer is advising a

70. Nathan B. Oman, "Temple, Talmud, and Sacrament: Some Christian Thoughts on Halakhah," *Villanova Law Review* 64 (2019): 756.

71. The image of the disenchanted world was first offered by Max Weber as a description of a society dominated by desacralized formal bureaucracies. See generally Max Weber, *The Vocation Lectures* (Indianapolis: Hackett Publishing Company, 2004). As several writers have pointed out, however, the disenchantment

client on what to do, the law purports to act as an exclusionary reason. In other words, it presses in on our normative deliberations and demands that we set aside our own all-things-considered judgments and abnegate ourselves before its superior claims.[72] To be sure, this claim to authority is suspect, and in many cases it will be pernicious. My point is about the phenomenology of law, not the legitimacy of its substantive claims. This is a claim about how we experience law, not a suggestion that human laws are divine or should be treated as such. However, as a necessary element of legal experience, it must be grappled with by any jurisprudence—perhaps especially one such as Cover's—that purports to explain how mere interpretation can become law. The necessity of some transcendent element beyond interpretation or commitment is the ultimate burden of Nephi's account of law.

V. Conclusion

The Book of Mormon had a scandalous birth. It came into the world surrounded by stories of angels and miracles, along with accusations of fraud and humbug. Too often it has been unable to escape the allure of its origin story. However, the text of the book reveals itself as far more subtle and complex than the polemics of belief and disbelief would suggest. It repays close reading. In the stories of conflict between Nephi and his brothers that open the book, we have an argument about rule-following that implicates basic questions of how we think about law. Strikingly, Nephi's account of law-following in terms of narrative re-enactment makes little sense within the traditional categories of analytical jurisprudence but fits well within Robert Cover's theory of jurisgenesis. The climax of Nephi's story, however, challenges Cover's account of how interpretation becomes law. Where Cover pointed toward the priority of commitment to narratives, Nephi points toward the direct intervention of the transcendent in narratives. This is a dramatic claim about the structure of legal experience. Law claims to come from beyond us. It is not something that we subjec-

---

has by no means been as total as Weber prophesized. See generally Yishai Blank, "The Reenchantment of Law," *Cornell Law Review* 96 (2011): 633–70; Richard Jenkins, "Disenchantment, Enchantment and Re-Enchantment: Max Weber at the Millennium," *Max Weber Studies* 1, no. 1 (2000): 11–32.

72. See Joseph Raz, *The Authority of Law: Essays on Law and Morality*, 2nd ed. (New York: Oxford University Press, 2009), 21–25 (arguing that law presents itself as a kind of exclusionary reason).

tively create through our commitment. Indeed, part of what makes it such a fruitful site for the mythmaking valorized by Cover is precisely the fact that it comes at us from a higher authority rather than arising from our subjective commitment. In religious legal systems, the divine provides the source of legal transcendence. This point is illustrated in different ways by both the Book of Mormon and the story of the Oven of Aknai. If Nephi's account of how interpretation and transcendence interact to create a nomos is correct, then Cover's account of legal interpretation must locate the source of legal authority outside of the process of interpretation and commitment. We must grapple with the way in which legal authority erupts into our lives from some place beyond subjective commitment.

CHAPTER 11

The Language and Tradition of Our Fathers: Some Book of Mormon Thoughts on Community and Identity

In modern societies, it is common to experience community as a threat to identity. This can become especially salient when we are members of communities that make strong claims to authority, as is often true of religious traditions. My thesis is that this sense of community as a threat is driven in large part by common models of the self, models that are so widespread as to be difficult to see as anything other than common sense. I want to bring these ideas into the foreground for a bit of examination. I hope to show that for all of their truth, these models all suffer from a similar conceptual failure. They do not fully appreciate the role of communities in making identity possible. I then want to suggest some resources in the Latter-day Saint tradition that might be used to salvage what is valuable in these models of identity while offering a more productive and realistic way of living as individuals in community.

My claim isn't triumphalist. Latter-day Saint thought and scripture does not offer a clear or simple answer to the conundrums of identity and community. The Book of Mormon, however, does offer one potentially useful way of orienting ourselves towards this problem. It suggests two ways in which community constitutes identity. One, which it labels "tradition," involves a static reception of an identity defined in terms of political resentments. The other, which it labels "language," sees community as providing resources from which we dynamically fashion identity. The normative divide between these approaches, however, does not breakdown into a tradition-bad, language-good dichotomy. Rather, for the Book of Mormon the moral fulcrum of our identity lies beyond the self in the demands of Christian love.

The concept of the self seems so obvious that reflecting on it can be strange. To be sure, understanding any individual takes a bit of work, but we assume that we know the kind of thing we are looking for when we go looking for an individual's identity. Let me suggest, however, that things are more complicated—and interesting—than they first appear. As soon as we say "I am . . .", we are invoking, if only implicitly, a model of the self—a way of thinking about what it means to be an "I" that could have an identity. Modernity offers us at least three models of the self: the self as a bearer of rights, the self as a fount of authenticity, and the self as a demander of recognition. These aren't the only modern approaches to the self, but between the three of them they cover a lot of conceptual ground. For my purposes, what makes them interesting is that all three of these models define the self in a way that makes community particularly threatening to identity. While these conceptions of the self form part of the common sense of our society, it's important to recognize that they are not timeless nor self-evident truths. Each of them has a particular history and a particular structure, and each of them is problematic and incomplete in various ways.

What I offer here is not a complete or accurate intellectual history, nor do I claim that these models provide the best interpretation of the thinkers that I discuss. Rather, what makes these models important is that something like them lies behind ideas of identity and community that are common in modern society.

The Self as a Bearer of Rights

Perhaps the most common model of the self in Western societies is the vision of individuals as bearers of rights. Rights began as a legal concept. The holder of a right has a veto power over the acts of another. The paradigmatic example of a right is private property. To have property rights is to be entitled to exclude others from possession or use of a particular thing for any reason whatsoever or for no reason at all. As William Blackstone defined it in his influential *Commentaries on the Laws of England*, property is "that sole and despotic dominion which one man claims and exercises over the external things of the world, in total exclusion of the right of any other individual in the universe."[1] Our modern conception of people as bearers of rights arose in the seventeenth and eighteenth centuries, when this conception of property was used to define our conception of ourselves and our relations to the rest of humanity. The key figures in this development were Thomas Hobbes and John Locke. Together they defined what subsequent historians have called the ideology of "possessive individualism," which has at its heart the idea of self-ownership.[2] Self-ownership implies that we should exercise "despotic dominion" over ourselves to the "total exclusion

1. William Blackstone, *Commentaries on the Laws of England*, ed. Wilfrid R. Prest (New York: Oxford University Press, 2016), II:2.

2. See C. B. Macpherson, *The Political Theory of Possessive Individualism: Hobbes to Locke*, reprint edition (New York: Oxford University Press, 2011).

of the right of any other individual in the universe." This is the liberal idea of freedom, what we often refer to as "autonomy." The term is telling, coming from Greek and meaning something like a "self-given law."

Today's rights-bearing self has two striking characteristics. The first is its universality. If we take property as the primordial model of rights, historically one of its main features was its limited distribution within the population. Women, children, slaves, and a myriad of dependent classes could not have property rights or had only limited rights to property, as in the *peculiam* of slaves under Roman law. Today, however, the class of rights-bearers in theory encompasses all human beings. In the words of the United Nations' Universal Declaration of Human Rights (notice the "universal"), "the inherent dignity and the equal and inalienable rights of all members of the human family is the foundation of freedom, justice and peace in the world."[3] This expansion is one of modernity's great moral accomplishments.

The second characteristic of the rights-bearing self is what we might call its thinness. To have rights doesn't imply any particular personal history, cultural identity, or individual morality. At best such aspects of the self tend to be reduced to the ideas of choice and preference. This is because the idea of the rights-bearing self offers no more guidance on such questions than on the choice between chocolate and vanilla ice cream. To use the language of economics, they are exogenous to the model. The influential arguments of the philosopher John Rawls provide a graphic illustration of the relative vacuousness of this model of the self. Rawls asks the basic question of what rights citizens ought to have in a well-ordered society.[4] He insists that to correctly answer this question, we must consider what we would do in the so-called "original position." In the original position, we specify rights behind a veil of ignorance. We know nothing about our personal history, religious beliefs, ethnic identities, gender, or the like. We do not even know our own ideas of what constitutes right and wrong. Rawls's point is that none of these characteristics should be relevant to whether a person has rights, so we shouldn't consider them when we deliberate over the scope of rights. They are irrelevant to the self as bearer of rights.

Another way of getting at the same point is to consider the Bill of Rights, which is an important expression of this model of the self in our society. For well over a century, corporations—which are wholly fictitious

3. Universal Declaration of Human Rights, G.A. Res. 217A(III), U.N. GAOR, 3d Sess., at 71, U.N. Doc. A/810 (1948).

4. See John Rawls, *A Theory of Justice*, revised edition (Cambridge: Belknap Press, 1999), chap. 3.

persons—have been able to claim constitutional rights.[5] Now there are very good reasons to grant legal rights to corporations. Fictitious legal personality is one of the great discoveries of western legal systems and is responsible for much of the material prosperity what makes modernity attractive.[6] In 2010, the Supreme Court held in *Citizens United v. Federal Election Commission* that campaign finance laws violated the First Amendment rights of a corporation.[7] Many commentators erupted in outrage. Surely First Amendment rights must be reserved only for flesh-and-blood persons and not legal fictions, insisted the critics.[8] This argument illustrates something important about the rights-bearing self. The very ease with which these fictional persons can become the bearers of rights testifies to the relative emptiness of the model of personhood assumed by the concept of rights. Indeed, Rawls suggests that it is precisely the messy, historically contingent, flesh-and-blood bits of our identity that are irrelevant for our rights.

Because of the thinness of the rights-bearing individual, communities can appear particularly threatening. Almost the only salient feature of this model of the self is that it is entitled not to have its boundaries crossed. Communities, however, press in on individuals. They cross boundaries. They make demands and claim to author obligations. Furthermore, as collectives they wield power, power that often exceeds that of the solitary rights-bearer. As such they must necessarily appear threatening. After all, that power might be used to challenge an individual's sole and despotic dominion over him- or herself.

---

5. See, e.g., Pembina Consol. Silver Mining & Milling Co. v. Com. of Pennsylvania, 125 U.S. 181, 189 (1888) ("Under the designation of 'person' there is no doubt that a private corporation is included [within the Fourteenth Amendment]. Such corporations are merely associations of individuals united for a special purpose, and permitted to do business under a particular name, and have a succession of members without dissolution").

6. For an account of the role of corporate personhood in the comparative economic advantage of certain countries, see Timur Kuran, *The Long Divergence: How Islamic Law Held Back the Middle East* (Princeton: Princeton University Press, 2011).

7. See Citizens United v. Federal Election Commission, 558 U.S. 310 (2010).

8. See, e.g., "The Court's Blow to Democracy," *The New York Times*, January 21, 2010, https://www.nytimes.com/2010/01/22/opinion/22fri1.html ("The majority is deeply wrong on the law. Most wrongheaded of all is its insistence that corporations are just like people and entitled to the same First Amendment rights").

The Self as a Source of Authenticity

The next model of the self is as a source of authenticity. Today, we are inclined to see the self as a deep well from which we can draw meaning and a "true" sense of identity. This authentic self drawn from within is contrasted with the inauthentic identities we are provided by society. This model of the self also has its own idiosyncratic history. Inner personal life has been an intense object of religious concern since at least the time of Augustine. But Augustine didn't turn his attention to this inner world in search of meaning or authenticity in the modern sense. Rather, Augustine's *Confessions* consist in large part of his observations of the workings of sin and faith within his own soul. This tendency toward what Charles Taylor has called the "inwardness" of identity accelerated with the Protestant Reformation, which followed Augustine in seeing self-examination as the primary means of discerning the state of the soul and God's working in the world.[9]

In the eighteenth century, this inward turn was secularized, most influentially by Jean-Jaques Rousseau. It is to him that we owe our current fascination with the conception of the inner self as a source of authenticity and ultimate meaning. It was Rousseau who first taught us to make grandiose claims about the moral and spiritual authority of the self. As the American philosopher and historian Robert Solomon has put it:

> Strolling in solitude through the lush forests of St. Germain [outside Paris] . . . Jean-Jacques Rousseau made a miraculous discovery. It was his self. . . . What Rousseau discovered in the woods of France was a self so rich and substantial, so filled with good feeling and half-articulated good thoughts, so expansive, natural, and at peace with the universe that he recognized it immediately as something much more than *his* singular self. It was rather the Self as such, the soul of humanity.[10]

In the American tradition, perhaps the most eloquent and forceful exponent of the authenticity of the inner self is Ralph Waldo Emerson. "Who so would be a man must be a nonconformist," he wrote. "He who would gather immortal palms must not be hindered by the name of goodness, but must explore if it be goodness. Nothing is at last sacred but the integrity of our own mind. Absolve yourself, and you shall have the

---

9. See Charles Taylor, *Sources of the Self: The Making of the Modern Identity* (Cambridge: Harvard University Press, 1989), part II.

10. Robert C. Solomon, *Continental Philosophy since 1750: The Rise and Fall of the Self*, A History of Western Philosophy 7 (New York: Oxford University Press, 1988), 1.

suffrage of the world."[11] For Emerson, obedience to the inner voice of "Intuition" or "Spontaneity" offers not simply the realization of one's true self but also promises heroism. "[I]t demands something godlike in him who has cast off the common motives of humanity, and has ventured to trust himself for a task-master."[12]

Emerson's formulation also reveals the way in which community threatens such an authentic self. Society assaults the self with its own messages, demanding conformity. The inner self calls us to authenticity, but its voice can be hard to hear amidst the babble and pressure of the community. He writes:

> These are the voices [i.e. the voices of the inner self] which we hear in solitude, but they grow faint and inaudible when we enter into the world. Society everywhere is in conspiracy against the manhood of every one of its members. Society is a joint-stock company, in which the members agree, for the better securing of his bread to each shareholder, to surrender liberty and culture of the eater. The virtue most requested is conformity, Self-reliance is its aversion. It loves not realities and creators, but names and customs.[13]

Rousseau is more succinct: "Nature made man happy and good, and society depraves him and makes him miserable."[14]

The Self as a Demander of Recognition

The third model of identity is of the self as a demander of recognition. If Rousseau was the prophet of personal authenticity, Hegel, writing a generation later, was the prophet of recognition. Since at least the seventeenth century, philosophers have used the idea of a state of nature. Hegel has his own state-of-nature story, although one told in almost completely impenetrable prose.[15] Very roughly speaking, it goes like this: Two individuals meet. Each sees the other as an independent person, and in the other's recognition of the self as a rational agent and vice versa, each comes to self-awareness of himself. At the same time, the presence of another person is threatening, and the two grapple in a death struggle. The battle ends only

---

11. Ralph Waldo Emerson, *Essays and Poems*, ed. Tony Tanner (London: Everyman, 1997), 26. All quotations are to Emerson's essay "Self-Reliance."

12. Emerson, 38.

13. Emerson, 25–26.

14. Quoted in Solomon, *Continental Philosophy*, 21.

15. See G. W. F. Hegel, *The Phenomenology of Spirit*, trans. A. V. Miller (New York: Oxford University Press, 1977), chap. 4. Good luck.

when one yields, becoming a slave and thus giving up the freedom that was so threatening to the other. The victory of the master over the slave, however, is hollow. Only in the free recognition of himself by another can the master be assured of his own identity. Indeed, it was the very confrontation with the other that led to the master's initial self-consciousness. Yet precisely because the slave is a slave, his recognition can never be the kind of free recognition that vouchsafes the identity of the master.

Hegel's is a strange story, but it gets at an important point. Emerson tells a monological story of the self's solitary discovery of its own authenticity. Hegel, in contrast, emphasizes that the self arises dialogically. While for Hegel the recognition of freedom and reason is key, subsequent thinking has expanded on his insight to include other aspects of our identities. Consider the example of the Civil Rights Movement in the United States. One way of looking at this movement is as a simple demand for equal rights. Widespread lynching denied the basic right to bodily security. Legal mechanisms denied rights to vote, rights to due process of law, and rights to equal protection of the laws. However, the Civil Rights Movement was about more than simply legal rights. Lynching is evil not only because it is murder, but because it is murder motivated by hatred and enmity based on race.[16] It's not simply that African Americans under Jim Crow were subject to violence, but that they were uniquely vulnerable based on an unchosen element of their identity. There is something going on here other than the mere assertion of legal rights or even psychological damage. Rather, it was about how identity is constituted.

The messy legal arguments over segregation illustrate this dynamic. In *Brown v. Board of Education*, the Supreme Court case repudiating the doctrine of separate-but-equal, the justices defined the evil of segregation using the language of psychology:

> Segregation of white and colored children in public schools has a detrimental effect upon the colored children. A sense of inferiority affects the motivation of a child to learn. . . . [This] has a tendency to [retard] the educational and mental development of negro children. . . .[17]

---

16. There are, of course, other ways of understanding the evil of lynching. Most obviously and importantly, lynching was a key element in the system of social subordination designed to keep an entire population fearful of violent retribution should any individual challenge his or her subordinate position in the racial caste system.

17. Brown v. Board of Education of Topeka, 347 U.S. 483, 494 (1954) (quoting a lower court opinion). The Court was also borrowing arguments

The court cited studies purporting to demonstrate this result. Its reliance on the supposed findings of mid-twentieth century behaviorism has long troubled legal thinkers.[18] This is in part because the results of these studies can be doubted. Many accomplished and highly motivated African American students nevertheless emerged from the segregated school system. More importantly, it seems mistaken to think that our assessment of the evil of segregation turns on individual psychology. Segregation wasn't evil because it made people feel bad. If anything, people felt bad because segregation was evil.

A better account is that the evil of segregation lay in its failure to recognize African Americans as fully human. The damage wrought was deeper than simply some particular psychological response. The strong-minded African American who refused to feel inferior despite the efforts of Jim Crow was still harmed by segregation. Her self continued to be constituted by a society that refused to recognize her full humanity and equality. It was not enough that she could look within for Emersonian authenticity. She also needed to be acknowledged by others, and her identity was battered by their misrecognition.

The Civil Rights Movement has become a paradigm for the so-called "politics of recognition."[19] Minorities of all kinds have made analogous demands, arguing that their misrecognition by the communities within which they reside threatens their identity. Feminists have pointed out the various ways in which women are "misrecognized" by society. Likewise, for its advocates, same-sex marriage is about far more than whether gay and lesbian couples can own real estate as a tenancy by the entirety or some

---

contained in amicus briefs in the case. See Kenneth B. Clark, Isidor Chein, and Stuart W. Cook, "The Effects of Segregation and the Consequences of Desegregation A (September 1952) Social Science Statement in the Brown v. Board of Education of Topeka Supreme Court Case," *American Psychologist* 59, no. 6 (2004): 495–501.

18. Criticisms of the Court's reasoning in *Brown* emerged early. See, e.g., Herbert Wechsler, "Toward Neutral Principles of Constitutional Law," *Harvard Law Review* 73 (1959): 1–35. For a summary of the contemporary and subsequent criticisms of the Court's reliance on psychological studies, see J. M. Balkin and Bruce A. Ackerman, eds., *What Brown v. Board of Education Should Have Said: The Nation's Top Legal Experts Rewrite America's Landmark Civil Rights Decision* (New York: New York University Press, 2001), 50–53.

19. See Charles Taylor, "The Politics of Recognition," in *Multiculturalism: Examining the Politics of Recognition*, ed. Amy Gutman (Princeton: Princeton University Press, 1995), 25–74.

other legal incident of marriage. Rather, when the Supreme Court held in 2003 that a Texas sodomy law violated the Constitution, Justice Kennedy wrote of the court's contrary prior holding that "its continuance as precedent demeans the lives of homosexual persons."[20] This is the language of recognition. Indeed, in an increasingly fragmented and pluralistic society, even those who are part of the supposed majority can engage in the politics of recognition. As Francis Fukuyama has recently written, "one of the great drivers of the new American nationalism that sent Donald Trump into the White House (and Britain out of the European Union) has been the perception of invisibility [by working class whites]."[21] The call to "Make America Great Again" is, perhaps, the echo of the Hegelian need for recognition.

It is also easy to see why, on this view, community would appear so threatening to identity. First, community is the arena in which we might be systematically targeted on the basis of our identity for humiliation or worse. However, the problem is deeper than simply the risk that we might be the target of hatred or bigotry. If Hegel is correct that identity and self-awareness arise dialogically out of the process of mutual recognition, then identity is almost unbearably exposed to the actions of the community. The very integrity of the self is threatened should the community fail to accord proper recognition to one's identity. Hence the sometimes frantic nature of identity politics. This exposure is even more threatening than the deadening and inauthentic social pressure feared by Emerson. Emerson at least held out the prospect of retreat to the inner authenticity of the self. Hegel, however, suggests that there is no self into which one can retreat that is not exposed to the baleful effects of misrecognition.

Identity and the Costs of Oikophobia

Where do these models of identity leave us? Each in its own way offers the promise of a liberated self, possessed of a coherent understanding of itself and the world around it. All of these models of identity have much to recommend themselves. We are fortunate—I might say blessed—to live in societies that have a public culture where individuals can seek redress for the violation of certain rights. As Judith Shklar has pointed out in response to glib attacks on the idea of individual rights by conservative

20. Lawrence v. Texas, 539 U.S. 558, 575 (2003).

21. Francis Fukuyama, *Identity: The Demand for Dignity and the Politics of Resentment* (New York: Farrar, Straus and Giroux, 2018), 87–88.

or communitarian critics, people in illiberal societies where such rights are not respected often live in the visceral fear of pain and suffering at the hands of the cruel and powerful.[22] Any criticism of the rights-bearing self must be aware of this fact. Likewise, the Emersonian search for the authentic inner self has produced some marvelous pieces of art and literature. Finally, the demand for recognition has done much to ameliorate the suffering and injustices suffered by many minorities. It has also given those at the cultural margins tools for understanding the ways in which their own thinking can become infected by distorted images of themselves. This point has been made in the Mormon context, for example, by Richard Bushman, who argues that too often Latter-day Saints—particularly those of an intellectual bent—have tended to view themselves through the distorting images of hostile or indifferent observers who can claim the authority of sitting closer to the cultural mainstream.[23]

All of these models, however, are ultimately unsustainable. The first two offer up visions of the self that imagine we can speak coherently of identity wholly independent of community. This can be seen most clearly in the model of the self as bearer of rights, which emerges from legal models that are explicitly designed to abstract out much of the detail that makes human life human. The late Justice Antonin Scalia once remarked, "The main business of a lawyer is to take the romance, the mystery, the irony, the ambiguity out of everything he touches."[24] Unsurprisingly, this is what ideas borrowed from lawyers do. The result is a radically incomplete vision of what it means to be a human being. Likewise, the authentic self of Emerson is chimerical. There is no way of escaping the influence of history and context on our own thinking. Thus, the authentic self that one discovers within will generally reflect a hackneyed social script. Think of the innumerable movie plots that revolve around the daring individual true to his or her inner self, each story following the cliched conventions of the genre. Worse, if we take Emerson's claim that "nothing is at last sacred but the integrity of our own mind,"[25] we are left without the re-

22. See Judith N. Shklar, "The Liberalism of Fear," in *Liberalism and the Moral Life*, ed. Nancy L. Rosenblum (Cambridge: Harvard University Press, 1989).

23. See Richard Lyman Bushman, "The Colonization of the Mormon Mind," in *Annual of the Association for Mormon Letters 2000*, ed. Lavina Fielding Anderson (Salt Lake City: Association for Mormon Letters, 2000).

24. "Justice Antonin Scalia: In His Own Words," BBC, February 14, 2016, https://www.bbc.com/news/world-us-canada-35571825.

25. Emerson, *Essays and Poems*, 26.

sources to engage in substantive moral deliberation, wallowing in a vacuous soft relativism where the only injunction is to "do your own thing."

Aristotle offers what I think is a more realistic assessment of the relationship between identity and community. He points out the various ways in which solitary human life is impossible, the most obvious example being the prolonged vulnerability of human infants. He writes, "It is evident that the *polis* [or community] is a creation of nature, and that man by nature is a political animal. And he who by nature and not by mere accident is without a community, is either a bad man or above humanity."[26] This doesn't mean that human beings are social animals in the way that bees or ants are social animals. Rather, what he means is that a distinctively human identity exists only because there is a pre-existing community that makes that identity possible. One of the most fundamental ways in which this is true is through language, which is what allows us to create the systems of meaning by which we are able to identify and conceptualize ourselves. Yet no language is a private creation. Indeed, a fully private language is an impossibility.[27] Language is always something that one inherits from a community. Hence, one cannot coherently conceptualize community purely in terms of something "out there" beyond the self, pressing aggressively in on our identities. Rather, community is always implicated in our identity. Indeed, if community can threaten identity, it is also the

---

26. Aristotle, *Politics* 1253a. The translation quoted in the text is taken from the Benjamin Jowett translation of the *Politics* printed in Aristotle, *Introduction to Aristotle*, ed. Richard McKeon (New York: Modern Library, 1992). However, I have taken the liberty of leaving the Greek word *polis* in the text, which Jowett translates as "state" but which could creatively be translated as "community," although that term is also not accurate. Aristotle was referring to a particular form of community, namely the Greek city-state of the classical period. See H. G. Liddell and R. Scott, "Polis," in *Greek-English Lexicon* (Oxford: Clarendon Press, 1996). One could argue that the Greek words *ethnos* or *koinounia* are better candidates for the English word "community." Certainly, the term *polis* implies living under a common set of laws and political institutions while sharing a civic identity in a way that these other Greek terms do not. I am grateful for discussions with Professor Mitch Brown of the William & Mary classics department on the nuances of the term *polis* and the plausibility of translating it as "community."

27. See Ludwig Wittgenstein, *Philosophical Investigations*, trans. G. E. M. Anscombe, 3rd edition (Englewood Cliffs: Pearson, 1973), §. 243; Stewart Candlish and George Wrisley, "Private Language," in *The Stanford Encyclopedia of Philosophy*, ed. Edward N. Zalta, Fall 2014 (Metaphysics Research Lab, Stanford University, 2014), https://plato.stanford.edu/archives/fall2014/entries/private-language/.

case that identity cannot exist without it. No man is an island, or to use the language of the New Testament, "you are not your own" (1 Cor. 6:19).

Aristotle took his insight in a direction where few of us would follow, insisting that the only way of being truly human was to live in the best possible way in the best possible community, which meant being a free male property owner in an ancient Greek city-state with a mixed constitution. Notice the way in which my refusal to follow Aristotle down the road to classical Greek society gestures toward ideas that we associate with the rights-bearing self and the individualism of the authentic Emersonian self, ideas rendered at least problematic by the Aristotelian insight into the nature of identity. We are left with powerful and apparently valid moral responses that seem to rest on, at best, incomplete and, at worse, incoherent models of the self. The self as a demander of recognition offers one possible solution to this conundrum. This model of the self rests on something very similar to Aristotle's insight. For Hegel and those that have wittingly and unwittingly followed him, identity emerges dialogically, which is precisely why the recognition of others is so important to the self. However, the concern for recognition as it is usually cashed out in our society tends to lead to alienation from community. This need not be the case. It has been suggested that in the past, the failure of recognition to arise as a moral concern was not the result of it being less important. Rather in societies in which social roles are relatively fixed and their meanings are well understood, to occupy a social role is to be recognized. In modern society, by contrast, social roles are fluid and contested. Hence community, rather than appearing as a foundation of identity as in Aristotle, is a constant threat, even if one acknowledges the dependence of identity on others.

All three of these models of identity can lead to what the philosopher Roger Scruton has usefully called *oikophobia*.[28] The term is a Greek neologism derived from the word *oikos*, meaning "home," and *phobos*, meaning "fear." What Scruton means by oikophobia is the persistent anxiety in which community appears primarily as an enemy of the self. In his own writings, Scruton tends to emphasize the hostility toward community that is bred by oikophobia. However, I think it may be more useful to look at its effects elsewhere. If Aristotle is right, then the largely solitary models of identity I've just discussed are unsustainable, and human beings, practi-

28. See Roger Scruton, *A Political Philosophy: Arguments for Conservatism* (New York: Continuum, 2007), 23–25.

cal souls that we are, will seek—if only implicitly and inarticulately—for some substitute for the communities that must sustain our identities.

The role of romantic love in our society illustrates this dynamic and its difficulties. Romantic intimacy seems to promise a solution to the alienation created by contemporary models of identity, a solution that doesn't challenge their basic assumptions. The ideal intimate relationship is consensual, and thus doesn't involve violation of rights. It is supposed to be almost wholly subjective, arising from an overwhelming emotion originating within the self. It thus appears in the guise of a kind of Emersonian authenticity. Indeed, we will often grant romantic love the kind of self-certifying moral authority Emerson reserves for the authentic self. Not only does love cover a multitude of sins, it may dispose of the idea of sin entirely (although not the idea of rights!). Finally, in the ideal intimate relationship, we have the promise of perfect recognition, a safe haven for the self from a threatening world.

There is great truth in this vision of romantic love. As a man who adores his wife, I feel its pull and power. However, I do not think that personal intimacy alone can redeem the alienation that too often flows from modern models of identity. Even romantic love requires a home, something that is difficult to find amidst oikophobia. For example, the sociologist Anthony Giddens has noted, "Sexuality has become imprisoned within a search for self-identity which sexual activity itself can only momentarily fulfil."[29] By increasing the psychic demands on intimacy, we render it more brittle. It is far easier for romantic love to fail when it is made to carry the entire burden of identity. As the English philosopher Simon May has written:

> [E]very increase in individualism fuels the prestige of love. The more independent our identity is of political, religious, national or community loyalties, so the more we turn to love as the ultimate source and sign of belonging—a sign that people displayed today as eagerly as in previous eras they displayed their fidelity to church or state. And the more individualistic we become the more we expect love to be a secular journey for the soul, a final source of meaning and freedom, a supreme standard of value, a key to the problem of identity, a solace in the face of rootlessness, a desire for the worldly and simultaneously a desire to transcend it, a redemption from suffering and, a promise of eternity. Or all of these at once.
>
> In short: love is being overloaded.[30]

---

29. Anthony Giddens, *The Transformation of Intimacy: Sexuality, Love and Eroticism in Modern Societies* (Stanford: Stanford University Press, 1992), 197.

30. Simon May, *Love: A History* (New Haven: Yale University Press, 2011), 239.

Let me suggest that, ultimately, the social demands of our identities require more than a romantic dyad, no matter how deep and sincere the dyad's love. Indeed, romantic love that is less existentially burdened may be more robust. Intimacy blossoms best in a larger garden of sociability.

We are thus left with models of identity that are both attractive and repellant. One response is a root-and-branch rejection of modern identity. This is the stance taken by some serious intellectual conservatives. It has been adopted by atheist philosophers such as the late Alan Bloom, and religious thinkers such as Notre Dame's Patrick Deneen, whose recent book *Why Liberalism Failed* offers a thorough going critique of contemporary individualism.[31] I am skeptical that a root-and-branch rejection of modern models of identity is possible at this point. While they are deeply suspicious of history, culture, and institutions, within modern societies those models have ironically enough become embedded in all three. It is difficult to imagine how they might be escaped even were we inclined to do so.[32] However, a kind of Goldilocks response in which we just try not to have too much modern identity seems vacuous. It gives us no guidance on how to orient our thinking about the self and its relationship to community. As Charles Taylor has written:

> I differ . . . from the various middle positions, which hold that there are some good things in this culture [built around modern models of identity] (like greater freedom for the individual), but that these come at the expense of certain dangers (like weakening of the sense of citizenship), so that one's best policy is to find the ideal point of trade-off between advantages and costs.[33]

The language of trade-offs or balancing assumes some clear metric that renders the allures and pathologies of community and modern identity commensurable. Without falling into a crude—and ultimately untenable—utilitarian calculus, I don't see how such balancing is supposed to occur. We lack a scale and a system of weights. Rather, what we need is a

---

31. See Patrick J. Deneen, *Why Liberalism Failed* (New Haven: Yale University Press, 2018); Allan Bloom, *Closing of the American Mind: How Higher Education Has Failed Democracy and Impoverished the Souls of Today's Students*, reissue edition (New York: Simon & Schuster, 2012).

32. This hasn't, of course, stopped some from trying to imagine what an escape might look like in practice. See Rod Dreher, *The Benedict Option: A Strategy for Christians in a Post-Christian Nation* (New York: Sentinel, 2017).

33. Charles Taylor, *The Ethics of Authenticity* (Cambridge: Harvard University Press, 1991), 23.

way of orienting ourselves toward the world that points us toward a more fruitful way of thinking about the relationship between community and identity. The Book of Mormon offers one such possible orientation.

Traditions of the Fathers and Language of the Fathers

The formation of identity in community is a major theme in the Book of Mormon.[34] The book's narrative centers on the conflict between two warring societies—Nephites and Lamanites.[35] It has been common to read this conflict in racial terms, and given some frankly disturbing racialist language in the book (e.g. Jacob 3:5, 8–9), this is unsurprising.[36] However, a closer reading of the text complicates this story. First, the narrator acknowledges that to a certain extent, the dichotomy between the two groups is an artificial narrative simplification, masking a much more complicated underlying reality (e.g. Jacob 1:13; Mormon 1:8–9). Second, the boundaries between Lamanites and Nephites turn out to be remarkably fluid. Lamanites frequently become Nephites and vice versa. Finally, the distinction between Nephites and Lamanites collapses entirely in the utopian society recounted in 4 Nephi only to be recreated as people turn away from God, suggesting that these identities are ultimately tied to something other than ethnic lineage.

Two themes emerge from these stories. The first is that within the Book of Mormon, what it means to have an individual identity is in large part tied up in belonging to one group or another. It's perhaps telling here that while the Book of Mormon is filled with vivid individual characters, such

---

34. There are a number of good academic introductions to the Book of Mormon. See Grant Hardy, *Understanding the Book of Mormon: A Reader's Guide* (New York: Oxford University Press, 2010); Terryl L. Givens, *By the Hand of Mormon: The American Scripture That Launched a New World Religion* (New York: Oxford University Press, 2003). For an account of the historical context surrounding the book and its publication, See Daniel Howe, *What Hath God Wrought: The Transformation of America, 1815–1848* (New York: Oxford University Press, 2007), 314–15; Richard Lyman Bushman, *Joseph Smith: Rough Stone Rolling* (New York: Alfred A. Knopf, 2005), 57–83.

35. For a summary of the contents of the Book of Mormon, see Bushman, *Rough Stone Rolling*, 84–108.

36. For an extensive account of the complex effect of the Book of Mormon on subsequent racial thinking by Latter-day Saints, see Armand L. Mauss, *All Abraham's Children: Changing Mormon Conceptions of Race and Lineage* (Urbana: University of Illinois Press, 2003), 41–157.

as Alma the Younger or Captain Moroni, the narrative contains no individual characters from the period in which the "-ites" disappear (see 4 Ne. 15–20). Indeed, the narrative repeatedly dwells on how an individual character is influenced by social context and individual history. Consider the story of Enos, who is perhaps the closest that the Book of Mormon comes to an Emersonian character. He goes into the woods alone and while there reaches, in his words, "deep into my heart" but what he finds there is not an authentic self but rather "the words which I had often heard my father speak" (Enos 1:3). Second, the process by which communities constitute identity are not uniform or morally neutral. There are different ways in which community interacts with identity. Some are beneficent and others are pernicious. It's wrong to suggest that the book always presents the Nephites as righteous and the Lamanites as wicked. The Book of Mormon is morally pessimistic rather than Manichean. With few exceptions, it does not present a cosmic battle between good guys and bad guys. Rather, most of the people—Lamanite and Nephite—are wicked most of the time, although occasionally both groups produce righteous remnants. That said, the book generally presents identity formation among the Lamanites negatively, which is contrasted with the positive model among the righteous minority of Nephite characters on which much of the narrative centers.

Although its language is not perfectly consistent, generally speaking the Book of Mormon refers negatively to "traditions." To be sure, sometimes "tradition" is used positively (e.g. Enos 1:14, Mosiah 10:12), but more commonly the term is coupled with negative terms like "incorrect" (e.g. Alma 3:8) or "wicked fathers" (Alma 24:7). It is frequently used to explain the wickedness of people in the story (e.g. Alma 17:9) and is sometimes used as a term of abuse by the wicked against the righteous, as when the people of Ammonihah tell Alma the Younger, "we do not believe in such foolish traditions" (Alma 8:11; see also Hel. 16:20). Furthermore, tradition is presented as a means of apostasy and descent into wickedness. Thus, Amalickiah and his followers "became more hardened and impenitent, and more wild, wicked, and ferocious than the Lamanites—drinking in with the traditions of the Lamanites" (Alma 47:36). In short, the book routinely links identity and moral formation to inherited traditions as a negative force. Indeed, the book suggests that at some point, identity becomes so tied up in tradition that it compromises moral agency and accountability. Thus, the Book of Mormon says of the Lamanites' wickedness that "it is because of the traditions of their fathers," and accordingly, "the Lord will be merciful to them and prolong their existence in the land" (Alma 9:16).

In contrast to the discussion of inherited traditions, the Book of Mormon generally presents inherited language in positive terms. Again, the book is not entirely consistent. For example, the "language of the people" is sometimes associated with the sophistry of wicked men (e.g. Jacob 7:4) or the corrupting of others (e.g. Mosiah 24:4). Generally, however, language is associated with a positive vision of inherited identity. Thus, the book opens with Nephi's account of being "born of goodly parents" and being taught "all of the learning of my father," which included the "language of my father" (see 1 Ne. 1:1–2). Likewise, much of the opening action in the book consists of the efforts to obtain the brass plates, which Nephi informs us are necessary that "we may preserve unto our children the language of our fathers" (1 Ne. 3:19). Later, Enos says of his father, "he was a just man—for he taught me in his language, and also in the nurture and admonition of the Lord" (Enos 1:1). Likewise, positive traditions are positive in part because of their association with inherited language. Hence, when the Book of Mormon identifies "the traditions of the Nephites" with the "knowledge of the Lord" it is because of "the records and prophecies which are handed down to the present time" (Alma 23:5). Likewise, a people's traditions become corrupted because "their language had become corrupted," a situation that can only be reversed by being taught correct language (Omni 1:17–18).

What are we to make of this divide between tradition and language? First, it is important to distinguish the Book of Mormon's negative use of the term from the line of thinking on tradition goes back to Edmund Burke and before him, to seventeenth-century thinkers such as Edward Coke, John Selden, and Matthew Hale.[37] These writers emphasized the idea of continuity rather than stasis. On this view, tradition is diffuse, evolutionary, and adaptive, a repository for collective wisdom. This is not how the Book of Mormon uses the term. Rather, in the Book of Mormon, traditions are presented as static and focused on social power. The clearest example of this is the presentation of the Lamanite version of the history recounted in the opening narratives of the Book of Mormon. In place of a righteous Nephi thwarted by murmuring brothers, the Lamanite narrative focused on how Nephi's brothers were "wronged in the land of their first

37. See Edmund Burke, *Reflections on the Revolution in France*, ed. J. C. D. Clark (Stanford: Stanford University Press, 2001); Gerald Postema, *Bentham and the Common Law Tradition* (New York: Oxford University Press, 1986); Roger Scruton, *The Meaning of Conservatism*, 3rd ed. (South Bend: St. Augustine's Press, 2014).

inheritance" by a power-hungry Nephi (see Mos. 10:13–14). This tradition represents the hard crystallization of a claim made earlier in the narrative by Laman himself (see 2 Ne. 5:3). Likewise, when "tradition" is used as a term of abuse, it is linked to oppression. Thus, Korihor claims that Alma the Younger uses tradition to "yoke them [i.e. the people] according to their [i.e. the priests] desires" (Alma 30:28). In contrast, language in the Book of Mormon appears in dynamic and empowering terms. One can use language to do good things, such as teaching the gospel, or to do wicked things, such as ridiculing the humble or enlisting others in projects for personal gain. Language is also a way in which identity changes. Hence, conversion—including most dramatically the shift from membership in one community to another community—is mediated through language.

We might read "traditions" as being bad because they are collective, political, and stagnant, while "language" is good because it is fluid, creative, and individualized. Notice that thinking about the dichotomy of tradition and language in these ways tends to inscribe modern models of identity into the text of the Book of Mormon. Language gestures toward respect for individual rights, the authenticity of personal expression, and recognition of the self. Tradition, however, is about rights-threatening grabs for political power, stultifying conformity, and demonizing the "other." Such a reading, however, freights the text with moral concerns that seem largely absent from its moral agenda. These concerns focus on the self and its individual liberation in a way that just doesn't seem to be of interest to Nephi, Mormon, or Moroni. The Book of Mormon narrators simply aren't focused on individual rights or personal authenticity. Such a reading amounts to a kind of ideological proof texting that obscures the issues that do concern the text.

Rather, the book makes Christian love the fulcrum on which differing models of identity and community are balanced. The chief evil of the incorrect traditions of the fathers is that they teach hatred. The Book of Mosiah, after summarizing the content of Lamanite traditions, says:

> And thus they have taught their children that they should hate them, and that they should murder them, and that they should rob and plunder them, and do all they could to destroy them; therefore they have an eternal hatred towards the children of Nephi. (Mos. 10:17)

Likewise, when "-ites" re-emerge from the failed utopia of 4 Nephi, the Book of Mormon presents this as the recovery of a lost tradition and with it, the recovery of hatred. "And they were taught to hate the children of God, even as the Lamanites were taught to hate the children of Nephi from the beginning" (4 Ne. 1:39). On the other hand, the chief positive effect of the language that is preserved and passed from generation to generation is that it allows for conversion to the Gospel (see 1 Ne. 3:19–21). There is, however, nothing inevitable about language leading to this result. The wicked can be "learned" and use their "perfect knowledge of the language of the people" to gain "much power of speech" over their fellows (Jacob 7:4). Rather, language only leads men and women to the love of God when their agency mingles with their inheritance and the shared inheritance of others (see Enos 1:2–4).

We are thus left with two ways in which communities interact with people to form identity. On one hand, "traditions of the fathers," when accepted passively, focus on maintaining political power and generating enmity toward others. On the other hand, "language of the fathers" provides a set of resources that morally accountable agents can use to turn toward the love of God. The object of this agency, however, is not the self but rather the love of God and of others. Inherited language takes its value from how it points toward the language of God. Thus, Enos writes of how his father "taught me in his language, and also in the nurture and admonition of the Lord" (Enos 1:1), and Nephi insists that "the Lord God giveth light unto the understanding; for he speaketh unto men according to their language, unto their understanding" (2 Ne. 31:3). We are, as Joseph Smith wrote, always confined within "the little, narrow prison, almost as it were, total darkness of . . . a crooked, broken, scattered and imperfect language."[38] This inherited prison is a creation of the community into which we are born, and we cannot help but be constituted in part by it. However, it has the power to point to something beyond both itself and the self that it constitutes for us.

Ludwig Wittgenstein wrote suggestively that:

> [F]aith is faith in what is needed by my heart, my soul, not my speculative intelligence. For it is my soul with its passions, as it were with its flesh and blood, that has to be saved, not my abstract mind. Perhaps we can only say: Only love can believe in the Resurrection. Or: it is love that believes the Resurrection.[39]

---

38. Quoted in Richard Lyman Bushman, "The 'Little, Narrow Prison' of Language: The Rhetoric of Revelation," in *Believing History: Latter-Day Saint Essays*, ed. Reid L. Neilson and Jed Woodworth (New York: Columbia University Press, 2004), 250.

39. Ludwig Wittgenstein, *Culture and Value*, trans. Peter Winch (Chicago: University of Chicago Press, 1980), 33e.

Let me suggest that in our identities, what is at stake is more than the various modern models of the self that seem so threatened by the force of community. For all their truth, what these models miss is "my soul with its passions, as it were with its flesh and blood." Our flesh, blood, and passions defy the neat categories of rights, self-created authenticity, and the anxieties of recognition. These are aspects of ourselves that are inherited and absorbed from our communities. They are both our traditions and our language.

In his 2018 Gifford Lectures, N. T. Wright expanded on Wittgenstein's claim that "it is love that believes the resurrection" to defend what Wright calls an epistemology of love.[40] The New Testament, he insists, teaches that the resurrection of Jesus Christ inaugurated a new creation. We are living within the Kingdom of God that was inaugurated by the death and resurrection of Jesus. The ordinary world of "godless geometric space,"[41] to borrow a favorite phrase of Neal A. Maxwell, appears that way only because of a failure of love toward God and his creations. It is love that believes the resurrection because it is love that reorients our understanding of the world to see God's new creation. The Book of Mormon suggests, I think, that love has a similar power to reorient our understanding of community and identity. Community constitutes our identity but also provides resources from which to construct and alter that identity. The point of these reconstructive projects, however, is not autonomy, authenticity, or recognition. Rather, it is "a perfect brightness of hope, and a love of God and of all men" (2 Ne. 31:20).

40. The lectures are available online at N. T. Wright, "Discerning the Dawn: History, Eschatology and New Creation," The Gifford Lectures, December 14, 2017, https://www.giffordlectures.org/lectures/discerning-dawn-history-eschatology-and-new-creation. See also N. T. Wright, *History and Eschatology: Jesus and the Promise of Natural Theology* (Waco: Baylor University Press, 2019).

41. See Neal A. Maxwell, "The Inexhaustible Gospel," BYU Speeches, August 18, 1992, https://speeches.byu.edu/talks/neal-a-maxwell/inexhaustible-gospel/.

CHAPTER 12

"Standing Betwixt Them and Justice": War and Atonement in the Book of Mormon

The doctrine of atonement lies at the center of the gospel of Jesus Christ as taught by Latter-day Saints. Yet, as many have pointed out, what that doctrine consists of is not always clear. If asked to explain the doctrine, most Latter-day Saints would likely respond that the Atonement refers to the process by which Jesus Christ takes upon himself the consequences of humanity's sins and thereby makes repentance and salvation possible for all of God's children. But upon reflection, difficulties immediately arise. Why must God punish someone for sin? Why not simply forgive without punishment? Why would God want to punish someone who wasn't guilty in order to forgive someone who was guilty? The most common formulation of atonement among Latter-day Saints is what historians of theology call the penal substitution model, but it is by no means the only or the earliest way of thinking about Christ's sacrifice and its import for salvation.[1] The scriptures abound with metaphors of atonement that do not rely upon substitutionary punishment. For example, when we say that Christ is our intercessor or that he makes intercession for the children of men (see 2 Ne. 2:9), the image is not that of substitutionary punishment. Rather, in such contexts Christ is conceptualized as a kind of advocate who intercedes with a judge on behalf of a client. Another common image is that of debt and ransom (see 1 Tim. 2:6), and this image is also legal in nature. Indeed, the very term "redemption" has a legal significance associated with the payment of debts. Redemption is the process by which a debtor pays a creditor and thereby obtains possession of a piece of pledged collateral. Hence, Christ can be seen as paying a debt to Satan, who holds the human race as collateral for the price of sin.

My purpose in this chapter is not to resolve conflicts among competing theories of atonement, or to offer a new theory of atonement of my own. Rather, I will work on the assumption that the various images of atonement in the scriptures should be taken as what they manifestly are, namely metaphors. The purpose of piling up metaphors is not to suggest

1. See Terryl L. Givens, *Wrestling the Angel: The Foundations of Mormon Thought: Cosmos, God, Humanity* (New York: Oxford University Press, 2014), 222–40 (discussing ideas of atonement in Mormon thought).

multiple theological theories, but rather to poetically provide the believer with a basic orientation toward what can ultimately only be understood from within the process of sin, repentance, forgiveness, and salvation. With that basic stance in mind, I wish to explore a metaphor for atonement that seemingly appears only in Abinadi's speech in Mosiah 15. Abinadi, I shall argue, compares the redeeming Christ to a warrior who defends the sinner from a personified and aggressive justice. This image is not only consistent with the earliest Christian theories of atonement and Abinadi's narrative context but is also nested within a larger Book of Mormon discussion of war—one in which the book, particularly through its main redactor, Mormon, ultimately comes to reject an Old Testament ideology of holy war that associates military victory with justice and righteousness. Against this background, Abinadi's new metaphor for atonement can be seen as part of a rejection of not only aggressive war, but the whole project of striving for righteousness through victory and domination of others.

Commenting on the suffering servant passages in Isaiah 54, Abinadi says:

> And thus God breaketh the bands of death, having gained the victory over death, giving the Son power to make intercession for the children of men, having ascended into heaven, having the bowels of mercy, being filled with compassion toward the children of men, standing betwixt them and justice, having broken the bands of death, having taken upon himself their iniquity and their transgressions, having redeemed them and satisfied the demands of justice. (Mosiah 15:8–9)

This passage contains many familiar metaphors of atonement. We have the language of "intercession for the children of men" and the familiar image of Christ taking upon himself our iniquities and transgressions, as well as the language of satisfaction and redemption. However, Abinadi also says of the Son and the children of men that he is "standing betwixt them and justice." This is the only place in scripture where the phrase "betwixt them and justice" appears, and it is the only place where this image is used as a metaphor for Christ's Atonement. The precise meaning of the image is unclear, but I want to suggest that it presents Christ as a warrior, one who defends the sinner against an advancing enemy; in this case, personified justice. As I shall argue below, such an interpretation of the image makes sense in light of the earliest Christian theories of atonement, the narrative context of Mosiah 15, and the theologies of warriors and war employed in the Old Testament and the Book of Mormon.

The earliest models of atonement in Christian thought are not based on the penal substitution theory. Substitution only became the dominant model of atonement during the middle ages when it received its classic formulation in Anselm's treatise *Cur Deus Homo*.[2] Even in the Middle Ages, Anselm's view competed with so-called subjective theories of atonement associated with Peter Abelard.[3] Subjective accounts of atonement emphasize the power of Christ's example of love and suffering to motivate the sinner to repent. Language supporting both views of atonement can be found in the Book of Mormon. In Alma 34, Amulek offers what seems to be a penal substitution model of atonement, testifying, "I know that Christ shall come among the children of men, to take upon him the transgressions of his people" (Alma 34:8).[4] In contrast, King Benjamin seems to offer a subjective account of atonement, suggesting that salvation comes through "the knowledge of the goodness of God, [which] at this time has awakened you to a sense of your nothingness, and your worthless fallen state" (Mosiah 4:5). Similarly, later in the Book of Mormon, Alma the Younger offers a subjective theory of the Atonement, one that focuses on the role of suffering in increasing Christ's capacity for empathy. "[H]e will take upon him their infirmities, that his bowels may be filled with mercy, according to the flesh, that he may know according to the flesh how to succor his people according to their infirmities" (Alma 7:12).

In contrast to the objective-subjective divide that crystalized in the Middle Ages, however, the earliest Christian models of atonement emphasized the victory of Christ over death and the devil. As Gustaf Aulen has written:

> The background of the idea [of victory] is dualistic; God is pictured as in Christ carrying through a victorious conflict against the powers of evil which are hostile to His Will. This constitutes atonement, because the drama is a cosmic drama, and the victory over the hostile powers brings to pass a new relation, a relation of reconciliation between God and the world; and, still

---

2. See St. Anselm, *Anselm of Canterbury: The Major Works*, ed. Brian Davies and G. R. Evans, reissue edition (New York: Oxford University Press, 2008).

3. See Thomas Williams, "Sin, Grace, and Redemption in Abelard," in *The Cambridge Companion to Abelard*, ed. Jeffrey Brower and Kevin Guilfoy (Cambridge: Cambridge University Press, 2004).

4. It may be possible to read these passages as not offering a penal substitution model, and LDS critics of that approach have tried to do so. See R. Dennis Potter, "Did Christ Pay for Our Sins?," *Dialogue: A Journal of Mormon Thought* 32, no. 4 (Winter 1999): 84–86.

> more, because in a measure of the hostile powers are regarded as in the service of the Will of God the judge of all, and the executants of his judgment.[5]

To later theologians, the image of Christ as a victor over opposing forces was a mythological embarrassment that ascribed too much power to Satan,[6] but it does seem to represent the earliest substratum of thinking about atonement in the period immediately after the close of the New Testament, what Aulen calls the image of *Christus victor*. Similar imagery of Christ as victor over the devil appears in the Book of Mormon:

> O the greatness of the mercy of our God, the Holy One of Israel! For he delivereth his saints from that awful monster the devil, and death, and hell, and that lake of fire and brimstone, which is endless torment. (1 Ne. 9:19)

Given this tradition, seeing Christ as a defending warrior is a plausible contribution to the story of atonement metaphors.

The image of Christ as a defending warrior also makes sense given the narrative context of Mosiah 15. Lurking in the background of Abinadi's denunciation of King Noah and his priests is the military victory of the

---

5. Gustaf Aulen, *Christus Victor: An Historical Study of the Three Main Types of the Idea of Atonement*, trans. A. G. Hebert (New York: The McMillan Company, 1961), 4–5.

6. Michael J. Murray and Michael Rea summarize the issue thus:

> Although the Christus Victor theory is of historical importance and has exerted a great deal of literary influence, it has been widely rejected since the middle ages, in no small part because it is hard to take seriously the idea that God might be in competition with or have obligations toward another being (much less a being like the Devil) in the ways described above. Critics object to the idea, which is typically part of this view, that salvation involves a sort of transaction between God and the Devil; they object to the idea, present particularly in Gregory of Nyssa's version of the view, that Christ's victory over the Devil comes partly through divine deception (with Christ's divinity being hidden from the Devil until after Christ's death, when he triumphantly rises from the grave); and they sometimes also object to the reification and personification of the forces of sin, death, and evil. For this reason, the Abelardian and Anselmian views have been far and away the more popular theories for the past millenium.

Michael J. Murray and Michael Rea, "Philosophy and Christian Theology," in *The Stanford Encyclopedia of Philosophy*, ed. Edward N. Zalta, Winter 2016 (Metaphysics Research Lab, Stanford University, 2016), https://plato.stanford.edu/archives/win2016/entries/christiantheology-philosophy/.

Zeniffite colony over the Lamanites recorded in Mosiah 11. Mormon recounts the victory thus:

> Then it came to pass the King Noah sent his armies against them; and they were driven back, or they drove them back for a time. And now because of this great victory they were lifted up in the pride of their hearts therefore they returned rejoicing in their spoil. They did boast in their own strength, saying that their fifty could stand against the thousands of the Lamanites. (Mosiah 11:18–19)

Tellingly, Abinadi first appears in the verse immediately following this passage. "Then it came to pass that there was a man among them whose name was Abinadi" (Mosiah 11:19). Notice that the most natural antecedent for the pronoun "them" in this sentence is the victorious Zeniffite army, suggesting that Abinadi may have been a soldier in the battle against the Lamanites. If this is the case, then the use of military metaphors would have been natural for Abinadi. Indeed, later in chapter 15 itself, Abinadi concludes his sermon by quoting military imagery from Isaiah 52 in the context of his atonement theology: "The Lord hath made bare his holy arm in the eyes of all nations; and all the ends of the earth shall see the salvation of our God" (Mosiah 15:31; cf. Isa. 52:10).

The Book of Mormon presents the Zeniffite victory as a purely military event whose only theological significance lies in the fact that it offered an opportunity for King Noah and his followers to be lifted up in pride. However, it is clear that King Noah and his priests endowed the victory with far greater theological significance. We can see traces of this in the narrative. The phrase "their fifty could stand against the thousands of the Lamanites" could contain an allusion to the victorious band of Gideon's warriors recounted in Judges (see Judg. 7–8), and perhaps to the victory hymn sung by the women of Israel after the victory of David and Saul over the Philistines (see 1 Sam. 18:7). These are paradigmatic examples of God granting military victory to his chosen people. Indeed, in Gideon's confrontation with the Midianites recounted in Judges 7, the Lord commands him to reduce the size of his forces "lest Israel vaunt themselves against me, saying, 'my own hand has delivered me'" (Judg. 7:2). Of course, such vaunting is precisely the sin of King Noah and his people. However, for King Noah and his priests, the meaning was different. For them, the victory was the "good tidings of good" (Mosiah 12:21; cf. Isa. 52:7) brought by the blessed messenger celebrated in Isaiah 52.

In seeing their military victory as evidence of divine favor, King Noah and his priests were using a well-worn theological trope from the Old

Testament.[7] Indeed, some of the earliest theological materials in the Old Testament related to fairly tight ritual formulas of holy war.[8] Likewise, many of the oldest passages in the Hebrew Bible are songs in which the Lord is presented as a victorious warrior (see, for example, Ex. 15; Deut. 33; Judg. 5; Hab. 3). These songs declare that "the Lord is a man of war" (Ex. 15:3) and that the Lord is "the shield of your help, and the sword of your triumph" (Deut. 33:29). As a warrior, the Lord manifests his justice through trial by ordeal, in which victory in combat is taken as evidence of God's judgment. Hence, for example, in Judges, when the Amorites object to the children of Israel occupying their land, the Israelites respond by saying:

> "I therefore have not sinned against you, and you do me wrong by making war on me; the Lord, the judge, decide this day between the people of Israel and the people of Ammon" . . . So Jephthah crossed over to the Amorites to fight against them; and the Lord gave them into his hand. (Judg. 12:27, 32)

While the moral reasoning in this passage sounds crude to modern ears, it is important to remember that for millennia, trial by combat was seen as a perfectly legitimate way of establishing the justice of one's claim. (It was only at the Fourth Lateran Council in 1215 that trial by ordeal was finally outlawed in the west, many centuries after the Bible was penned.)[9] The idea was not that might makes right, but rather that right makes might. Victory was evidence of divine favor. In this ideology of holy war, victory and righteousness or justice are inextricably intertwined.[10]

The ideology of holy war also appears in the Book of Mormon.[11] Perhaps the clearest statement appears in Mormon's description of King

---

7. See Stephen D. Ricks, "The Sacred Ideology of War in the Ancient Near East: The Basic Pattern," in *Warfare in the Book of Mormon*, ed. Stephen D. Ricks and William J. Hamblin (Salt Lake City: FARMS and Deseret Book, 1990), 103–17.

8. See Gerhard Von Rad, *Holy War in Ancient Israel*, trans. Marva J. Dawn (Grand Rapids: Eerdmans Publishers, 1991).

9. See Harold J. Berman, *Law and Revolution: The Formation of the Western Legal Tradition* (Cambridge: Harvard University Press, 1983), 251.

10. Indeed, the Hebrew term for righteousness, *sadaq*, tends to be associated less with God's character than with his actions. Thus, there is a sense in which God's victory of his enemies *is* his righteousness in these earliest theologies. See B. Johnson, "Sadaq," in *Theological Dictionary of the Old Testament*, ed. G. Johannes Botterweck, Helmer Ringgren, and Heinz-Josef Fabry, trans. David E. Green (Grand Rapids: William B. Eerdmans Publishing Company, 2001).

11. See generally Stephen D. Ricks and William J. Hamblin, eds., *Warfare in the Book of Mormon* (Salt Lake City: FARMS and Deseret Book, 1990).

Benjamin's victories. For contemporary Latter-day Saints, King Benjamin is known almost exclusively for the long sermon that he delivers in the opening chapters of Mosiah, which focuses on the themes of God's unconditional love and human redemption. King Benjamin was also a war leader. The Words of Mormon state:

> And it came to pass that the armies of the Lamanites came down out of the land of Nephi to battle against his people. But behold, King Benjamin gathered together his armies, and he did stand against them, and he did fight with the strength of his own arm with the sword of Laban. And in the strength of the Lord they did contend against their enemies until they had slain many thousands of the Lamanites. And it came to pass that they did contend against the Lamanites until they had driven them out of the lands of their inheritance. (W of M 13–14)

The earliest manuscript evidence suggests that what is currently Mosiah 1 was actually the beginning of "Chapter III," the first two chapters of Mosiah having been the final portion of the lost 116 pages.[12] These lost chapters likely contained a lengthier account of King Benjamin's wars alluded to in Words of Mormon. This material may have also contained a longer discussion of the holy war ideology alluded to in Words of Mormon 13–14.[13] This victory of the righteous King Benjamin would have then been an obvious contrast with King Noah's victory and the Zeniffite boasting in Mosiah 11:18–19, which forms the immediate backdrop to Abinadi's critical inversion of the ideology of holy war in his atonement image.

Although the Book of Mormon affords other instances where military victory is ascribed to divine intervention (e.g. Alma 58:33; 46:7), Mormon himself ultimately became pessimistic about the ideology of holy war. It is against this background of ultimately rejecting holy war that

12. See Jack M. Lyon and Kent R. Minson, "When Pages Collide: Dissecting the Words of Mormon," *BYU Studies Quarterly* 51, no. 4 (2012): 122–24.

13. Indeed, the verse included at the end of the Words of Mormon in the published text may have actually been part of the original book of Mosiah and then mistakenly included in the Words of Mormon when Oliver Cowdery prepared the "printer's manuscript," a copy of the manuscript originally dictated by Joseph Smith. Unfortunately, the original manuscript for the entirety of Mosiah was lost, so it is difficult to determine the precise status of the end of the Words of Mormon. See generally Lyon and Minson, "When Pages Collide." This view, however, is controversial. See Brant A. Gardner, "When Hypotheses Collide: Responding to Lyon and Minson's 'When Pages Collide,'" *Interpreter: A Journal of Mormon Scripture* 5 (2013): 105–19.

Abinadi's image of Christ standing betwixt the sinner and justice makes the most sense. Mormon is only willing to entertain the idea that victory is evidence of divine approval when discussing wars that happened many centuries before his time, in what he often presents as a lost golden age.[14] When discussing the wars in which he actually fought himself, however, Mormon is unrelentingly disheartened, seeing only the continual violence of godless men. Even when the Nephites are victorious, Mormon himself takes credit for the victory rather than ascribing it to the Lord. "And thrice have I delivered them out of the hands of their enemies, and they have repented not of their sins" (Morm. 3:13). I don't think that this passage should be read as an instance of military boasting by Mormon. Rather, in it, Mormon rejects the idea that military victory should be seen as evidence of divine favor.

In the end, Mormon offers a very different theology of war than that contained in the earliest passages of the Hebrew Bible and implicitly relied upon by King Noah and his priests. He writes, "But behold, the judgments of God will overtake the wicked. And it is by the wicked that the wicked are punished. For it is the wicked that stirreth up the hearts of the children of men unto bloodshed" (Morm. 4:5). There are still vestiges of the old theology of war in this passage. War can be the judgments of God overtaking the wicked. However, mainly the logic of misery seems to be self-sustaining. War, rather than being a manifestation of God's agency in history, seems to largely be a matter of the wicked consequences of wicked

---

14. Perhaps the clearest example of this comes in Alma 48, where Mormon discusses Captain Moroni and his battles against the Nephites' enemies. There he writes:

> And this was their faith, that by so doing God would prosper them in the land, or in other words, if they were faithful in keeping the commandments of God that he would prosper them in the land; yea, warn them to flee, or to prepare for war, according to their danger; and also, that God would make it known unto them whither they should go to defend themselves against their enemies, and by so doing, the Lord would deliver them; and this was the faith of Moroni, and his heart did glory in it; not in the shedding of blood but in doing good, in preserving his people, yea, in keeping the commandments of God, yea, and resisting iniquity. (Alma 48:15–16)

Notice, however, that while this passage clearly imagines the Nephites of Mormon's day in less morally pessimistic terms, the discussion of God's intervention in military affairs even here is ambiguous, sometimes warning the chosen people to flee rather than aiding them to victory.

actions. In the end, Mormon's is the voice of a man disillusioned with the idea that war has any redeeming moral or religious content. We can see Mormon's disillusionment with war in other aspects of his rhetoric. Grant Hardy, for example, has noted: "As a military man himself, Mormon never speaks of war figuratively or makes it a metaphor for Christian living. There is no mention of putting on the armor of God, fighting the good fight of faith, or spiritual warfare against temptation (in contrast to some recent Latter-day Saint readings of the war chapters in Alma)."[15]

Against this background, Abinadi's metaphor takes on a richer theological significance. The burden of the image of Christ standing betwixt the sinner and justice is the idea that justice is an enemy that might be rightly resisted. Indeed, in presenting Christ as defender, Abinadi's image fits squarely within the teachings on just war articulated by Mormon in Alma 43:45–47. The standard for a just war given there is high and places overwhelming emphasis on defensive war. A war for "monarchy" and "power" (Alma 43:45) is unacceptable, and one cannot be "guilty of the first offense, neither the second" (Alma 43:46). It is only when one's family is attacked that war becomes legitimate: "And again, the Lord has said that: Ye shall defend your families even unto bloodshed" (Alma 43:47). Thus, Jesus as a defender presents the image of justice as an aggressive attacker. Like all images of atonement, justice is at best ambiguous in its view. For example, one can compare Abinadi with Paul, who frames justice primarily in terms of the law and atonement as a response to the law's inadequacies (see Rom. 8:2–4). In the ideology of holy war, on the other hand, we associate justice with warfare rather than law. Unlike in the *Christus victor* image of the early church fathers, Abinadi does not see the Atonement as a matter of Christ's victory over the devil. Rather, he casts the enemy from which Christ defends us as justice itself. This inverts the ideology of holy war. It continues to see war as a site of justice, but that war is now rejected, an evil from which Christ saves us. Where Paul problematizes justice by denigrating the law, or at least pointing toward is incompleteness, Abinadi and the Book of Mormon problematize the idea of justice by rejecting the ideology of holy war, which sees military victory as a sign of righteousness.

Abinadi's image of atonement in terms of the Son as a defending warrior makes sense given the arc of the Book of Mormon's theological attitude toward the ideology of holy war. His image's essentially negative

---

15. Grant Hardy, *Understanding the Book of Mormon: A Reader's Guide* (New York: Oxford University Press, 2010), 108.

picture of justice resonates with the Book of Mormon's broader rejection of the ideology of holy war, an ideology that saw God's justice primarily in terms of military victory. For the Book of Mormon, especially as presented in the mature writings of Mormon, military victory is hollow, a matter of wickedness inflicting misery upon the wicked for its own sake. Justice as war, when seen through a prophetic understanding that rejects war, becomes the destructive effort of human beings to achieve righteousness through victory over, and domination of, others. Repentance thus becomes a way, to use another Book of Mormon image of justice defeated, "to bring about the bowels of mercy, which overpowereth justice" (Alma 34:15). Through his mercy and love, the Son shows us an alternative to the ultimately fruitless search for righteousness in human victory. This is the justice from which Christ defends us, calling us to live an entirely different kind of life based on his example.

Index

G

H

I

J

K

N

O

P

Q

R

Also available from

GREG KOFFORD BOOKS

Common Ground—Different Opinions: Latter-day Saints and Contemporary Issues

Edited by Justin F. White and James E. Faulconer

Paperback, ISBN: 978-1-58958-573-7

There are many hotly debated issues about which many people disagree, and where common ground is hard to find. From evolution to environmentalism, war and peace to political partisanship, stem cell research to same-sex marriage, how we think about controversial issues affects how we interact as Latter-day Saints.

In this volume various Latter-day Saint authors address these and other issues from differing points of view. Though they differ on these tough questions, they have all found common ground in the gospel of Jesus Christ and the latter-day restoration. Their insights offer diverse points of view while demonstrating we can still love those with whom we disagree.

Praise for *Common Ground—Different Opinions*:

"[This book] provide models of faithful and diverse Latter-day Saints who remain united in the body of Christ. This collection clearly demonstrates that a variety of perspectives on a number of sensitive issues do in fact exist in the Church. . . . [T]he collection is successful in any case where it manages to give readers pause with regard to an issue they've been fond of debating, or convinces them to approach such conversations with greater charity and much more patience. It served as just such a reminder and encouragement to me, and for that reason above all, I recommend this book." — Blair Hodges, Maxwell Institute

Future Mormon: Essays in Mormon Theology

Adam S. Miller

Paperback, ISBN: 978-1-58958-509-6

From the Introduction:

I have three children, a girl and two boys. Our worlds overlap but, already, these worlds are not the same. Their worlds, the worlds that they will grow to fill, are already taking leave of mine. Their futures are already wedged into our present. This is both heartening and frightening. So much of our world deserves to be left. So much of it deserves to be scrapped and recycled. But, too, this scares me. I worry that a lot of what has mattered most to me in this world—Mormonism in particular—may be largely unintelligible to them in theirs. This problem isn't new, but it is perpetually urgent. Every generation must start again. Every generation must work out their own salvation. Every generation must live its own lives and think its own thoughts and receive its own revelations. And, if Mormonism continues to matter, it will be because they, rather than leaving, were willing to be Mormon all over again. Like our grandparents, like our parents, and like us, they will have to rethink the whole tradition, from top to bottom, right from the beginning, and make it their own in order to embody Christ anew in this passing world. To the degree that we can help, our job is to model that work in love and then offer them the tools, the raw materials, and the room to do it themselves.

These essays are a modest contribution in this vein, a future tense apologetics meant for future Mormons. They model, I hope, a thoughtful and creative engagement with Mormon ideas while sketching, without obligation, possible directions for future thinking.

Dead Wood and Rushing Water: Essays on Mormon Faith, Culture, and Family

Boyd Jay Petersen

Paperback, ISBN: 978-1-58958-658-1

For over a decade, Boyd Petersen has been an active voice in Mormon studies and thought. In essays that steer a course between apologetics and criticism, striving for the balance of what Eugene England once called the "radical middle," he explores various aspects of Mormon life and culture—from the Dream Mine near Salem, Utah, to the challenges that Latter-day Saints of the millennial generation face today.

Praise for *Dead Wood and Rushing Water*:

"*Dead Wood and Rushing Water* gives us a reflective, striving, wise soul ruminating on his world. In the tradition of Eugene England, Petersen examines everything in his Mormon life from the gold plates to missions to dream mines to doubt and on to Glenn Beck, Hugh Nibley, and gender. It is a book I had trouble putting down." — Richard L. Bushman, author of *Joseph Smith: Rough Stone Rolling*

"Boyd Petersen is correct when he says that Mormons have a deep hunger for personal stories—at least when they are as thoughtful and well-crafted as the ones he shares in this collection." — Jana Riess, author of *The Twible* and *Flunking Sainthood*

"Boyd Petersen invites us all to ponder anew the verities we hold, sharing in his humility, tentativeness, and cheerful confidence that our paths will converge in the end." — Terryl. L. Givens, author of *People of Paradox: A History of Mormon Culture*

For Zion: A Mormon Theology of Hope

Joseph M. Spencer

Paperback, ISBN: 978-1-58958-568-3

What is hope? What is Zion? And what does it mean to hope for Zion? In this insightful book, Joseph Spencer explores these questions through the scriptures of two continents separated by nearly two millennia. In the first half, Spencer engages in a rich study of Paul's letter to the Roman to better understand how the apostle understood hope and what it means to have it. In the second half of the book, Spencer jumps to the early years of the Restoration and the various revelations on consecration to understand how Latter-day Saints are expected to strive for Zion. Between these halves is an interlude examining the hoped-for Zion that both thrived in the Book of Mormon and was hoped to be established again.

Praise for *For Zion*:

"Joseph Spencer is one of the most astute readers of sacred texts working in Mormon Studies. Blending theological savvy, historical grounding, and sensitive readings of scripture, he has produced an original and compelling case for consecration and the life of discipleship." — Terryl Givens, author, *Wrestling the Angel: The Foundations of Mormon Thought*

"*For Zion: A Mormon Theology of Hope* is more than a theological reflection. It also consists of able textual exegesis, historical contextualization, and philosophic exploration. Spencer's careful readings of Paul's focus on hope in Romans and on Joseph Smith's development of consecration in his early revelations, linking them as he does with the Book of Mormon, have provided an intriguing, intertextual avenue for understanding what true stewardship should be for us—now and in the future. As such he has set a new benchmark for solid, innovative Latter-day Saint scholarship that is at once provocative and challenging." — Eric D. Huntsman, author, *The Miracles of Jesus*

www.ingramcontent.com/pod-product-compliance
Lightning Source LLC
Chambersburg PA
CBHW021719210326
41599CB00013B/1701

* 9 7 8 1 5 8 9 5 8 8 0 8 0 *